D0702405

Johann Wolfgang von Goethe

PLAYS

Egmont
Iphigenia in Tauris
Torquato Tasso

Jack O'Connell
21. Januar 1994
Seattle

The German Library: Volume 20
Volkmar Sander, General Editor

EDITORIAL BOARD
Peter Demetz (Yale University)
Reinhold Grimm (University of Wisconsin)
Jost Hermand (University of Wisconsin)
Patricia A. Herminghouse (University of Rochester)
Walter Hinderer (Princeton University)
Victor Lange (Princeton University)
Frank G. Ryder (University of Virginia)
Volkmar Sander (New York University)
Egon Schwarz (Washington University)
A. Leslie Willson (University of Texas)

Johann Wolfgang von Goethe

PLAYS

Egmont
Iphigenia in Tauris
Torquato Tasso

Edited by Frank G. Ryder

CONTINUUM · NEW YORK

1993

The Continuum Publishing Company
370 Lexington Avenue, New York, NY 10017

The German Library
is published in cooperation with Deutsches Haus,
New York University.
This volume has been supported by a grant
from the Marie Baier Foundation.

Copyright © 1993 by The Continuum Publishing Company
Introduction © 1993 by Frank G. Ryder

All rights reserved. No part of this book may be reproduced,
stored in retrieval system, or transmitted, in any form or by
any means, electronic, mechanical, photocopying, recording,
or otherwise, without the written permission of
The Continuum Publishing Company.

Printed in the United States of America

Library of Congress Cataloging-in-Publication Data

Goethe, Johann Wolfgang von, 1749–1832.
  [Plays. English. Selections]
  Plays / Johann Wolfgang von Goethe ; edited by Frank G. Ryder.
    p. cm. — (The German Library ; v. 20)
  Translated from the German.
  Contents: Egmont — Iphigenia in Tauris — Torquato Tasso.
  ISBN 0-8264-0716-1 (alk. paper) — ISBN 0-8264-0717-X
  (pbk. : alk. paper)
  1. Goethe, Johann Wolfgang von, 1749–1832—Translations
into English. 2. Egmont, Lamoraal, Graaf van, 1522–1568—Drama.
3. Tasso, Torquato, 1544–1595—Drama. 4. Iphigenia (Greek
mythology)—Drama. I. Ryder, Frank Glessner, 1916–
II. Goethe, Johann Wolfgang von, 1749–1832. Egmont. English.
1992. III. Goethe, Johann Wolfgang von, 1749–1832. Iphigenie auf
Tauris. English. 1992. IV. Goethe, Johann Wolfgang von,
1749–1832. Torquato Tasso, English. 1992. V. Series.
PT2026 1992
832′. 6—dc20
                                              92-25103
                                                 CIP

Contents

CONCORDIA UNIVERSITY LIBRAR
PORTLAND, OR 97211

Introduction

History

Goethe has been called "the greatest of the Germans." That he is one of the greatest poets in world literature is beyond argument. It used to be a commonplace to speak of the triad Dante, Shakespeare, Goethe as the summit of literary eminence. Yet Goethe was not simply a writer, certainly not a "writer by profession." He was a lawyer and a scientist—he may well have regarded the *Farbenlehre*, a study in optics, as his most significant work—and he was also an amateur artist, an actor and theater director, above all a high government official.

The three plays of this volume were written in the one period of his life when such extra-literary activities and demands weighed most heavily upon him. It was the first decade of his career as adviser, companion, and Privy Councillor to the sovereign of a small German state—and the two years of "escape" that followed. It is remarkable that, amid such distractions and pressures, he was able to finish these plays as well as a significant number of other works.

The biographical setting is important. Goethe's novel *The Sufferings of Young Werther* (1774; volume 19 of The German Library) had gained him sudden, widespread fame and specifically the attention of Karl August, the young scion of the Duchy of Weimar. In 1775, at the duke's invitation, he left Frankfurt, its family ties and the literary environment of Sturm und Drang to take up a new life as the duke's adviser and companion. (Their escapades caused a great wagging of tongues.) He threw himself immediately into the

courtly environment of a small eighteenth-century absolute state—
and not unwillingly. Aristocracy and "benevolent absolutism" became, and would remain, his preferred model for good government.

Nor was he just a spectator or only the duke's companion in
frivolity. Over the years he came to occupy a bewildering variety
of government positions: everything from Privy Councillor to the
ministries of mines, highways and public works, finance, war and
recruiting, indeed practically every post except the ministry of justice, the one his law degree and admission to the bar would seem
to have prepared him for. In each of these jobs he was responsible
for the smallest details. He even had to take the physical measure-
ments of possible recruits. Besides this he ran the active amateur
theater of the duchy. Not surprisingly, he finally fled Weimar and
all his involvements there, taking "administrative leave" and not
saying when he would be back. In 1786 he took a coach to Italy.
He returned in 1790, a quite different man, to a differently defined
life in Weimar. There, in 1789–90, the three plays were at last
finished and published. There, too, he died in 1832, at the age of
82.

The close ties of Frankfurt and the comparative isolation of studies in Leipzig and legal service in Wetzlar (site of the Holy Roman
Empire's "supreme court") had yielded to complex responsibilities
of government and a radical change in social and cultural sur-
roundings. These were also years marked by uncertainties: deep
concerns as to his intended—or possible—audience; questioning of
the proper balance of literary activity and public service; doubts
as to how he should select and portray his heroes and heroines;
uncertainty even as to the optimal form of his dramatic works—
Prose? Verse? If verse, what meters? These years of change and
challenge are most lucidly described by Nicholas Boyd in his massive new study *Goethe: The Poet and the Age.*

There is another and more positive side to such uncertainty,
especially in the matter of form. It lies in the special kind of creative
impulse which drove Goethe to the long and often complicating
quest of appropriateness. Throughout his career he experimented
constantly, altered and amended constantly. Of all the great poets
he is the most insistent reviser. The process and the result are
apparent in the multiple recasting of the three plays included in

this volume. *Iphigenia* went through three or four versions. *Tasso* was composed first in prose, then in blank verse. *Egmont* was conceived first in rhythmic language, even verse, finally in prose, with its poetic origin showing through in passages that scan and in long sequences of elevated discourse. These radical revisions are part of the history, but only the history, of each text. They have little bearing on the literary stature of the finished works. Apart from *Faust,* they are Goethe's greatest dramatic achievements.

Egmont is by several years and in its conceptual background the earliest. Much of the initial writing was done by 1775, the year Goethe left Frankfurt. During the first months in Weimar he continued to work on the play, but the disparity between its Sturm und Drang thematics and the social and cultural patterns of the absolute state which Goethe now served made the work acutely difficult. It would also in the end determine a sea change in the treatment of the background of the play. The grand scale of history (the Low Countries under the Spanish yoke) owes much of its prominence in the play to a kind of tribute exacted by Goethe's new political environment. In its original conception *Egmont* was far more personal in scope, the love affair with Clara more intense and central, with little of its later allegorical aspect. The problem of reconciling these two conceptions of the play's balance obviously led to Goethe's difficulty in finishing it, his long delay in reworking it at all, and ultimately to his confession that he often wished he had never started it. By 1782, however he had the general plan under control. He took the manuscript with him to Italy and in 1787 he finally brought the play to its conclusion.

Iphigenia was begun in 1779, its first acts dictated—Goethe often worked this way—on a recruiting trip for the ducal army. Goethe was then a member of the War Commission. The first acts were presented on stage later the same year, with Goethe as Orestes and (in a subsequent performance) the duke as Pylades. The play was rewritten, now fully in verse, during 1786. Like *Egmont* it was finished in Italy.

As with *Egmont,* so with *Tasso:* the new circumstances of Goethe's life posed a dilemma. How was he to portray a brilliant but hypersensitive poet in an uncomfortable and frustrating relationship to a court, its ruling family, and its minions? The equation was too close for comfort. Work on the play, begun in 1780, ceased in 1781. The play had originally been composed in a kind of rhythmic prose, like that of the early *Iphigenia*. Goethe took the manuscript to Italy and finally returned to the project, finishing it in 1787. Thus these three plays, diverse in origin and textual development, come together in the same year and in a foreign land.

The development of Goethe's dramatic language has its own history in the three plays. The distance in time of initial conception from *Egmont* to the other two is perhaps most unmistakable in the external form. It is not just a matter of prose and poetry. In *Egmont*, as in *Götz* before it, there is an individuation of speech according to character, background, and class that resembles what we know from Shakespeare—for good reason, given Goethe's early and ardent study of his English model. In *Iphigenia* and *Tasso* he turns to the virtually undifferentiated poetic language of classical drama. When all characters speak alike, the idiosyncratic aspects of a personality, given us on the surface in "realistic" plays like *Egmont*, must be searched out beneath the surface.

Such, in brief, is the genesis and history of the three plays.

However remarkable the biographical background, however important the temporal context, they harbor a subtle danger. Paying too much attention to them may lead to a diminished focus on the works as they stand in their final form, and it is in their final form that they have made their mark on the world's consciousness. In fact the best course for the reader would be to turn to the plays first and consider this introduction later. The reader also has the right to form his own judgments, independently and even skeptically, in the face of any critical analyses, including those offered here. It would be strange indeed if the complexities of any great literary work could be fixed beyond debate in any single interpretation. Goethe himself complained that people were always asking him for the "idea" of his *Faust*, as if, he said, such a complex life could be strung on the meager string of a single idea.

In what follows I shall accordingly try to avoid expansive generalizations on the total meaning of each work, turning rather to salient features of structure, themes and motifs, character portrayal, and so on. The presence of such features is clear, and their relevance to the understanding of the works will be clear. But their interpretation is—to say it once again—open to discussion.

Immediately apparent in such an approach is an evolving pattern in the depiction of character and background from play to play. There is, however, also a remarkably stable pattern of themes and motifs within each play and a consistent deployment of such elements across the three works, indeed through much of the range of Goethe's oeuvre. Such distinctive structures bear witness to the workings of one of the most powerful and prolific creative minds in Western literature. They are an essential constituent of a profound literary statement about the human condition. Through them we may also return to the poet with a larger, though certainly not unambiguous understanding of his literary imagination, his intellectual and psychological make-up. The insight thus gained is often more reliable than the autobiographical writings, even of so generous an autobiographer. It is also more satisfying than much of the secondary literature.

Nowhere in biography or autobiography is—to take a prime example first—the seemingly arbitrary subordination of "reality" in favor of illusion so clear as in Orestes's rescue from madness and guilt through his vision of reconciliation in the Underworld, made possible by the contagion of Iphigenia's transcendent goodness. Or in Egmont's triumphant self-delusion in the literal ecstasy of the last moments before his death. Or in Tasso's ultimate surrender to the hope, tenuous in "real" terms, of rescue by his quondam antagonist Antonio. (By "real" and "reality" I shall refer to the totality of events in a commonsense world, the course of things as they would be without Goethe's introduction of illusion and visions.)

Strangely enough it is in *Tasso* that the vision is so long delayed and the contending forces of "reality" so long confronted as to lead, almost, to the logical conclusion of total frustration and collapse—logical, that is, in terms of ordinary reality. Here the later play reveals a paradoxical kinship with an earlier play, *Götz von Berlichingen*, to which reference will be frequently made. (This is a Sturm und Drang play with a main plot, a major subplot, and two or three sub-subplots. The central figure is Götz. He is a "free knight" of the Holy Roman Empire, answerable only to the emperor, who is the political warrant for Götz's passionate ideal of a life in liberty. When the emperor is persuaded by self-serving advisers to move against him and subdue him, ostensibly on account of his forays against traveling merchants, Götz faces an absolute dilemma. He must abandon freedom or abandon the emperor, the icon of that freedom. Unable to bear the house arrest to which he is condemned, Götz breaks out, becomes culpably involved with peasant revolutionaries, is captured, and confined to prison. Cut off from his cherished life in freedom, he will die.)

Occasional comparisons backward in time to *Götz* and forward to *Faust* will serve to place our three plays in the broader picture of Goethe's development as a dramatist.

Concepts of Tragic Conflict

Inescapable and evenly balanced ideal goals are a commonplace of everyday life. Pay the extra tuition for a specially gifted child or give in equal shares to all three children? Each course embodies an ideal goal. It may be impossible to do both. Doing either, one does wrong. In the whole range of Western literature, even and inescapable conflict is remarkably rare. The corpus of Greek drama, origin and inspiration of Western tragic literature, is almost devoid of it. Inner conflict is generally adulterated or transformed by external complications or by flaws of character. Antigone denies or averts inner doubt. What could have been her dilemma is plain: Give burial rites to her fallen brother at the cost of diminishing the welfare of the city-state? She obscures the conflict by her stubborn and self-centered insistence on playing the exclusive role in familial and ritual duty. Her fault is perceived as such and reproached as such by her own sister, Ismene.

The true clash between ideal goals in an otherwise guiltless person who must, by taking action, become guilty, is exemplified (despite the deus ex machina ending) in another of Sophocles's plays, the *Philoctetes*. Here Neoptolemus faces a dilemma not unlike Iphigenia's. Sent to the island of Lemnos to trick Philoctetes (owner of the bow and arrows of Hercules) into coming to Troy to save the otherwise doomed Greek forces, he first agrees and lies to Philoctetes, saying the Greek leaders have quarreled, hence the impasse. Philoctetes, in terrible pain from a serpent bite, begs to be taken back to Greece. He collapses but before that entrusts his bow to Neoptolemus. When he wakes, Neoptolemus, unable to bear lying to a noble friend, reveals the plot. He cannot persuade Philoctetes to come to Troy so he will hold to his promise and take Philoctetes home (thus ostensibly dooming the Greek forces). This resolution would be disastrous for the Greeks. Hercules appears from the Underworld, however, and saves everybody. Philoctetes will go to Troy.

Irreconcilable conflict is explicitly recognized as such by a beleaguered hero in the medieval German epic the *Nibelungenlied*. Ruedeger, who has in all innocence and for good reason sworn blood brotherhood with the Burgundians, is called upon by his liege-lord, Etzel (Attila the Hun) to fight these very friends, who have now become Etzel's foes: the hopeless dilemma of friendship versus fealty. In his desperation he cries:

> Whichever course before me I reject,
> To do the other, I've done a cursed act.

There is no more perfect statement of inescapable dilemma.

The evolution of Goethe's treatment of tragedy is in part the history of his escape from this inevitability. Yet the inevitability is explicitly recognized in his first significant statement on the tragic situation. This is the formulation in the *Shakespeare-Rede* of 1772: "the point where the characteristic quality of our being, our presumed free will, collides with the inevitable course of the whole." The true nature of the point has been almost uniformly misunderstood. "Free will" is taken to imply the individual as an independent volitional entity, while the "inevitable course of the whole" is said to imply the forces of society, historical trends, class differences—whatever kind of determinism one wishes. This is too facile. It distorts and cheapens the definition. As Benjamin Bennett has pointed out, the "whole" is also an aspect of the individual. It refers to his whole being, and it is within the whole pattern of his being that the idea of freedom conflicts with what he recognizes as his duty or obligation. *That* situation engenders tragic conflict. It immobilizes the individual and may lead to his destruction. *Götz*, a work contemporary with the *Shakespeare-Rede*, embodies the dilemma exactly.

Among our plays we see the stages to which Goethe moved as he was, so to speak, no longer able to bear the notion of irreconcil-

able and terminal conflict within the mind and heart of his protagonist. The earlier definition is first superseded by another
formulation, memorably stated in *Egmont,* the notion of the *Daemon.* This is not our garden-variety "demon," of course. It is rather
the inescapable essence of our personality, by which we are impelled, through inspiration or compulsion, to act our roles. Speaking to his secretary—in an earlier version it may have been to
Clara—Egmont says,

> Child! Child! No more! As if they were whipped by invisible spirits,
> the sun-steeds of time bolt, and run off with the light chariot of our
> destiny; and there is nothing we can do but take heart and grasp
> the reins firmly and turn the wheels now to the right, now to the
> left, away from the precipice here, the rock wall there. Where he is
> heading, who knows? The truth is, he scarcely remembers whence
> he came.

This is a Sturm und Drang concept, vital to *Egmont,* much less
powerful in *Tasso* because to some extent diluted by paranoia,
hardly present in *Iphigenia*—though conceivably in Orestes, but
there transcended by the anguish and reality of guilt. (Only in
Egmont could a reasonable case be made for viewing the hero in
the light of another kind of tragedy: the fatal overextension of a
great merit. Oedipus was misled and destroyed because he set too
much store in his own power of intellect. Egmont is betrayed by
his very humanity, his amiability, his generous and trusting nature.
He walks, naively confident and unsuspecting, into the murderous
trap set by Alba.)

The final and most characteristically Goethean stage is a recogni-
tion of the inner conflict but the subsequent transcending of it
either through the exercise of will and human kindness or, more
characteristically, through visions of salvation. Both possibilities
are realized in *Iphigenia.* In Iphigenia herself the conflict is played
out in reality, that is, overtly and consciously, as she manages her
involvement with Thoas and Arcas, Orestes and Pylades. When
she can no longer "manage" she still acts, in desperation and at
great risk, but consciously and heroically, to place her faith in the
power of truth and in Thoas's decency. On the other hand, when
reality becomes too much for Orestes, under the pressure of mem-

ory, of guilt, of pursuit by the Furies, he collapses and in his unconscious state dreams a vision of reconciliation and absolution, and awakens whole and cured.

So this is the progression as far as the Goethean hero is concerned: Götz himself is neither rescued nor redeemed, except for the suggestion that future ages may come to see his greatness. Werther is not rescued from death, indeed he inflicts death upon himself, and he is redeemed only in a desperate, self-constructed illusion. Egmont is not rescued from death but he is redeemed, first, like Götz though more explicitly, in the eyes of posterity as hero and patron spirit of his country; secondly, in a decisive advance from the earlier play, in his own dream as well. Götz had no such benefaction. Egmont, as an individual, perishes, yet he is sustained by his vision. Orestes is rescued, redeemed, and cured. Iphigenia herself is rescued—or, unlike her male counterparts, rescues herself—from the dual imprisonment of exile and inner conflict, since her ideal of truth and humanity is confirmed. Tasso is rescued from literal and psychological imprisonment, but redemption, either as artist or as person, is only an implied possibility, and one that Tasso creates for himself. Curiously, perhaps, *Tasso* comes closest to a tragic or desperately pathetic outcome and is in this respect nearer to *Götz* than are the other two. *Faust Part I,* though outside our readings, is part of our time frame. To speak of *Faust II* goes beyond it but serves to show where the progression is heading. In *Faust II,* the rescue and the redemption are at their height, because the depicted reality is at its most uncompromising, extensive, and harsh. The long burden of his flaws—the hubris of universal knowledge, the seduction of a basically innocent girl, complicit responsibility for the death of her (and his) child, direct responsibility for the murder of her brother—occasions only frustration and the briefest remorse. His guilt is wiped away in a vastly symbolic night of sleep. What follows is an allegorical venture in cultural synthesis—the ancient world and the modern, no less—and of statecraft at the highest level. It is an extraordinary pageant, ending in resolution, reconciliation, and redemption. All this is provided him by his author. But the ultimate vision of a free people in a world of freedom is, in a sense, a repetition of *Egmont:* death (in *Faust* by natural causes, in *Egmont* by human design) followed by ascension (in *Faust* literally to a heavenly realm, in *Egmont* to the status of folk hero.) And yet in both cases, Goethe undermines the illusion with irony: in *Egmont* the subtle irony, not that he is in fact beheaded—he knew he would be—but by the fact that his vision of his people rising to expel the foreigner is oddly undercut by the contradictory nature, invariably overlooked, of his own metaphor of the process of liberation: "and as the sea breaks through your dikes, just so tear down the wall of tyranny." That is a metaphor of destruction, not of reconquest. In *Faust* the irony is obvious and stark. The sound of digging that Faust greets as the work of building his new world is in fact the sound of the Lemures digging his grave.

At the crux of all these plays after *Götz*, the ones in which rescue supervenes, lies the leap of faith, whether confirmed in reality or not, the transcending of reason or reasoned action, even in the face of obdurate conflict, guilt, and threatening disaster. The movement is always *toward* the desired effect of salvation. Nowhere is the process more pervasive, more fully elaborated, than in *Iphigenia*. It is perhaps of all Goethe's works, including even *Faust,* the most compelling drama of the human *mind*—where Faust may remain, if the semantic distinction is warranted, the most powerful evoking of the human condition.

The Truth, the Whole Truth . . .

Goethe may try to avoid tragedy but he does not, so to speak, withhold evidence in order to do so. Consider the case of Iphigenia. She is legitimately taken, in the common view, as a paragon of goodness and *Humanität*. Yet under pressure she resorts to invention, diversionary action, and manipulation. In the end she sets things right. But the lapses should at least be noted. They are part of the picture of Iphigenia as a human being.

Trying to persuade Thoas to give her freedom, she first seeks (honestly enough, perhaps) to frighten him by the narration of her family's horrifying past. But when he makes his wonderful response, "I give no more preferment, no more trust to the king's daughter than I do the stranger. I repeat my first proposal: Come, follow me and share in what I have," she tries to evade his urgency and his steadfast open-mindedness by taking refuge in her position and obligation as priestess. It is at least a partial truth, but it is also an evasion. Thoas's frustrated anger triggers the crucial threat of return to blood sacrifice, which would entail the killing of her own brother. The fact that to gain time she lies about the desecration of the temple by the Furies is not truly consequential. The lie was imposed upon her by Pylades. But when she defends her failure to carry the deception of Thoas and Arcas to the full and Pylades rebukes her, saying she should have cloaked herself in priestly privilege, she replies, "Never have I used it as a cloak," and that is not strictly true. In first putting off Thoas and his wish that she be his bride, she does not say that she cannot do so since she cannot love him as a husband. Instead she says, "Has not the goddess . . . sole right to this, my consecrated life?" A similar stain lies upon her later protestation to Thoas, warning him that the weak (meaning especially women) have learned tricks of their own: "Outflank, delay, evade." When he in turn warns her that "precautions can be taken against cunning," and she replies, "The pure in heart will neither need nor use it," Thoas's rejoinder is justified: "Be careful! Don't pass sentence on yourself."

On the other hand, Iphigenia twice averts misunderstanding or disaster by recourse to the truth. Having collaborated—and not for the last time—with Pylades's fabrication, in this instance his lie concerning his and Orestes's background, she must now, with the deceit unmasked, confront the terrible suffering of her brother, his wish for death, his despair, his morbid exultation at what he sees as the annihilation of his family. Moments before, she had revealed her identity, crying, "Between us let there be truth." Later, unable further to prolong the deluding of Thoas through Pylades's carefully planned fabrication, she says in effect the same thing:

> Now my heart rises and falls with a bold undertaking. . . . Yes, Sire, hear what I say: a secret chain of guile is being forged. You'll ask about the prisoners in vain; both are gone. . . . So now I have delivered up to you two survivors of the house of Tantalus. Destroy us— if you can.

Then, in the sudden confusion and burst of action occasioned by the return of Pylades with the Greek force, Thoas makes the mistake (in the context of his self-interest) of simply questioning Orestes's identity: "How can you prove that you are Agamemnon's son, the brother of this woman?" Iphigenia seizes upon this opening to move swiftly into what seems a quite manipulative mode: "See here on his right hand the birthmark. . . . and the scar that cuts across his eyebrow. . . ." She has (artfully?) narrowed the issue to a mere case of mistaken identity, now set right. Before, her revelation of the truth was in effect a shifting of responsibility for the crucial decision, from herself to the king. That was no dereliction— what could she do alone?—and she did have evidence to suggest to her that Thoas is sufficiently a man of principle, one who holds her in both affection and high regard. Arcas has said, "I tell you this: the whole is in your hands. The King's indignant state of mind alone condemns these strangers to their bitter death," a plea that he follows with a moving description of what she has done for the humanizing of Scythia. That the desperate hope to do justice to two conflicting obligations of such magnitude should lead a high-minded woman to bend the truth is scarcely implausible—or demeaning. And the risk she takes in telling the greater truth makes her all the more credible as a model of human virtue.

The almost universal temptation has been to regard Tasso as the embodiment of poetic gift, the epitome of the sensitive poet, different, misunderstood, much put upon, but vastly talented. This involves a serious overlooking of other evidence that Goethe provides in abundance. Talented he is, but he is also a virtual case study in eccentricity carried to pathological extremes, indeed a case study of near paranoia.

He does not merely forget to bring back half the things he takes on trips, though that modest eccentricity is mentioned. He is a hypochondriac and makes ridiculous demands on his doctor: "Give me medicine to cure me; that's your business. And see that I don't have to give up what I like to eat and drink" (V. 1). He believes, erroneously, that people are breaking into his rooms (I. 2). Antonio says (V. 1): "He thinks he is surrounded by enemies," and that his letters are intercepted.

Leonore lectures him on his self-destructive delusions: "You have spun the strangest web, for your own harm" (IV. 2). In the next scene he becomes overtly paranoid: "Am I supposed to think that no one persecutes me?" His soliloquy in IV. 3 is a litany of self-pity and visions of rejection, indeed of a death more welcome than such rejection. He sees Leonore, who had tried to help him, as a little serpent hissing "with a honeyed tongue." Later (IV. 5) he envisions even his beloved princess as his enemy. He vows to slip away. Yet when there is the slightest chance of staying, he abjectly begs to be the humble caretaker for her summer house and gardens (V. 4). He commits the faux pas of embracing her, and when the princess rejects him he is plunged into self-serving despair (V. 5). His long tirade in V. 5 is paranoid to the point of near madness: "They crowned me, to be led before the altar . . . like any sacrificial victim."

At the other extreme he has sufficient egotism to compare himself with the Titans (II. 4) and to think he should be consulted in affairs of state, instead of "always Antonio" (IV. 2). He revels in the premature ecstasy of being much more to the princess than an intellectual companion; "I am yours" (II. 2). Antonio is brusque and unnecessarily cold, but Tasso relentlessly presses him to accept friendship and love, accuses him of jealousy, and when he is definitely rejected, challenges him to a duel, an undertaking quite beyond his experience (II. 3). This is more than impetuousness. And when the spat comes to Alfonso's attention, Tasso grossly exaggerates the wrong done him (II. 4).

Tasso also lies. He lies to cover his planned defection and he lies in the attempt to retrieve the manuscript of his poem (IV. 4). He even admits to his own dissembling and takes pride in it (V. 3). All this is a far, far cry from the shortcomings of Iphigenia, but it renders both the protagonist and the play fascinatingly complex. *Tasso* remains one of literature's most penetrating explorations of the psychopathology of genius.

Contradictions and complexities in Egmont's character lie open on the prose surface, but they require examination. He is not merely the folk hero of his people, extroverted and impulsive. The ambivalence of his attitude toward the politics of his own situation is subtly revealed in his dazzling appearance before Clara. His dress is of the ornate Spanish cut. He is not merely one of the leaders of the opposition to Spain but a candidate for the very regency that has served as the representative of the occupying power. His flair for the new style has been remarked by the commoners. In act 2, after Egmont's departure, Jetter says, "Did you notice how he was dressed? It was the newest fashion—the Spanish cut." He becomes explicitly conscious of the affection, even love, which the Regent, Margaret of Parma, feels for him. Seemingly little burdened by self-awareness, he comes to analyze his own character in the surprising introspection of the famous words (later in act 2) about the chariot of destiny. In act 4, confronting Alba, who has secretly prepared his arrest, he touches upon issues still fundamental to political discourse and expounds a vision of political and personal liberty that is anything but naive. After the trap is sprung he yields to a final moment of vacillation. Speaking with the last major character who admires and loves him, he is torn between the admission of hopelessness and the flickering of hope. He urges, almost begs Ferdinand to intercede with his father the duke of Alba. And when that light is in turn extinguished, he implores Ferdinand to join forces with those who would support him if they could and march against Alba. Only when that avenue is blocked does he regain his composure and fortitude. This is no simple, uncomplicated personality.

So, as always, Goethe refrains from concealing the lines of contradiction and stress, the fault lines of character. As always, and much more than he is given credit for, he himself supplies the evidence for human flaws and failings, even in his protagonists. This openness gives Goethe's work the plausibility and vividness of life and keeps him from being as blandly Olympian and relentlessly uplifting as many of his admirers seem compelled to claim.

Themes and Motifs

The theme of redeeming illusion is paramount in the structure of Goethe's major plays. Yet it is only one of a considerable number that, taken together, help to define the substance of the three works presented here. Some have already been touched on: the pairing of the single-minded practical man with the complex "visionary"; the essential role of women; the contagion of goodness. There is more to say on all of these.

The saving vision has its own special timing, nature, and mechanisms. Some of its features are nearly constant from work to work.

It comes at the point of actual or threatened collapse, when inner conflicts and stresses are no longer bearable, at the point of unconsciousness or its antecedent crisis. It is *not* an epiphany. An epiphany comes as an unanticipated—though welcome—revelation. The Goethean vision is causally and in its consistent elements clearly derived from the protagonist's previous situation and, as it were, addresses that situation point by point. It is often closely associated with sleep and the regeneration sleep offers, literally and by extension symbolically. The reader who knows *Faust II* is familiar with the theme in its highest development. But Egmont is "saved" in his sleep, even though he will die. Not one word in the play touches on the time between the vision and the death. Orestes, too, collapses into sleep and it is in sleep or unconsciousness that his rescue is effected. (Stretching the notion a bit, one could say that Tasso is portrayed as about to fall into the "sleep" of total psychic collapse.)

The importance of both the redeeming illusion and the special mechanisms of its genesis is underscored by the measure of guilt, or the degree of inability to cope with reality, that precedes it and makes the redemptive vision "necessary." For Goethe the need for rescue becomes, as we know, almost a given. Guilt and failure must be, not atoned, but transcended. He proves his case a fortiori by depicting in his plays a virtuoso range of moral trespass. Even without counting *Faust*, the list includes murder; seduction with fatal consequences; hubris; incaution bordering on folly and leading to disaster for others; deceit; disloyalty; and betrayal.

The three plays contribute variously to the sum of these transgressions. To them must be added, in *Iphigenia*, inherited guilt, the guilt that out of the past and into the present burdens Orestes and makes him wish for his own death—at the hand of his sister, which would serve to extend and confirm the awful pattern.

If there is an intended or implied message in all this it is surely that life can go on because guilt can be overcome, but not by "good works" or not by them alone. It is both a hopeful and a seductive message. The only person in three plays who is saved by integrity of purpose and appropriate action is Iphigenia. That such betterment by force of will is the work of a woman is an essential facet in the Goethean pattern. For the men, what it takes is the magical vision, the saving illusion, the miraculous contagion of goodness.

The mental state that leads to impasse, to the point where all this wonderful apparatus must be set in motion, has its own particular symbol: imprisonment. It is astonishing how nearly omnipresent the symbol is. Götz was under house arrest. Egmont was first imprisoned without knowing it (in the interview with Alba), then in prison to be prepared for execution. In fact the whole action of the play can be viewed as a process of ever-tightening constriction, from the openness of the scenes with the commoners and the expansive freedom of Egmont, in love and politics, to the ultimate isolation of the prison cell.

Iphigenia refers to her life in Tauris as a form of imprisonment: "Thoas keeps me here . . . in solemn, holy bonds—of slavery." She begs Diana to save her from this "second death."

Tasso is banished to his quarters on his own recognizance, as we should now put it. He is under no delusion as to his situation: "Here you find your friend in jail," he says to Leonore. Having offended the court by his impetuous embrace of the princess, he waxes paranoid in his verbal assault on Antonio: "Fulfill your office, torture me to death. . . . Be prison keeper, be the torturer."

In *Faust I* it is different. Gretchen is the imprisoned one, and for the crime of infanticide. Faust had once apostrophized Gretchen's bare, cramped room as a blessed and happy prison. Now he can only express pity and frustration (for which he is taunted by Mephistopheles) when he is taken to her real prison by Mephistopheles. When he presses her to escape with him (and Mephistopheles), she rejects such a tainted rescue, which would threaten what remains of her once-innocent soul: "From here to my bed of eternal rest, and not one step beyond."

An interesting sub-chapter of the theme of redemption through visions is the issue of the origin of those visions. Speaking roughly, is the illusion to be seen as something supplied by the author or as something courted and created by the protagonist? Egmont's final vision of Freedom-cum-Clara, a vision that brings him an illusion of rescue and a failed denial of reality, is certainly supplied by his author, not by his own creation or through his own initiative. Granted, he was predisposed to seize upon such consolation, and his dream may be viewed as the glorified embodiment of his hope and desire. But that is at best our own "psychologizing." Consider the opposite pole, the illusion in which Tasso envisions his personal salvation through the uncertain possibility of support and comfort by Antonio. This is a creation of his own will and imagination, in a fully conscious state. He makes his own gesture of faith, just as does Werther in extremis. In most respects, Faust is the ultimate case of authorial benefaction, as he has been the ultimate exemplar of transgression. The case is most subtle in *Iphigenia*. Orestes cannot be said to create the illusion that saves him, because he is unconscious. Yet the illusion is the transference into dream reality of his deepest inner need. In that sense it *is* his own creation, made possible by the reality of Iphigenia's goodness, which embodies and proves the possibility of the very reconciliation and peace for which he yearns. His case is not unlike that of Egmont. What Egmont must transcend is death and the destruction of all his hopes. What Orestes had to transcend was massive guilt and generations of horror. The parallel is not exact; joining the two, however, is a great common denominator: the role of the loving woman.

It is by now abundantly clear that for Goethe the role of woman is special and central, and clear not just because of the last words of his last great play: "Das Ewig-Weibliche zieht uns hinan" (Woman, eternally, shows us the way). Almost from the beginning the only characters who are firm and positive and dependable are women: Elisabeth, Götz's wife, above all; Clara to some degree; Iphigenia with, from this point of view, inconsequential reservations. There is no equivalent in *Tasso*.

This is not to say that the relationship of women to men can be reduced to a simplistic statement. Its pattern is highly complex, and its elements may veer off in unexpected directions. Thematic in Goethe's works is the predicament of women under pressure: induced compliance, seduction, force. Again the sequence starts with *Götz*. Maria, Götz's sister, is virtually under siege by the vacillating and faithless Weislingen (with whom Goethe explicitly identified himself). Under the spell of the expert seductress Adelheid, Weislingen breaks his engagement to Maria. She will marry a much better man. It is important to mention this work not just because, as so often, it starts the chain of themes and motifs that mark the present plays, but because here Goethe made the (auto)-biographical connection so overtly: send a copy of Götz to poor

Friederike, so that she may console herself with the fact that the faithless man (Weislingen) is poisoned. Later he would say, "I had to leave her at a moment when it almost cost her her life."

Egmont makes Clara his (willing) mistress, ignoring the possible consequences for her, which are exhaustively portrayed. In this she is a forerunner of Gretchen.

Iphigenia fears that Thoas will use duress against her: "Would he take me by sheer force from my altar to his bed?" Arcas denies it, but he cites another danger, the king's likely renewal of the sacrifice of strangers. Iphigenia is dealing with a Scythian not yet tempered by her *Humanität*.

Tasso gets into definitive trouble by acting on his delusion (?) that the princess loves him. He suddenly embraces her, a faux pas of great moment in an aristocratic court. She turns him away and flees. (The motif of the woman attracted by adoration, then indignantly rejecting the amatory consequence, is directly paralleled in *Werther*.)

More elusive is the motif of love shunted off to the surrogate domain of father or brother. Poor Brackenburg, hopelessly in love with Clara, is told to content himself with being loved as a brother. On top of that, he is assigned the melancholy duty of taking care of Clara's mother after Clara is gone. It is no impiety to suggest that this has a touch of the contrived or unintentionally amusing about it. The themes and motifs of even the greatest writers occasionally go off on their own. Even Iphigenia tries to console Thoas by proposing that he be her surrogate father: "Dear to me and valued as my father was, so are you now."

To speculate on what such patterns imply as to Goethe's own sexuality would be a venture into tabloid psychohistory, except for the evidence of some of the poems and of the curious play *Brother and Sister* (1776). Nicholas Boyd and, more assertively, Kurt Eisler (*Goethe: A Psychoanalytical Study*) have a great deal to say about such matters.

The frequently noted pairing of the active with the contemplative person, or better, of the visionary personality with the practical, is also far from formulaic. With Egmont-Orange and Pylades-Orestes the differentiation seems straightforward. Egmont, the man with the *Daemon*, would have been better off to have followed the advice of Orange. Here the cautious but highly perceptive practical man is, in an ordinary view, right. To abandon the historical time frame for a moment: if we were to choose a leader we would do well to choose a man like Orange. Consider, however, the implications of the path offered by Pylades. Ostensibly the obvious and sensible course, it would surely lead to disaster. In fact, it almost does. The end point of Pylades's carefully calculated deception is war and death. One might argue that without Iphigenia's unwillingness to play the game of deceit, Pylades's well intentioned and well engineered plan might have succeeded. This is obviously speculation beyond the borders of the play, but it is relevant and justified because it is debated in the play. And the fact is that Pylades knew well enough what Iphigenia was like and—as at one point he admits—ought to have taken her special nature into account. This is another "what if" argument and in a sense extraneous to the work, but it is a real part of the motivational structure.

In *Iphigenia,* reconciliation and resolution depend not on the naively aggressive "practical" man so much as on the man who must suffer and almost perish until he is purged of his agony. And that in turn depends on the woman who effects this purgation. It is Orestes who, in his last long speech, puts the case for the liberation of the Greeks. His argument centers on the expiation Iphigenia will be able to accomplish at home *and* on what she has done for the cause of humanity in Tauris as well as for the king: "Repay the blessing she bestowed on you."

One is tempted to say that Antonio is the practical man after the model of Orange and that in "reality" things would have been all right if he could have prevailed, but that is at best a half-truth. For one thing Antonio is, unlike Orange, a flawed personality. He is to some degree a jealous man, aggressive and overbearing, envious of Tasso's talent. Certainly Tasso is not the sort of man to whom one would trust the welfare of the state, or even of one's household. But before Antonio could become Tasso's last hope, the "rock" to which Tasso will cling lest he founder, he has had to be chastened by Leonore and ultimately set straight by Alfonso.

In sum, the only wise, honest, effective "practical man" in the plays, the only one who can offer sound counsel, is Orange. The other counterpart figures are variously flawed and offer mixed blessings. A world of Wagners (*Faust*) would be honest and sincere enough but officiously circumscribed and boring to the point of pain; a world of men like Pylades, unpredictable and dangerous; a world of Antonios, unstable unless its leader were duly constrained—then, to be sure, decent and reliable.

The dichotomy of practical man and visionary finds a striking "diagnostic" summation and an implied resolution in the words of Leonore as she speaks of Tasso and Antonio:

> Who must be enemies because great Nature
> Did not form one man from the two of them.

The implied resolution is nowhere better resolved than in Goethe's own life.

At the end of this treatment of recurrent features we must add an element that may disturb the modern reader. The Goethe we see in life and writings is an unrepentant aristocrat, an elitist. He is interested primarily in persons of substance and stature, moving in a world of great decisions. That in real life he found this world in a small German principality may seem a bit odd. But Weimar really grew to be a sort of Ferrara, an extraordinary center of culture, the home not only of Goethe but also of Wieland, Herder, and (in Jena) Schiller, in other words of four of the five stars in the cultural firmament of German "Classicism." Much of this was Goethe's doing.

Goethe remained firm in the belief that the benevolent absolutism embodied in Weimar was the best form of government, and he conceived his major works against that backdrop. Characters from the middle and lower classes, the likes of which populate the histories of Shakespeare, abound in *Götz*. But they occur, among our plays, only in *Egmont*. It is the earliest of the three, and in this and other respects it reflects the tradition of Sturm und Drang, with its interest in the "little man," his life, and his problems. Still, the center of gravity in *Egmont* has moved from the broader spectrum to the higher reaches. The characters of *Iphigenia* are conceived on the grandest possible scale, those of *Tasso* are the members of a ruling caste. (Tasso, to be sure, is of humble origin.) It is hard to make Goethe into a democrat, although it has been tried. The texts say otherwise. Egmont's first words in the play are frankly suppressive of any objection to the status quo, and the status quo is pretty bad. To the restive citizens he says, "Peace! Peace! good people. . . . Disperse and go about your business. . . . An honest citizen who provides for himself, honorably and industriously, has as much freedom as he needs anywhere." There is no use being alienated by this. It is Goethe's personal stance, and we are likely to disagree with it. But it detracts very little from the profundity of his depiction of the human condition.

Finally, a word on another kind of motif: what might be called a negative occurrence. What is not there is often as interesting as what is—only more difficult to notice. If all we read were *Iphigenia* and *Tasso,* for example, we would probably be struck by the fact that there is hardly a commoner present. Other lacunae suggest themselves, but the reader may want to discover them on his own. Perhaps the most generalized non-occurring element in Goethe's work is an overt or explicit "message." His works do not teach, though we may learn from them. At the opposite pole are genres such as socialist realism. A more substantial and more nearly universal non-occurrence is, as has been touched on before, the tragic ending, or at least the unmitigated loss of the central figure. This lacuna is highly specific to Goethe and sets him apart from most of our great writers.

A final caveat: it has been clear that this introduction does not hestiate to relate characters and situations in drama to life as we live it. This can of course be overdone. A character in literature is not a real person. He exists in and is to some degree defined by elements of structure, symbol, metaphor, motif. (We have touched on such matters.) But if writers did not wish us to see their characters in terms of our reality, they would not—this is more than just facetious—bother to give them names. Nor would they make them act like people. To deny the "relevance" of literary figures and situations, to avoid learning from them, is to reduce the study of literature to an artificial and bloodless exercise. The claim of relevance does not mean that anyone can tell precisely what Goethe meant by *Egmont* or *Iphigenia* or *Tasso,* or what we should learn from them. Readers will judge for themselves the bearing of the plays on their own experience.

A Final Note

The texts are not provided with footnotes. The story of the House of Atreus is fully recounted by Iphigenia. Footnoting of the historical background of *Egmont* would only mean explaining the liberties Goethe took with history. *Tasso* is self-contained; Ferrara, Florence, and the Medicis can all be looked up in reference works.

In translating *Iphigenia* I have avoided the regularity of German iambs, preferring to take advantage of the many freedoms of English blank verse. The play seems to me stronger this way. With *Tasso* I have largely held to more regular meter.

In the adaptation of Anna Swanwick's prose and of Charles Passage's verse, much liberty has been taken, especially in eliminating archaisms and artificial inversions. However, long segments of both translations are not merely accurate, they are effective and eloquent, and more than deserving of retention. Extensive checking confirms that Swanwick's work is in the public domain. Copyright to Passage's resides with the publisher of the present volume, whose permission is gratefully acknowledged.

In the introduction, citations of verse passages have been run on without the use of virgules to separate lines.

F. G. R.

EGMONT

CAST OF CHARACTERS

Margaret of Parma, daughter of Charles V, king of Spain; Regent
  of the Netherlands
Count Egmont, Prince of Gaure
William of Orange
Duke of Alba
Ferdinand, his natural son
Machiavelli, on the staff of the Regent
Richard, Egmont's private secretary
Silva and Gomez, in service to the Duke of Alba
Clara, Egmont's beloved
Clara's mother
Brackenburg, a young man of the middle class
Soest, a shopkeeper; Jetter, a tailor; a master carpenter; a
  soapboiler—all citizens of Brussels
Buyck, a soldier in Egmont's command
Ruysum, a veteran and hard of hearing
Vansen, a clerk
Citizens, retainers, guards, etc.

The action takes place in Brussels.

Act 1

Crossbow competition.
Soldiers *and* Citizens, *with crossbows;*
Jetter, *citizen of Brussels,* tailor,
steps forward and bends his crossbow;
Soest, *citizen of Brussels,* shopkeeper.

SOEST: Come on now, shoot, and get it over with! You won't beat me! Three black rings—you never made a shot like that in all your life. And so I guess I'm master for this year.

JETTER: Master and king to boot; who's jealous? You'll have to pay double the tab; it's only fair you should pay for your skill.

Buyck (from Holland, soldier under Egmont).

BUYCK: Jetter, I'll buy your turn from you, share the prize, and treat the company. I've already been here so long, and I'm in your debt for so many courtesies. If I miss, we'll just say it was your shot.

SOEST: I ought to get a word in, in fact I'll be the loser. No matter! Come on, Buyck, shoot.

BUYCK (*shoots*): Now, Corporal, look out!—One! Two! Three! Four!

SOEST: Four rings? So be it!

ALL: Hurrah! Long live the King! Hurrah! Hurrah!

BUYCK: Thanks, sirs, even "master" would be too much! Thanks for the honor.

JETTER: You have no one to thank but yourself.

Ruysum (Frisian, a veteran, hard of hearing).

RUYSUM: Let me tell you!—

SOEST: How now, graybeard?

RUYSUM: Let me tell you!—He shoots like his master, he shoots like Egmont.

BUYCK: Compared with him, I'm only a poor bungler. He aims and hits with the rifle like no one else in the world. Not only when he's lucky or in the mood; no! he levels and it's in the black. I've learned from him. Any fellow who could serve under him and learn nothing would really have to be a blockhead!—But, sirs, let's not forget! A king provides for his followers; and so, bring wine and charge it to the King!

JETTER: We've agreed among ourselves that each—

BUYCK: I'm a foreigner and a king, and I don't worry about your laws and customs.

JETTER: Why, you're worse than the Spaniards; they haven't dared meddle with them yet.

RUYSUM: What does he say?

SOEST *(loud to Ruysum):* He wants to treat us; he won't hear of our clubbing together, and the King paying only a double share.

RUYSUM: Let him! But under protest! It's his master's fashion, too, to be generous and let the money flow in a good cause. *(Wine is brought.)*

ALL: Here's to His Majesty! Hurrah!

JETTER *(to Buyck):* That means *Your* Majesty, of course.

BUYCK: My hearty thanks, if that's how it is.

SOEST: Indeed! A Netherlander doesn't find it easy to drink the health of His Spanish Majesty—and do so from his heart.

RUYSUM: Who?

SOEST *(aloud):* Philip the Second, King of Spain.

RUYSUM: Our most gracious King and master! Long life to him!

SOEST: Didn't you like his father, Charles the Fifth, better?

RUYSUM: God bless him! He was a real king! His hand reached over the whole earth, and he was all in all. Yet, when he met you, he'd greet you just as one neighbor greets another—and if you were frightened, he knew so well how to put you at your ease—understand me—he'd go out walking or riding, just as it came into his head, with very few followers. We all wept when he resigned the government here to his son. Understand me—he is another sort of man, he's more majestic.

JETTER: When he was here, he never appeared in public, except in pomp and royal state. He doesn't talk much, they say.

SOEST: He's no king for us Netherlanders. Our princes must be happy and free like ourselves, live and let live. We'll neither be despised nor oppressed, good-natured fools though we be.

JETTER: The King, I think, would be a gracious sovereign, if only he had better counsellors.

SOEST: No, no! He has no affection for us Netherlanders; he has no heart for the people; he doesn't love us; how can we love him? Why is everybody so fond of Count Egmont? Why are we all so devoted to him? Why, because we can read in his face that he loves us; because happiness, openheartedness, and good nature, speak in his eyes; because he possesses nothing that he doesn't share with anyone who needs it—and with anyone who doesn't need it. Long live Count Egmont! Buyck, it's for you to give the first toast! Give us your master's health.

BUYCK: With all my heart; here's to Count Egmont! Hurrah!

RUYSUM: Conqueror of St. Quentin.

BUYCK: The hero of Gravelines.

ALL: Hurrah!

RUYSUM: St. Quentin was my last battle. I could hardly move, could hardly carry my heavy rifle. I still managed to singe the skin of the French once more, and as a parting gift I got a shot that grazed my right leg.

BUYCK: Gravelines! Ha, my friends, we had a time of it there! The victory was all ours. Didn't those French dogs carry fire and desolation into the very heart of Flanders? But I tell you, we gave it to them! Their tough old veterans held out bravely for a while, but we pushed on, fired away, and laid about us, till they screwed up their faces in pain, and their lines gave way. Then Egmont's horse was shot out from under him; and for a long time we fought back and forth, man to man, horse against horse, troop with troop, on the broad, flat sea-sand. Suddenly down it came as if from heaven, from the mouth of the river, boom, boom, one cannon shot after the other right into the midst of the French. They were English under Admiral Malin, who happened to be sailing past from Dunkirk. They didn't help us much, it's true; they could only approach with their smallest vessels, and that not near enough—besides, their shots sometimes fell among our troops. Still it helped, it broke the French lines, and raised our courage. On it went, helter-skelter! back and forth!

all struck down, or forced into the river; the fellows were drowned the moment they tasted the water, while we, being Hollanders, dashed in after them. Now, since we're amphibious, we really felt at home, like frogs, and hacked away at the enemy, and shot them down as if they'd been ducks. The few who struggled through were struck dead in their flight by peasant women, armed with hoes and pitchforks. His Gallic majesty was compelled at once to humble himself, and make peace; and that peace you owe to us, to the great Egmont.

ALL: Hurrah, for the great Egmont! Hurrah! Hurrah!

JETTER: If only they'd appointed *him* Regent, instead of Margaret of Parma!

SOEST: Not so! Truth is truth! I'll not hear Margaret abused. Now it's my turn. Long live our gracious lady!

ALL: Long life to her!

SOEST: Truly, there are excellent women in that family. Long live the Regent!

JETTER: She is prudent and moderate in all she does; if only she wouldn't stick so closely to the priests. It's partly her fault, too, that we have the fourteen new bishop's mitres in the land. What use are they, I'd like to know? Why, so that foreigners may be shoved into the good benefices, where formerly abbots were chosen out of the chapters! And we're to believe it's for the sake of religion. We know better. Three bishops were enough for us; things went decently and honorably. Now each one must act as if he were needed; and this gives rise to dissensions and ill will at every point. And the more you rattle and shake things, the worse it gets. *(They drink.)*

SOEST: But it was the will of the King; she can't change it, one way or another.

JETTER: And then we mustn't even sing the new psalms; and they're so beautifully rhymed and the tunes are truly inspiring. We're not supposed to sing them, but vulgar songs, as many as we please. And why? There's heresy in them, they say, and heaven knows what. But, I've sung some of them; they are something new, to be sure, but I see no harm in them.

BUYCK: I'm not about to ask their leave! In our province we sing what we please. That's because Count Egmont is our provincial governor and he doesn't trouble himself about such matters. In Ghent, Ypres, and through the whole of Flanders, anybody sings them that wants to. *(Aloud to Ruysum)* There's nothing more harmless than a spiritual song. Is there, Father?

RUYSUM: Indeed, that's true. It's a godly work, and truly edifying.

JETTER: But they say that they're not the right sort, not their sort, and, since it *is* dangerous, we had better leave them alone. The officers of the Inquisition are always lurking about and spying, and many an honest fellow has already met his fate. They haven't yet gone so far as to meddle with conscience. If they won't allow me to do what I like, they might at least let me think and sing as I please.

SOEST: The Inquisition won't succeed here. We are not made like the Spaniards, to let our consciences be tyrannized over. The nobles must look to it, and clip its wings.

JETTER: It is a great bore. If it occurs to our dear friends to break into my house, and I'm sitting there at my work, humming a French psalm, thinking nothing about it, neither good nor bad, singing it just because it's in my throat—immediately I'm a heretic, and I'm clapped into prison. Or if I'm passing through the country, and stand near a crowd listening to a new preacher, one of those who've come from Germany, instantly I'm called a rebel, and I'm in danger of losing my head! Have you ever heard one of these preachers?

SOEST: Brave fellows! Not long ago, I heard one of them preach in a field, before thousands and thousands of people. He served up a different sort of dish from our preachers, who drum about the pulpit and choke their listeners with scraps of Latin. He spoke from his heart; told us how, till now, we'd been led around by the nose, how we'd been kept in darkness, and how we might get more light—and he proved it all out of the Bible.

JETTER: There may be something in it. I always said as much and I've often pondered the matter. It's been running through my head for a long time.

BUYCK: All the people chase after them.

SOEST: No wonder, when they can hear something good and something new as well.

JETTER: And what's it all about? Surely they might let every one preach after his own fashion.

BUYCK: Come, sirs! While you're talking you forget the wine and the Prince of Orange.

JETTER: We must not forget him. He's a regular wall. Just thinking of him, you fancy that you could just hide behind him, and the devil himself couldn't get at you. Here's to William of Orange! Hurrah!

ALL: Hurrah! Hurrah!

SOEST: Now, graybeard, let's have your toast.

RUYSUM: Here's to old soldiers! To all soldiers! War forever!

BUYCK: Bravo, old fellow! Here's to all soldiers! War forever!

JETTER: War! War! Do you know what you're shouting about? That it should slip easily from your lips is natural enough; but what wretched work it is for us. I have no words to tell you. To listen the whole year round to the beating of the drum; to hear nothing except how one troop marched here, and another there; how they came over this height, and halted near that mill; how many were left dead on this field, and how many on that; how they both pressed forward, and how one wins, and another loses, without anyone's being able to understand what they're fighting about; how a town is taken, how the citizens are put to the sword, and how it fares with the poor women and innocent children. It makes you fear and tremble, thinking every moment: "Here they come! It will be our turn next."

SOEST: That's why every citizen must be practiced in the use of arms.

JETTER: Practice, indeed, for him who has a wife and children. Yet I would rather hear of soldiers than see them.

BUYCK: I should take offense at that.

JETTER: It was not intended for you, countryman. When we got rid of the Spanish garrison, we breathed freely again.

SOEST: They pressed on you heavy enough, right?

JETTER: Mind your own business.

SOEST: Pretty sharp being quartered with you.

JETTER: Hold your tongue.

SOEST: They drove him out of kitchen, cellar, chamber—and bed.
(*They laugh*)

JETTER: You're a blockhead.

BUYCK: Peace, sirs! Must the soldier cry peace? Since you don't want to hear anything of us, let's have a toast of your own—a citizen's toast.

JETTER: We're all ready for that! Safety and peace!

SOEST: Freedom and order!

BUYCK: Bravo! We're happy with that too.

(They ring their glasses together, and joyously repeat the words, but in such a manner that each utters a different sound, and it becomes a kind of canon; the old man listens, and at length joins in.)

ALL: Safety and peace! Freedom and order!

> *Palace of the Regent.*
> *Margaret of Parma, in hunting dress;*
> *Courtiers, Pages, Servants.*

REGENT: You will put off the hunt, I shall not ride today. Tell Machiavelli to report to me. *(Exeunt all but the Regent.)*

The thought of these terrible events leaves me no repose! Nothing can amuse me, nothing can divert my mind. These images, these worries are always before me. Now the King will say that these are the natural fruits of my kindness, of my clemency; yet my conscience assures me at every moment that I have adopted the best and most prudent course. Ought I rather to have fanned these flames and spread them abroad with the breath of my wrath? My hope was to contain them, to let them smoulder in their own ashes. Yes, what I tell myself and what I know to be true justifies my conduct in my own eyes, but in what light will it appear to my brother? Can it be denied that the insolence of these foreign teachers has grown by the day? They have desecrated our sanctuaries, unsettled the dull minds of the people, and conjured up among them the spell of delusion. Impure spirits have mingled among the insurgents, deeds horrible to think of have been perpetrated, and of these a detailed account must be transmitted instantly to court. My communication must be prompt and detailed lest rumor outrun my messenger and the King suspect that even more has been purposely withheld. I can see no means, severe or mild, by which to stem the evil. Oh, what are we of great power on the billows of human life? We think we control them, and they toss us up and down, back and forth.

(Enter Machiavelli.)

REGENT: Are the dispatches to the King prepared?

MACHIAVELLI: In an hour they will be ready for your signature.

REGENT: Have you made the report sufficiently extensive?

MACHIAVELLI: Extensive and circumstantial, as the King loves to have it. I relate how the rage of the iconoclasts first broke out at St. Omer. How a furious multitude, with stones, hatchets, hammers, ladders, and cords, accompanied by a few armed men, first assailed the chapels, churches, and convents, drove out the worshipers, forced the barred gates, threw everything into confusion, tore down the altars, destroyed the statues of the saints, defaced the pictures, and smashed and tore and trampled underfoot whatever came in their way that was consecrated and holy. How the crowd increased as it advanced, and how the inhabitants of Ypres opened their gates at its approach. How, with incredible rapidity, they laid waste to the cathedral, and burned the library of the bishop. How a vast multitude, possessed by the same frenzy, spread out through Menin, Comines, Verviers, Lille, encountering opposition nowhere; and how, through almost the whole of Flanders, in a single moment the monstrous conspiracy broke forth, and accomplished its objective.

REGENT: Alas! With your recital I am seized again by the grief I felt, and added to it is the fear that the evil will only increase. Tell me your thoughts, Machiavelli!

MACHIAVELLI: Pardon me, Your Highness, my thoughts will seem like idle fancies; and though you were always satisfied with my services, you have seldom felt inclined to follow my advice. How often you have said in jest: "You see too far, Machiavelli! You should be a historian; he who acts must provide for the immediate moment." And yet, didn't I recite this history before it happened? Have I not foreseen it all?

REGENT: I too can foresee many things without being able to avert them.

MACHIAVELLI: One word in lieu of a thousand, then:—you will not be able to suppress the new faith. Let it be recognized, separate its followers from the true believers, give them churches of their own, include them within the social order, place limits on them—do this, and you will at once quiet the insurgents. All other measures will prove abortive, and you will devastate the country.

REGENT: Have you forgotten with what aversion my brother rejected the mere suggestion of tolerating the new doctrine? Have you forgotten how in every letter he urgently recommends to me the upholding of the true faith? That he will not hear of tranquillity and order being restored at the expense of religion? Even in the provinces, does he not maintain spies, unknown to us, in order to ascertain who inclines to the new doctrines? Has he not, to our astonishment, named to us this or that individual, in close proximity to us, who secretly incurred the charge of heresy? Does he not enjoin harshness and severity? And I am to be lenient? I am to recommend for his adoption measures of indulgence and toleration? Would I not lose all his faith and confidence?

MACHIAVELLI: I know it. The King commands and puts you in full possession of his intentions. You are to restore tranquillity and peace by measures which will embitter men's minds, and which will inevitably kindle the flames of war from one end of the country to the other. Consider what you are doing. The principal merchants are infected—nobles, citizens, soldiers. What good is it, persisting in one's opinion, when everything is changing around us? If only some good genius would make Philip see that it better becomes a monarch to govern subjects of two different creeds, than to excite them to mutual destruction!

REGENT: Never let me hear such words again. I know full well that politics can rarely maintain truth and fidelity; that it excludes from our heart candor, charity, toleration. In secular affairs, this is, alas! only too true; but shall we trifle with God as we do with each other? Shall we be indifferent to our established faith, for the sake of which so many have sacrificed their lives? We are to abandon it to these vagrant, obscure, and self-contradicting heresies?

MACHIAVELLI: Don't think the worse of me for what I've said.

REGENT: I know you and your fidelity, and I know that a man may be both honest and wise, even though he has missed the best and nearest way to the salvation of his soul. There are others, Machiavelli, men whom I esteem, yet with whom I must find fault.

MACHIAVELLI: To whom do you refer?

REGENT: I must confess that Egmont caused me deep and heartfelt annoyance today.

MACHIAVELLI: How so?

REGENT: By his usual demeanor, his indifference and levity. I received the terrible news as I was leaving church, attended by him and several others. I did not restrain my anguish, I complained aloud and, turning to him, exclaimed, "See what's happening in your province! And you tolerate this, Count, you, in whom the King placed such high hopes?"

MACHIAVELLI: And what was his reply?

REGENT: As if it were nothing, a secondary matter, he answered: "If only the Netherlanders were satisfied as to their constitution, the rest would soon follow."

MACHIAVELLI: There was perhaps more truth than discretion or piety in his words. How can we hope to acquire and maintain the confidence of the Netherlander, when he sees that we are more interested in his possessions than in his welfare, temporal or spiritual? Does the number of souls saved by the new bishops exceed that of the fat benefices they have swallowed up? And are they not for the most part foreigners? As yet, the office of provincial governor has been held by Netherlanders; but do not the Spaniards betray all too clearly their great and irresistible desire for these positions? Will people not prefer being governed by their own countrymen, in their own fashion, rather than by foreigners who, from their first entrance into the land, seek to acquire possessions at everyone else's expense, who bring with them foreign standards, and who exercise their authority in a hostile fashion, without sympathy?

REGENT: You side with our opponents?

MACHIAVELLI: Assuredly not in my heart. I wish that in my mind I could be wholly on our side!

REGENT: If that's what you want, I would be forced to resign the regency to them; for both Egmont and Orange entertained great hopes of occupying this position. Then they were adversaries, now they are leagued against me, and have become friends, inseparable friends.

MACHIAVELLI: A dangerous pair.

REGENT: To speak candidly, I fear Orange—I fear for Egmont—Orange is up to no good; his thoughts are far-reaching, he is secretive, appears to agree to everything, never contradicts, and with the deepest respect and deference, with clear foresight and the greatest caution, accomplishes his own designs.

MACHIAVELLI: Egmont, quite on the contrary, walks with a bold step, as if he owned the world.

REGENT: He bears his head as proudly as if the hand of majesty were not suspended over him.

MACHIAVELLI: The eyes of the people are fixed upon him, and he is the idol of their hearts.

REGENT: He has never avoided giving the impression that no one had a right to call him to account. He still bears the name of Egmont. Count Egmont is the title by which he loves to hear himself addressed, as though he did not wish to forget that his ancestors were masters of Guelderland. Why does he not assume his proper title, Prince of Gaure? Why does he do that? Does he want to revive antiquated claims?

MACHIAVELLI: I consider him a faithful servant of the King.

REGENT: If he were so inclined, how essential he could be to the government; whereas now, without benefiting himself, he has caused us unspeakable vexation. His banquets and entertainments have done more to unite the nobles and to knit them together than the most dangerous secret meetings. With his toasts, his guests have got themselves into a permanent state of intoxication, a giddiness that never subsides. How often have his jesting words stirred up the minds of the populace? And how startled the mob was by the new livery and the extravagant insignia of his followers!

MACHIAVELLI: I am convinced there was no intent behind it.

REGENT: Bad enough! It's as I say, he injures us without benefiting himself. He treats serious matters as a jest, and not to appear negligent and remiss, we are forced to treat his jests seriously. Thus one incites the other; and what we are trying to avert happens all the sooner. He is more dangerous than the acknowledged head of a conspiracy; and I am much mistaken if it is not all remembered against him at court. I cannot deny that scarcely a day passes in which he does not trouble me, deeply trouble me.

MACHIAVELLI: He appears to me to act in all matters according to the dictates of his conscience.

REGENT: His conscience has a convenient mirror. His demeanor is often offensive. He often looks as if he were completely convinced that he is the master here, and were restrained by courtesy alone from making us feel it; as if he would not exactly drive us out of the country—there'll be no need for that.

MACHIAVELLI: I beg you, don't interpret as dangerous his open

and joyous temper, which treats lightly all matters of importance. You only injure yourself and him.

REGENT: I interpret nothing. I speak only of inevitable consequences, and I know him. His patent of Netherlandic nobility,
and the Golden Fleece upon his breast, strengthen his confidence,
his audacity. Both can protect him against any sudden, capricious outbreak of royal displeasure. Examine the matter closely,
and he alone is responsible for all the misfortune that is afflicting
Flanders. From the first, he tolerated the foreign teachers, didn't
take a very serious view of things, and perhaps rejoiced in secret
that they kept us so busy. Don't stop me! This is my chance to
be freed of what weighs on my heart. I will not shoot my arrows
in vain. I know where he is vulnerable. For he is vulnerable.

MACHIAVELLI: Have you summoned the council? Will Orange
attend?

REGENT: I have sent for him, to Antwerp. I will lay upon their
shoulders the burden of responsibility; they shall join with me
in serious measures to quell the evil, or declare themselves as
rebels too. Let the letters be completed without delay, and bring
them for my signature. Then hasten to dispatch our trusty Vasca
to Madrid; he is loyal and tireless; let him use all diligence to
see that my brother receives the intelligence first through him,
so that he may not be anticipated by common report. I will speak
with him myself before he departs.

MACHIAVELLI: Your orders shall be obeyed quickly and precisely.

Citizen's house.
(Clara, her Mother, Brackenburg.)

CLARA: Won't you hold the yarn for me, Brackenburg?

BRACKENBURG: I beg you, excuse me, Clara.

CLARA: What ails you? Why refuse me this little service of love?

BRACKENBURG: When I hold the yarn, I stand before you, spell-
bound, and cannot escape your eyes.

CLARA: Nonsense! Come and hold!

MOTHER (*in her armchair, knitting*): Give us a song! Brackenburg
sings such a good tenor. You used to be so merry once, and I
always had something to laugh at.

BRACKENBURG: Once!

CLARA: Let's sing.

BRACKENBURG: As you please.

CLARA: Let's be nice and cheerful, then, and here we go! It's a soldier's song, my favorite.

(She winds yarn, and sings with Brackenburg.)

> Now beat the drums loudly
> And let the pipes play!
> My love in his armor
> Holds all in his sway.
> He lifts his lance proudly
> And leads his men boldly.
> I feel my heart beating,
> My blood is on fire.
> Oh, give me a helmet,
> A soldier's attire!
>
> I'd leave the gates with him,
> My step would be strong.
> We'd ride every province,
> And I'd ride along.
> The foe is retreating;
> We shoot as they flee.
> What joy without equal
> A man's life would be!

(During the singing Brackenburg has frequently looked at Clara; at length his voice falters, his eyes fill with tears, he lets the skein fall and goes to the window; Clara finishes the song alone; her mother motions to her, half-displeased; she rises, advances a few steps toward him, turns back as if irresolute, and again sits down.)

MOTHER: What's going on in the street, Brackenburg? I hear soldiers marching.

BRACKENBURG: It's the Regent's bodyguard.

CLARA: At this hour? What can it mean! *(She rises and joins Brackenburg at the window.)* That's not the daily guard; there are too many of them, almost all the troops! Oh, Brackenburg, do go! Find out what it means. It must be something unusual. Go, dear Brackenburg, do me this favor.

BRACKENBURG: I'm going! I'll return immediately.

(As he leaves, he offers his hand to Clara, and she gives him hers.)

MOTHER: You're sending him away so soon!

CLARA: I'm curious; and, besides—don't be angry, mother—his presence pains me. I never know how I ought to behave towards him. I've done him a wrong, and it goes to my heart to see how deeply he feels it. Well, it can't be changed now!

MOTHER: He is such a loyal fellow!

CLARA: I can't help it, I have to treat him with kindness. Often, without thinking, I return the gentle, loving pressure of his hand. I reproach myself that I'm deceiving him, that I'm nourishing in his heart a vain hope. I feel very bad. God knows, I don't mean to deceive him. I don't wish him to hope, yet I still can't let him despair!

MOTHER: That's not as it should be.

CLARA: I liked him once, and in my soul I like him still. I could have married him, yet I believe I was never really in love with him.

MOTHER: You would always have been happy with him.

CLARA: I would have been provided for, and would have led a quiet life.

MOTHER: And it's your fault that it's all been trifled away.

CLARA: I'm in a strange position. When I think how it's come to pass, I know—and I don't know. But I only need to look at Egmont, and it's all perfectly clear. I understand it all; yes, and even more than that would still seem understandable. Oh, what a man he is. All the provinces worship him. And in his arms—do you think I wouldn't be the happiest creature in the world?

MOTHER: And how will it be in the future?

CLARA: I only ask, does he love me? And is there any doubt about that?

MOTHER: One has nothing but anxiety with one's children. Always care and sorrow! How will it all end? It can come to no good! Alas, you've made yourself unhappy! You've made me unhappy too.

CLARA *(quietly):* Yet you allowed it in the beginning.

MOTHER: Alas, I was too indulgent, I'm always too indulgent.

CLARA: When Egmont rode by, and I ran to the window, did you rebuke me then? Didn't you come to the window yourself? When he looked up and smiled and nodded and greeted me—did it displease you? Didn't you feel honored in your daughter?

MOTHER: Go on, reproach me.

CLARA *(with emotion):* When he passed by more frequently, and we felt sure that it was on my account that he came this way, didn't you notice it yourself, and secretly enjoy it? Did you call me away when I stood at the window waiting for him?

MOTHER: Could I imagine that it would go so far?

CLARA *(with faltering voice and repressed tears):* And then, in the evening, when he came, wrapped in his mantle, and surprised us as we sat at our lamp—who was so busy receiving him, while I remained lost in astonishment, as if I were chained to my chair?

MOTHER: Could I imagine that my prudent Clara would be carried away so soon by this unhappy love? I must now face the fact that my daughter—

CLARA *(bursting into tears):* Mother! How can you? You take pleasure in tormenting me.

MOTHER *(weeping):* Weep—on top of everything else! Make me even more wretched by your grief. Isn't it misery enough that my only daughter is disgraced?

CLARA *(rising, and speaking coldly):* Disgraced? Egmont's lover disgraced?—What princess wouldn't envy poor little Clara her place in his heart? Oh, Mother,—my own mother, you never used to talk like this! Dear mother, be kind! Whatever people think, whatever the neighbors whisper—this room, this little house is a paradise since Egmont's love has been part of it.

MOTHER: One can't help liking him, that's true. He's always so friendly and frank and openhearted.

CLARA: There's not a drop of false blood in his body. And yet, Mother, he's still the great Egmont; but when he comes to me, how gentle and kind he is! How gladly he would conceal from me his rank, his bravery! How anxious he is about me! so purely and completely the man, the friend, the lover.

MOTHER: Do you expect him today?

CLARA: Haven't you noticed how often I go to the window? How I listen to every noise at the door? Though I know that he won't come before nightfall, still from the time when I rise in the morning, I keep expecting him at any moment. If only I were a boy, to follow him always, to court and everywhere! If only I could carry his colors on the battlefield!

MOTHER: You were always such a lively, restless creature; even as a little child, sometimes wild, sometimes pensive. Won't you try to dress a little better?

CLARA: Perhaps I may, if I get bored. Yesterday, imagine, some of his people went by, singing songs in his honor. At least, his name was in the songs! I couldn't understand the rest. My heart leaped into my throat—I would have liked to call them back if I had not been ashamed.

MOTHER: Take care! Your impetuous nature may still spoil everything. You obviously give yourself away before people; as you did, not long ago, at your cousin's, when you found the woodcut with the inscription and exclaimed with a cry: "Count Egmont!"—I turned as red as fire.

CLARA: Shouldn't I have cried out? It was the battle of Gravelines, and at the top of the picture I found the letter C and then looked for it in the inscription below. There it was: "Count Egmont, with his horse shot from under him." I shuddered, and afterwards I couldn't help laughing at the woodcut figure of Egmont, as tall as the tower of Gravelines right beside him, and the English ships at the side.—When I remember sometimes how I used to picture battles, and what an idea I had, as a girl, of Count Egmont, when I listened to people talking about him, and about all the other counts and princes;—and think how it is with me now!

Enter Brackenburg.

CLARA: Well, what's going on?

BRACKENBURG: Nobody knows for sure. It's rumored that an insurrection has recently broken out in Flanders; they say the Regent is afraid of its spreading here. The castle is strongly garrisoned, the citizens are crowding around the gates, and the streets are buzzing with people. I just want to hurry and be with my old father. (*As if about to go.*)

CLARA: Shall we see you tomorrow? I want to dress up a little. I'm expecting my cousin, and I really look too shabby. Mother, help me a moment. Take the book with you, Brackenburg, and bring me another story like that.

MOTHER: Farewell.

BRACKENBURG (*extending his hand*): Your hand!

CLARA (*refusing hers*): When you come again.

(*Exeunt Mother and Daughter*)

BRACKENBURG *(alone):* I had resolved to go away again at once, and yet, when she takes me at my word and lets me leave, I feel as if I could go mad.—What a wretched man you are! And the fate of your fatherland, the growing turmoil doesn't move you?—And countryman and Spaniard—are they the same to you?—Don't you care who rules, and who's in the right?—I was a different sort of fellow as a schoolboy!—Then, when an essay was assigned, "Brutus's Speech for Liberty, an Exercise in Rhetoric" for instance, Fritz was always the first, and the rector would say: "If it were only more orderly, the words not stumbling all over one another."—Then my blood boiled, and I longed for action.—Now I just drag along, bound by the eyes of this girl. I still cannot leave her! She still cannot love me!—ah—no—she—she can't have rejected me entirely—not entirely—yet half a love is no love!—I can't stand it any longer!—Can it be true, what a friend whispered in my ear recently, that she secretly admits a man into the house by night, when she always sends me away modestly before evening? No, it's not true! It's a lie! A base, slanderous lie! Clara is as innocent as I am wretched.—She has rejected me, thrust me from her heart—and shall I live on this way? I cannot, I will not endure it. Already my native land is convulsed by internal discord, and all I do is wither away abjectly in the midst of all the tumult! I won't endure it! When the trumpet sounds, when a shot falls, it thrills through my bone and marrow! But, alas, it does not rouse me! It does not summon me to join the fray, to rescue, to dare.—Miserable, degrading condition! Better to end it at once! Not long ago, I threw myself into the water; I sank—but nature in her agony was too strong for me; I felt that I could swim, and saved myself against my will. If only I could forget the time when she loved me, seemed to love me!—Why has this happiness suffused my very bone and marrow? Why have these hopes, disclosing to me a distant paradise, consumed all the pleasure in life?—And that first, that only kiss!—Here *(laying his hand upon the table),* here we were alone—she had always been kind and friendly toward me—then she seemed to soften—she looked at me—my brain reeled—I felt her lips on mine—and—and now?—Die, poor man! Why do you hesitate? *(He draws a vial from his pocket.)* Healing poison, I don't want to have stolen you from my brother's medicine chest in vain! You shall free me from this anxious fear, this dizziness, this sweat of death, dissolving and consuming them.

Act 2

Square in Brussels.
(Jetter and a Master Carpenter, meeting.)

CARPENTER: Didn't I predict it? A week ago, at the guild, I said there would be serious trouble.

JETTER: Is it true that they've plundered the churches in Flanders?

CARPENTER: They've completely destroyed churches and chapels. All they've left standing are the four bare walls. They're nothing but rabble! And that damages our good cause. We ought rather to have laid our claims before the Regent, in proper form and with firmness, and then have held to them. If we speak now, if we assemble now, it will be said that we are joining the rebels.

JETTER: Yes, so everyone thinks at first. Why should you thrust your nose into the mess? After all, the nose is very closely connected with the neck.

CARPENTER: I'm always uneasy when disturbances arise among the mob, among people who have nothing to lose. What we ourselves must also appeal to, they use as a pretext, and plunge the country into misery.

(Enter Soest.)

SOEST: Good day, sirs! What news? Is it true that the iconoclasts are coming in this very direction?

CARPENTER: They'll not touch anything here!

SOEST: A soldier came into my shop just now to buy tobacco; I questioned him. This time the Regent, as brave and prudent as she has always been, has for once lost her presence of mind. Things must be really bad when she takes refuge behind her guards. The castle is strongly garrisoned. They even say she means to flee the town.

CARPENTER: She shall not leave! Her presence protects us, and we will ensure her safety better than her mustachioed gentry. If only she maintains our rights and privileges, we will treat her with the greatest care and respect.

(Enter Soapboiler.)

SOAPBOILER: An ugly business this! a bad business! Troubles are beginning; things are going wrong! Mind you keep quiet, or they'll take you for rioters, too.

SOEST: Here come the seven wise men of Greece.

SOAPBOILER: I know there are many who secretly hold with the Calvinists, rail at the bishops, and have no respect for the King. But a loyal subject, a sincere Catholic!—

(Gradually, others join the speakers and listen.)

(Enter Vansen.)

VANSEN: God save you, sirs! What news?

CARPENTER: Have nothing to do with him, he's a bad fellow.

JETTER: Isn't he secretary to Dr. Wiets?

CARPENTER: He's already had several masters. First he was a clerk, and since one patron after another drove him off, what with the tricks he pulled, he now meddles in the business of notaries and advocates and he's a brandy keg to boot.

(More people gather round and stand in groups.)

VANSEN: So here you are, putting your heads together. Well, it is worth talking about.

SOEST: I think so too.

VANSEN: Now if only one of you had the heart and another one the head for it we might break the Spanish chains all at once.

SOEST: Sir! You mustn't talk like that. We have taken our oath to the King.

VANSEN: And the King to us. Mark that!

JETTER: That makes sense! Tell us what you think.

OTHERS: Listen to him; he's a smart fellow. He's very sharp.

VANSEN: I had an old master once who owned some letters and parchments, charters of ancient constitutions, contracts, and privileges. He set great store by the rarest books. One of these contained our whole constitution; how, at first, we Netherlanders had individual princes who governed according to hereditary laws, rights, and usages; how our ancestors paid full honor to their sovereign so long as he governed them the way he ought to, and how they were immediately on their guard the moment he was for overstepping his bounds. The Estates were after him at once; because every province, however small, had its own Parliament.

CARPENTER: Hold your tongue! We knew that long ago! Every honest citizen is as much informed about the constitution as he needs to be.

JETTER: Let him speak; there's always more to be learned.

SOEST: He's quite right.

SEVERAL CITIZENS: Go on! Go on! You don't hear such things every day.

VANSEN: That's just like you citizens! You live only in the present; and just as you tamely follow the trade you inherited from your fathers, so you let the government do with you just as it pleases. You make no inquiry into the origin, the history, or the rights of a Regent; and in consequence of this negligence, the Spaniard has drawn the net over your ears.

SOEST: Who thinks about that, if one only has his daily bread?

JETTER: The devil! Why doesn't someone come forward in time and tell us this?

VANSEN: I'm telling you now. The King of Spain, who by sheer good luck holds sway over the provinces, all of them, has no right to govern them otherwise than the petty princes did, who formerly possessed them separately. Do you understand that?

JETTER: Explain it to us.

VANSEN: Why, it's as clear as the sun. Mustn't you be governed according to your own provincial laws? How does that come about?

A CITIZEN: That's right!

VANSEN: Aren't the laws of Brussels different from those of Antwerp? The laws of Antwerp different from those of Ghent? How does that come about?

ANOTHER CITIZEN: By heaven!

VANSEN: But if you let matters run on like this, they'll soon tell you a different story. Shame on you! Now Philip, through a woman, does what neither Charles the Bold, Frederick the Warrior, nor Charles the Fifth could accomplish.

SOEST: Yes, yes! The old princes tried it too.

VANSEN: But our ancestors kept a sharp lookout. If they developed a grudge against their sovereign, maybe they would get his son and heir into their hands, and surrender him only on the most favorable conditions. Our fathers were real men! They knew where their own interests lay! They knew how to get hold of what they wanted, and to establish it permanently. Real men! And that's why our privileges are so clearly defined, our liberties so well secured.

SOAPBOILER: What are you saying about our liberties?

PEOPLE: Our liberties! Our privileges! Tell us something about our privileges.

VANSEN: All the provinces have their particular advantages, but we of Brabant are the most splendidly provided for. I have read it all.

SOEST: Tell us.

JETTER: Let's hear more.

A CITIZEN: Please do.

VANSEN: First, it's there in writing: The Duke of Brabant shall be to us a kind and faithful sovereign.

SOEST: Kind? Is it so written?

JETTER: Faithful? Is that true?

VANSEN: It's as I tell you. He's bound to us as we are to him. Secondly: not exhibit, or allow the appearance of, or think of permitting the use of force or arbitrary action—not in any way.

JETTER: Bravo! Bravo! Not exert force.

SOEST: Not allow the appearance of it.

ANOTHER: And not think of allowing it to others. That's the main point. Not allow it to anyone, in any way.

VANSEN: In so many words.

JETTER: Get us the book.

A CITIZEN: Yes, we must have it.

OTHERS: The book! The book!

ANOTHER: We will go to the Regent with the book.

ANOTHER: Doctor, you shall be our spokesman.

SOAPBOILER: Oh, the dolts!

OTHERS: Something more out of the book!

SOAPBOILER: I'll knock his teeth down his throat if he says another word.

PEOPLE: We'll see who dares to lay hands on him. Tell us about our privileges! Have we any more privileges?

VANSEN: Many; very good and very wholesome ones too. It's also written; the sovereign shall neither benefit the clergy, nor increase their number, without the consent of the nobles and the

Estates. Mark that! Nor shall he alter the constitution of the country.

SOEST: Is that true?

VANSEN: I'll show it to you—in writing, from two or three centuries ago.

A CITIZEN: And we tolerate the new bishops? The nobles must protect us, or we'll make trouble!

OTHERS: And we allow ourselves to be intimidated by the Inquisition?

VANSEN: It's your own fault.

PEOPLE: We still have Egmont! We still have Orange! They'll protect our interests.

VANSEN: Your brothers in Flanders are beginning the good work.

SOAPBOILER: You dog! *(Strikes him.)*

OTHERS *(oppose the* Soapboiler *and exclaim):* Are you a Spaniard too?

ANOTHER: What! This honorable man?

ANOTHER: This learned man?

(They attack the Soapboiler.)

CARPENTER: For heaven's sake, peace!

(Others mingle in the fray.)

CARPENTER: Citizens, what's the meaning of this?

(Boys whistle, throw stones, set on dogs; citizens stand and gape, people come running up, others walk quietly back and forth, others play all sorts of pranks, shout and cheer.)

OTHERS: Freedom and privileges! Privileges and freedom!

(Enter Egmont, with followers.)

EGMONT: Peace! Peace! Good people. What is the matter? Peace, I say! Separate them.

CARPENTER: My good lord, you come like an angel from heaven. Quiet! Do you see nothing? Count Egmont! Homage to Count Egmont!

EGMONT: Here, too? What are you doing? Citizen against citizen! So near to our royal Regent—and even that can't restrain this madness? Disperse and go about your business. It's a bad sign when you vacation on working days. What was the trouble?

(The tumult gradually subsides, and the people gather around Egmont.)

CARPENTER: They're fighting about their privileges.

EGMONT: Which they'll forfeit yet, through their own folly—and who are you? You seem honest people.

CARPENTER: We try to be.

EGMONT: What's your trade?

CARPENTER: Carpenter, and master of the guild.

EGMONT: And you?

SOEST: Shopkeeper.

EGMONT: And you?

JETTER: Tailor.

EGMONT: I remember, you were one of the workers on my men's livery. Your name is Jetter.

JETTER: To think of Your Grace remembering it!

EGMONT: I don't easily forget anyone I have seen or conversed with. Do what you can, good people, to keep the peace; you stand in bad enough repute already. Don't provoke the King still farther. The power, after all, is in his hands. An honest citizen who provides for himself, honorably and industriously, has as much freedom as he needs anywhere.

CARPENTER: That's just our misfortune! With all due deference, Your Grace, it's the idlers, the drunkards, and vagabonds, who quarrel for want of something to do, and clamor about privileges because they are hungry; they make up lies to impress the curious and the credulous, and in order to get treated to a mug of beer they start trouble that will bring misery upon thousands. That's just what they want. We keep our houses and coffers too well guarded; so they would like to drive us away with firebrands.

EGMONT: You shall have every assistance; forceful measures have been taken to stem the evil. Make a firm stand against the new doctrines, and do not imagine that privileges are secured by sedition. Remain at home, don't let crowds mass in the streets. Sensible people can accomplish much.

(In the meantime the crowd has for the most part dispersed.)

CARPENTER: Thanks, your Excellency—thanks for your good advice. We will do all we can! *(Exit Egmont.)* A gracious lord! A true Netherlander! Nothing of the Spaniard about him.

JETTER: If only we had him for a regent! It would be a pleasure to follow him.

SOEST: The King won't hear of that. He takes care to appoint his own people to the position.

JETTER: Did you notice how he was dressed? It was the newest fashion—the Spanish cut.

CARPENTER: A handsome gentleman.

JETTER: His head would be a dainty morsel for a hangman.

SOEST: Are you mad? What gives you that idea?

JETTER: It's stupid enough that such an idea should come into one's head! But that's the way it is with me. Whenever I see a long handsome neck, I can't help thinking how well it would suit the block. These cursed executions! You can't get them out of your head. When the lads are swimming, and I see a naked back, I immediately think of the dozens I've seen beaten with rods. If I meet a portly gentleman, I imagine I already see him roasting at the stake. At night, in my dreams, I tremble in every limb; one can't have a moment's enjoyment; I've forgotten all amusement and all fun, long since. The most terrible images seem etched on my brow.

Egmont's residence.

(His Secretary at the desk with papers; he rises impatiently.)

SECRETARY: He still doesn't come! And I've been waiting two hours, pen in hand, the papers before me; and just today I was anxious to be out early. The floor burns under my feet. I can hardly stay here, I'm so impatient. "Be there punctually." That was his last command; and now he doesn't come. There is so much business to get through, I won't have finished before midnight. He overlooks one's faults, it's true; I think it would be better, though, if he were more strict, and let one leave at the appointed time. Then one could arrange one's plans. It's now two hours since he left the Regent; who knows whom he's run into on the way?

(Enter Egmont.)

EGMONT: Well, how do things look?

SECRETARY: I am ready, and three couriers are waiting.

EGMONT: I've detained you too long; you look somewhat out of humor.

SECRETARY: In obedience to your command I have already been waiting for some time. Here are the papers!

EGMONT: Donna Elvira will be angry with me when she learns that I've detained you.

SECRETARY: You are jesting.

EGMONT: No, don't be ashamed. I admire your taste. She's pretty, and I have no objection to your having a friend at court. What do the letters say?

SECRETARY: Much, my lord, but little that is very pleasing.

EGMONT: It's well that we have pleasures at home; we have less occasion to seek them from abroad. Is there much that requires attention?

SECRETARY: Enough, my lord; three couriers are in attendance.

EGMONT: Go ahead—whatever's most urgent.

SECRETARY: It's all urgent.

EGMONT: One after the other; but quickly.

SECRETARY: Captain Breda sends an account of further developments in Ghent and the surrounding districts. The tumult has mostly subsided.

EGMONT: No doubt he reports individual acts of impropriety and folly?

SECRETARY: Yes, there are still many such things going on.

EGMONT: Spare me.

SECRETARY: Six more of the ones who tore down the image of the Virgin at Verviers have been arrested. He inquires whether they are to be hanged like the others?

EGMONT: I am weary of hanging; let them be flogged and discharged.

SECRETARY: There are two women among them; are they to be flogged also?

EGMONT: He may warn them and let them go.

SECRETARY: Brink, of Breda's company, wants to get married; the Captain hopes you will not allow it. There are so many women among the troops, he writes, that when we march it will look less like a column of soldiers than like a ragtag train of gypsies.

EGMONT: We must overlook it in his case. He is a fine young fellow, and moreover he asked me so earnestly before I left. This must be the last time, however; as much as it pains me to refuse the poor fellows their best fun; they have enough to torment them without that.

SECRETARY: Two of your people, Seter and Hart, have ill-treated a girl, the daughter of an innkeeper. They got her alone and she could not escape from them.

EGMONT: If she's an honorable girl and they used force, let them be flogged three days in succession; and if they have any property, let Breda retain as much of it as will give the girl a dowry.

SECRETARY: One of the foreign preachers has passed secretly through Comines and was discovered. He swore that he was on the point of leaving for France. According to regulations, he should be beheaded.

EGMONT: Let him be conducted quietly to the frontier, and assure him that the next time he won't escape so easily.

SECRETARY: A letter from your tax collector. He writes that very little money is coming in, and he will have difficulty sending you the required sum within the week; the disturbances have thrown everything into the greatest confusion.

EGMONT: The money must be had! It is for him to look to the means.

SECRETARY: He says he will do his utmost, and proposes finally to sue Raymond, who has been so long in your debt, and have him arrested.

EGMONT: But he has promised to pay!

SECRETARY: The last time he set a two weeks' deadline for himself.

EGMONT: Well, grant him another two weeks; after that he may proceed against him.

SECRETARY: You do well. It's not inability to pay; it's ill will on his part. He'll take it seriously when he sees you're not playing games. The collector further proposes to withhold for half a month the pensions you give to old soldiers, widows, and some others. In the meantime we may figure out something; they must make their arrangements accordingly.

EGMONT: But what arrangements can they make? These people need the money more than I do. He mustn't do that.

SECRETARY: Where then, my lord, will you tell him to get the money from?

EGMONT: It's his business to think of that. He was told so in our previous letter.

SECRETARY: And that's why he makes these proposals.

EGMONT: They will never do; he must think of something else. Let him make proposals that are acceptable and above all let him procure the money.

SECRETARY: I have once again included the letter from Count Oliva. Pardon my reminding you. More than all the others, the old

Count deserves a detailed reply. You were going to write to him yourself. He certainly loves you as a father.

EGMONT: I'll never get around to it; and of all detestable things, I find writing the most detestable. You imitate my hand so admirably, write in my name. I'm expecting Orange. I can't get around to it, and I do wish that something soothing might be written, to allay his fears.

SECRETARY: Just give me a notion of what you wish to say; I will at once draw up the answer and lay it before you. It shall be so written that it might pass for your hand in a court of justice.

EGMONT: Give me the letter. *(After looking at it.)* Dear, honest old man! Were you so cautious in your youth? Did you never mount a breach? In battle, did you remain in the rear, as prudence advises? Good old anxious friend! He has my safety and happiness at heart, but doesn't consider that he who lives to protect his life is already dead.—Tell him not to be anxious on my account; I act as I should and shall be on my guard. Let him use his influence at court in my favor, and be assured of my warmest thanks.

SECRETARY: Is that all? He expects more.

EGMONT: What more can I say? If you choose to write more fully, that's up to you. The matter turns upon a single point; he would have me live as I cannot live. That I am happy, live at a rapid pace, take things lightly, that is my good fortune; nor would I exchange it for a tomblike safety. Every drop of my blood rebels against the Spanish way of life, nor have I the least inclination to regulate my movements by the new and cautious measures of the court. Do I live only to think of life? Am I to forego the enjoyment of the present moment in order to secure the next? And must that moment in its turn be consumed in anxieties and idle fears?

SECRETARY: I entreat you, my lord, don't be so cruel and harsh toward the good man. You are accustomed to be friendly toward everyone. Say a kindly word that may allay the anxiety of your noble friend. See how considerate he is, with what delicacy he warns you.

EGMONT: Yet he harps continually on the same string. He knows from the past how I detest these admonitions. They serve only to perplex; they don't help in any way. What if I were a sleepwalker, and walked the giddy peak of a house,—would it be the part of friendship to call me by my name, to warn me of my danger, to waken me and kill me? Let each choose his own path and watch out for his own safety.

SECRETARY: It may be fitting, my lord, for you to be without fear, but those who know and love you—

EGMONT *(looking over the letter):* Then he recalls the old tales of our sayings and doings, one evening, in a modest excess of conviviality and wine. And what conclusions and inferences people drew from that and dragged all over the whole kingdom! Well, we had a cap and bells embroidered on the sleeves of our servants' liveries, and afterwards exchanged this mad device for a bundle of arrows;—a still more dangerous symbol for those who want to find meaning where nothing is meant. These and similar follies were conceived and brought forth in a moment of merriment. We are responsible for the fact that a noble troop, with beggars' wallets, and a self-chosen nickname, with mock humility, reminded the King of his duty. We were also responsible for—well, what does it signify? Is a carnival jest the same as high treason? Are people to begrudge us the scanty, colorful rags, with which a youthful spirit and a lively imagination hoped to adorn the poor nakedness of life? Take life too seriously, and what is it worth? If the morning wake us to no new joys, if in the evening we have no pleasures to hope for, is it worth the trouble of dressing and undressing? Does the sun shine on me today, so that I may reflect on what happened yesterday? So that I may try to foresee and control what can be neither foreseen nor controlled, the fate of the coming day? Spare me these reflections; we will leave them to scholars and courtiers. Let them ponder and contrive, walk and sneak about, get where they can, steal what they can.—If you can make use of all this, without swelling your letter into a whole volume, it's all right with me. Everything seems too important to the good old man. Just as a friend, who has long held our hand, grasps it again, more warmly, before he is about to let go of it.

SECRETARY: Forgive me. A man on foot grows dizzy when he sees a man drive past in noisy haste.

EGMONT: Child! Child! No more! As if they were whipped by invisible spirits, the sun steeds of time bolt, and run off with the light chariot of our destiny; and there is nothing we can do but take heart and grasp the reins firmly and turn the wheels now to the right, now to the left, away from the precipice here, the rock wall there. Where he is heading, who knows? The truth is, he scarcely remembers whence he came.

SECRETARY: My lord! my lord!

EGMONT: I stand high, but I can and must rise higher still. I feel courage, strength, and hope within me. I have not yet attained the peak of my growth, and if once I stand on that summit I mean to stand there firmly and without fear. Should I fall, then let a thunderclap, a storm blast, or yes, a false step of my own, cast me down into the abyss! I shall lie there with thousands of others. I have never disdained, even for small stakes, to throw the bloody dice with my good comrades; and shall I hesitate now, when all the free worth of life is at issue?

SECRETARY: Oh, my lord! You do not know what you are saying! May heaven protect you!

EGMONT: Collect your papers. Orange is coming. Finish what is most urgent, so that the couriers get away before the gates are closed. The rest may wait. Leave the Count's letter till tomorrow. Don't fail to visit Elvira, and greet her from me. See if you can find out how the Regent is feeling. She is said not to be well, though she conceals it. *(Exit Secretary.)*
(Enter Orange.)

EGMONT: Welcome, Orange; you don't seem entirely at ease.

ORANGE: What do you say to our conference with the Regent?

EGMONT: I found nothing extraordinary in her manner of receiving us. I have often seen her this way before. She seemed to me to be somewhat indisposed.

ORANGE: Didn't you notice that she was more reserved than usual? She began by cautiously approving our conduct during the late insurrection; afterward she remarked on the false light in which it still might be viewed; and she finally turned the discourse to her favorite topic of old: that her kind and gracious ways, her friendship for us Netherlanders, had never been sufficiently recognized, never appreciated as it deserved to be, that it had been treated too casually; that nothing seemed to come to the desired end; that for her part she was beginning to grow weary of it; that the King would have to decide on other measures. Did you hear that?

EGMONT: Not all of it; at the time I was thinking of something else. She is a woman, good Orange, and women would always like to have everyone submit passively to their gentle yoke; to have every Hercules lay aside his lion's skin and join their sewing circle, and, because women are themselves peaceably inclined, they imagine that the ferment which seizes a nation, the storm which powerful rivals excite against one another, may be allayed by one soothing word, and the most discordant elements be brought to unite in tranquil harmony at their feet. That's the case with her; and since she can't bring this about, she has no recourse but to lose her composure, threaten us with terrible prospects for the future—and complain about ignorance and folly and threaten to leave.

ORANGE: Don't you think that this time she may carry out her threat?

EGMONT: Never! How often I've seen her all prepared for the journey! Where should she go? Governor of a province here, a queen—do you think that she could bear to spend her days in insignificance at her brother's court? Or to go to Italy and drag out her days with old family connections?

ORANGE: People think she is incapable of this decision because you have already seen her hesitate and draw back; nevertheless, it is in her to take this step. New circumstances may impel her to the long delayed resolve. What if she were to depart, and the King to send another?

EGMONT: Why, he would come, and he also would find plenty to do. He would arrive with vast plans, projects, and ideas to reduce all things to order, to subjugate, and unify; and today he would have to deal with this trifle, tomorrow with that, and the day following discover some unexpected obstacle. He would spend one month in forming plans, another in mortification at their failure, and half a year in worries over a single province. With him too, time would pass, his head grow dizzy, and things continue on their way as before, till instead of sailing into the broad sea, according to the course he had previously set, he might thank God, if, amid the tempest, he were able to keep his vessel off the rocks.

ORANGE: What if the King were advised to try an experiment?

EGMONT: Namely?

ORANGE: To see what the body would do without the head.

EGMONT: How?

ORANGE: Egmont, I have for years borne our interests within my heart; I always stand as if over a chessboard, and regard no move of my adversary as insignficant; and as some men, with the leisure to do so, carefully investigate the secrets of nature, so I hold it to be the duty, the vocation of a prince, to acquaint himself with the dispositions and intentions of all parties. I have reason to fear an outbreak. The King has long acted according to certain principles; he finds that they do not serve his purpose; what is more probable than that he should seek it some other way?

EGMONT: I don't believe it. When a man grows old, has attempted much, and finds that the world will never get straightened out, he must at last grow weary and resigned.

ORANGE: One thing he has not yet attempted.

EGMONT: Well?

ORANGE: To spare the people, and destroy the princes.

EGMONT: How many have long feared that! There is no cause for such worries.

ORANGE: Once it was worry I felt; gradually I became suspicious; suspicion has at length grown into certainty.

EGMONT: And has the King more faithful servants than ourselves?

ORANGE: We serve him after our own fashion; and between ourselves we must confess that we understand pretty well how to make the interests of the King square with our own.

EGMONT: And who does not? He has our loyalty and compliance, in so far as they are his due.

ORANGE: But what if he should arrogate still more authority, and regard as disloyalty what we call the maintenance of our rights?

EGMONT: We shall know how to defend ourselves. Let him assemble the knights of the Golden Fleece; we will submit ourselves to their decision.

ORANGE: What if the sentence were to precede the trial and punishment precede the sentence?

EGMONT: It would be an injustice of which Philip is incapable, a folly which I cannot impute either to him or to his counsellors.

ORANGE: And what if they were both foolish and unjust?

EGMONT: No, Orange, it's impossible. Who would dare lay hands on us? The attempt to capture us would be a vain and fruitless enterprise. No, they dare not raise the banner of tyranny so high. The breeze that brought these tidings over the land would kindle a mighty conflagration. And what would they propose to do? The King has no power by himself to judge or condemn us; and would they attempt our lives by assassination? They cannot want to. A terrible league would unite the people in a moment. Hostility and eternal separation from the Spanish name would be forcibly declared.

ORANGE: Then the flames would rage over our grave, and the blood of our enemies flow—a vain oblation. Let us think, Egmont.

EGMONT: But how could they do it?

ORANGE: Alba is on the way.

EGMONT: I don't believe it.

ORANGE: I know it.

EGMONT: The Regent claimed not to know anything.

ORANGE: That convinces me all the more. The Regent will give place to him. I know his bloodthirsty disposition, and he brings an army with him.

EGMONT: To harass the provinces anew? The people will make a lot of trouble.

ORANGE: Their leaders will be taken into custody.

EGMONT: No! No!

ORANGE: Let us retire, each to his own province. There we will strengthen our position; the Duke will not begin with open violence.

EGMONT: Must we not greet him when he comes?

ORANGE: We will delay.

EGMONT: What if, on his arrival, he should summon us in the King's name?

ORANGE: We will answer evasively.

EGMONT: And if he presses us?

ORANGE: We will excuse ourselves.

EGMONT: And if he insists?

ORANGE: We shall be all the less disposed to come.

EGMONT: And war is declared, and we are rebels. Don't let prudence mislead you, Orange. I know it's not fear that makes you yield. Consider this step.

ORANGE: I have considered it.

EGMONT: Consider what you will be responsible for if you are wrong. For the most ruinous war that ever devastated a country. Your refusal is the signal that will immediately summon the provinces to arms, that justifies every cruelty for which Spain has hitherto so anxiously sought a pretext. With a single gesture you will inflame into the most terrible disorder all that we have long and patiently kept under control. Think of the towns, the nobles, the people; think of commerce, agriculture, trade! Imagine the murder, the devastation! On the battlefield, no doubt, the soldier calmly sees his comrade fall beside him. But toward you, down the river, will float the corpses of citizens, of children, of young women, till you stand there in horror, not knowing whose cause you are defending, since you shall see those for whose liberty you drew the sword perish around you. And how will you feel when you must quietly say to yourself, "It was for my own safety that I drew it."

ORANGE: We are not isolated individuals, Egmont. If it becomes us to sacrifice ourselves for thousands, it becomes us no less to spare ourselves for thousands.

EGMONT: He who spares himself becomes an object of suspicion to himself.

ORANGE: He who knows himself can safely advance or retreat.

EGMONT: The evil you fear is rendered certain by your own actions.

ORANGE: Wisdom and courage alike prompt us to face up to an inevitable evil.

EGMONT: When the danger is so great the faintest hope should be taken into account.

ORANGE: We have not even the slightest footing left; we are on the very brink of the precipice.

EGMONT: Is the King's favor such narrow footing?

ORANGE: Not narrow, perhaps, but slippery.

EGMONT: By heavens, people judge him wrongly. I cannot stand his being thought of so unfairly! He is Charles' son and incapable of meanness.

ORANGE: Kings, of course, do nothing mean.

EGMONT: People should know him better.

ORANGE: It is precisely our knowledge of him that counsels us not to wait until we face a dangerous test.

EGMONT: No test we have the courage to meet is dangerous.

ORANGE: You are losing your composure, Egmont.

EGMONT: I must see with my own eyes.

ORANGE: Oh if only this time you saw with mine! My friend, because your eyes are open, you imagine that you see. I am going. Await Alba's arrival, and God be with you! My refusal to do so may perhaps save you. The dragon may not think he's caught much if he cannot swallow us both. Perhaps he may delay, in order to carry out his plan more surely; in the meantime you may see matters in their true light. But then be quick, be quick! Save,—oh, save yourself! Farewell!—Let nothing escape your attention: how many troops he brings with him; how he garrisons the town; what power the Regent retains; how your friends are taking things. Send me news—Egmont—

EGMONT: What do you want?

ORANGE (*grasping his hand*): Be persuaded! Go with me!

EGMONT: What's this? Tears, Orange!

ORANGE: To weep for a lost friend is not unmanly.

EGMONT: You think I'm lost?

ORANGE: You are. Consider! Only a brief respite is left you. Farewell. (*Exit.*)

EGMONT (*alone*): Strange that the thoughts of other men should exert such an influence over us. These fears would never have entered my mind; and this man infects me with his worrying. Away with it! It's a foreign drop in my blood! Kind Nature, cast it out again! And there's still a friendly means to bathe the furrowed lines from my brow.

Act 3

Palace of the Regent.
(Margaret of Parma)

REGENT: I might have expected it. Ha! when we live along, immersed in anxiety and toil, we imagine that we are achieving the utmost that is possible; while he who looks on from a distance and gives orders believes that he is asking no more than what is possible. Kings! I would not have thought it could have galled

me so. It is so sweet to reign!—and to abdicate? I do not know
how my father could do it; but I will too.

[*Machiavelli appears in the background.*]

REGENT: Come here, Machiavelli. I am thinking over this letter
from my brother.

MACHIAVELLI: May I know what it contains?

REGENT: As much tender consideration for me as anxiety for his
states. He praises the firmness, the industry, the fidelity, with
which I have hitherto watched over the interests of His Majesty
in these provinces. He is sorry for me and regrets that this unruly
people causes me so much trouble. He is so thoroughly convinced of the depth of my insight, so extraordinarily satisfied
with the prudence of my conduct, that I must almost say the
letter is too politely written for a king—certainly for a brother.

MACHIAVELLI: It's not the first time he has given you a sign of his
just satisfaction.

REGENT: But the first time it has been a rhetorical figure.

MACHIAVELLI: I don't understand you.

REGENT: You soon will.—For after this preamble, he expresses the
opinion that without soldiers, without a small army, I shall always cut a sorry figure here! He intimates that we did wrong to
withdraw our troops from the provinces in order to meet the
complaints of the people. He thinks that a garrison which weighs
on the shoulders of the citizen will prevent him, by its pressure,
from making any lofty leaps.

MACHIAVELLI: It would inflame public opinion to the utmost.

REGENT: The King thinks, however—listen to this—he thinks that
a capable general, one who is never open to argument, will be
able to deal promptly with all parties—people and nobles, citizens and peasants; he therefore sends, with a powerful army, the
Duke of Alba.

MACHIAVELLI: Alba?

REGENT: You are surprised.

MACHIAVELLI: You say, he sends; doubtless he asks whether he
should send.

REGENT: The King does not ask, he sends.

MACHIAVELLI: Then you will have an experienced soldier in your
service.

REGENT: In my service? Be frank, Machiavelli.

MACHIAVELLI: I don't want to anticipate you.

REGENT: And I wish I could pretend! It wounds me—wounds me to the quick. I would rather my brother speak his mind than attach his signature to formal epistles, drawn up by a secretary of state.

MACHIAVELLI: Do you think they can't comprehend?—

REGENT: I know them in and out. They would like to have a clean sweep made; and since they cannot set about it themselves, they give their confidence to anyone who comes with a new broom in his hand. Oh, it seems to me as if I saw the King and his council worked into this tapestry.

MACHIAVELLI: So vividly?

REGENT: No feature is missing. There are good men among them. The honest Roderigo, so experienced and so moderate, who does not aim too high, yet lets nothing sink too low; the forthright Alonzo, the diligent Freneda, the steadfast Las Vargas, and others who join them when the good party is in power. But there sits the hollow-eyed Toledan, with his steely brow and his deep and fiery eyes, muttering between his teeth about women's softness, their ill-timed yielding; and saying that women can ride trained steeds well enough, but are themselves bad horse breakers, and similar pleasantries, which, in former times, I have been compelled to hear from political gentlemen.

MACHIAVELLI: You have chosen good colors for your portrait.

REGENT: Admit it, Machiavelli, among the tints from which I might, if need be, select, there is no hue so livid, so jaundicelike, as Alva's complexion, or as the color he is wont to paint with. He regards every one as a blasphemer or traitor; for under this heading they can be racked, impaled, quartered, and burnt at pleasure. The good I have accomplished here appears as nothing, seen from a distance, just because it is good. Then he dwells on every outbreak, long past, recalls every disturbance that has already been quieted, and what the King sees is such a picture of mutiny, sedition, and audacity, that he imagines we are actually devouring one another, when with us the fleeting boorishness of a rude people has long been forgotten. Thus he conceives a cordial hatred for the poor people; he views them with horror, as beasts and monsters, looks around for fire and sword, and imagines that human beings are subdued by such means.

MACHIAVELLI: You seem to me too vehement; you take the matter too seriously. Aren't you still Regent?

REGENT: I am aware of that. He will bring his instructions. I have grown old enough in affairs of state to understand how people can be supplanted without being actually deprived of office. First, he will produce instructions, couched in obscure and equivocal terms; he will stretch his authority, for the power is in his hands; if I complain, he will hint at secret instructions; if I desire to see them, he will answer evasively; if I insist, he will produce a paper of totally different import; and should this fail to satisfy me, he will go on precisely as if I hadn't been saying anything. Meanwhile he will have done what I dread, and turned aside what I hope for.

MACHIAVELLI: I wish I could contradict you.

REGENT: His harshness and cruelty will again stir up what, with endless patience, I have succeeded in quieting; I shall see my work destroyed before my eyes, and have to bear in addition the blame for what he has done.

MACHIAVELLI: Wait until it happens, Your Highness.

REGENT: I have sufficient self-command to remain quiet. Let him come; I will make way for him with the best grace before he pushes me aside.

MACHIAVELLI: So important a step so quickly?

REGENT: It's harder than you imagine. He who is accustomed to rule, to hold daily in his hand the destiny of thousands, descends from the throne as into the grave. But better thus than linger like a ghost among the living, and with hollow mien try to maintain a place which another has usurped and now possesses and enjoys.

Clara's dwelling.
(Clara and her Mother.)

MOTHER: Such a love as Brackenburg's I've never seen; I thought it was only in tales of heroes.

CLARA *(walking up and down the room, humming a tune):*
Happy alone
Is the person in love.

MOTHER: He suspects your attachment to Egmont; and yet if you would only be a little bit kind to him I do believe he would marry you still, if you would have him.

CLARA *(sings):*
Cheerful
And tearful
Then pensive again.
Yearning
And burning
In quivering pain;
Soaring to heaven,
Cast down from above
Happy alone
Is the person in love.

MOTHER: Stop the silly lullaby nonsense.

CLARA: Don't find fault with it. It's a song of great power. Many a time I've lulled a grown child to sleep with it.

MOTHER: You have nothing in your head but your love. If only you wouldn't forget all other things for the sake of the one. You should have more regard for Brackenburg, I tell you. He can make you happy again.

CLARA: He?

MOTHER: Oh, yes! A time will come! You children never look ahead, you give no ear to our experience. Youth and happy love, all has an end; and there comes a time when you thank God if you have a corner to creep into.

CLARA *(shudders, is silent, rises quickly):* Mother, let that time come—like death. To think of it beforehand is horrible! And if it comes! If we must—then—we will conduct ourselves as best we can. Live without you, Egmont! *(weeping.)* No! It's not possible, not possible.

> *(Enter Egmont, in the mantle of a cavalry officer,*
> *his hat pulled over his face.)*

EGMONT: Clara!

CLARA *(utters a cry and draws back):* Egmont! *(She hurries to him).* Egmont! *(She embraces and rests against him.)* O, you good, kind, sweet man! Have you come? Is it you?

EGMONT: Good evening, Mother!

MOTHER: God save you, noble sir! My little girl has almost pined away because you've been gone so long; she's been talking and singing about you all day.

EGMONT: You'll give me some supper?

MOTHER: You do us too much honor. If we only had anything—

CLARA: Certainly! Just be calm, Mother; I've anticipated everything; I've prepared something. Do not betray me, Mother.

MOTHER: There's little enough.

CLARA: Just wait! When he's with me I'm never hungry; so he can't have any great appetite when I am with him.

EGMONT: Do you think so?

CLARA *(stamps her foot and turns away in annoyance.)*

EGMONT: What's the trouble?

CLARA: Why are you so cold today? You haven't offered me a kiss yet. Why do you keep your arms folded in your mantle, like a newborn baby? It's not right for a soldier or a lover to keep his arms all covered up.

EGMONT: Sometimes, dearest, sometimes. When the soldier stands in ambush and means to outwit his foe, he collects his thoughts, gathers his mantle around him, and chews over his plan until it's ripe; and a lover—

MOTHER: Will you not take a seat and make yourself comfortable? I must go to the kitchen. Clara thinks of nothing when you are here. You must put up with what we have.

EGMONT: Your goodwill is the best seasoning. *(Exit Mother.)*

CLARA: And what then is my love?

EGMONT: As much as you please.

CLARA: Liken it to anything, if you have the heart.

EGMONT: But first—*He flings aside his mantle, and stands there in magnificent attire.)*

CLARA: Oh, heavens!

EGMONT: Now my arms are free. *(Embraces her.)*

CLARA: Don't! You'll ruin your clothes. *(She steps back.)* How magnificent! I dare not touch you.

EGMONT: Are you satisfied? I promised to come sometime dressed in the Spanish fashion.

CLARA: I had stopped reminding you of it; I thought you didn't want to—ah, and the Golden Fleece!

EGMONT: So now you see it.

CLARA: And did the Emperor really hang it around your neck?

EGMONT: He did, my child! And this chain and the symbol of the

Order invest the wearer with the noblest privileges. On earth I acknowledge no judge over my actions, except the Grand Master of the Order, with the assembled chapter of knights.

CLARA: Oh, you could let the whole world sit in judgment over you. The velvet is too splendid! and the braiding! and the embroidery! One doesn't know where to begin.

EGMONT: There, look your fill.

CLARA: And the Golden Fleece! You told me its history; you said it was the emblem of everything great and precious, of everything that can be merited and won by diligence and toil. It's very precious—I may liken it to your love—I wear that the same way, close to my heart—and then again—

EGMONT: Well—what then?

CLARA: And then again it's not the same.

EGMONT: How so?

CLARA: I have not won it by diligence and toil, I did not earn it.

EGMONT: With love it is different. You deserve that because you didn't seek it—and, for the most part, only those obtain it who don't set out in pursuit of it.

CLARA: Is it from your own experience that you have learned this? Did you make that proud remark in reference to yourself? You, whom all the people love?

EGMONT: Would that I had done something for them! That I could do anything for them! It is their own good pleasure to love me.

CLARA: You've doubtless been with the Regent today?

EGMONT: I have.

CLARA: Are you on good terms with her?

EGMONT: So it would appear. We are kind and helpful to each other.

CLARA: And in your heart?

EGMONT: I wish her well. True, we have each our own intentions. But that's not the point. She is an excellent woman, knows the people she has to deal with and would be perceptive enough if she weren't quite so suspicious. I give her plenty to do, because she is always suspecting some secret behind my actions when there is none.

CLARA: Really none?

EGMONT: Well, with one little exception. All wines deposit lees in the cask in the course of time. Orange furnishes her still better entertainment and is a perpetual riddle. He has got the reputation of harboring some secret design; and she studies his brow to discover his thoughts and his steps to learn in what direction they are bent.

CLARA: Does she hide her real purposes?

EGMONT: Regent—and you ask?

CLARA: Pardon me; I meant to say, is she false?

EGMONT: Neither more nor less than anyone who has his own objectives to attain.

CLARA: I should never feel at home in that world. But she has a masculine spirit, and is a different sort of woman from us housewives and seamstresses. She is great, steadfast, resolute.

EGMONT: Yes, when things are not too complicated. This time she's a little disconcerted.

CLARA: How so?

EGMONT: She also has a mustache on her upper lip and occasionally an attack of gout. A regular Amazon.

CLARA: A majestic woman! I'd be afraid to appear before her.

EGMONT: Yet you're not accustomed to be timid! It would not be fear, only maidenly bashfulness.

(Clara casts down her eyes, takes his hand,
and leans against him.)

EGMONT: I understand you, dear girl! You may raise your eyes. *(He kisses her eyes.)*

CLARA: Let me be silent! Let me hold you! Let me look into your eyes and find everything there—hope and comfort, joy and sorrow! *(She embraces and gazes at him.)* Tell me! Oh, tell me! It seems so strange—are you really Egmont? Count Egmont! The great Egmont, who causes such a stir in the world, who figures in the papers and to whom the provinces are so attached?

EGMONT: No, Clara, that's not who I am.

CLARA: How so?

EGMONT: You see, Clara—Let me sit down! *(He seats himself, she kneels on a footstool before him, rests her arms on his knees, and looks at him.)* That Egmont is a morose, cold, unbending Egmont, obliged to be on his guard, to put first one face on things and then another; harassed, misunderstood and perplexed, when the crowd consider him light-hearted and gay; loved by a people who do not know their own minds; honored and lifted on high by a mass of people you can do nothing with; surrounded by friends in whom he dares not confide; observed by men who are on the watch to get the better of him; toiling and striving, often without a goal, generally without a reward. O let me conceal how that man fares, let me not speak of his feelings! But this Egmont, Clara, is calm, open, happy, loved, and understood by the best of hearts, which he also knows fully and which he presses to his own with full confidence and love. *(He embraces her.)* That is your Egmont.

CLARA: So let me die! The world has no joy beyond this!

Act 4

A street.
(Jetter; Carpenter.)

JETTER: Hey! Pst! Hey, neighbor—a word with you, neighbor!

CARPENTER: On your way, and be quiet.

JETTER: Just a word. No news?

CARPENTER: Nothing, except that we are once more forbidden to speak.

JETTER: How so?

CARPENTER: Step over here, close to this house. Be careful. As soon as he arrived, the Duke of Alba had an order issued, by which two or three people found talking together on the street are declared guilty of high treason, with no trial.

JETTER: Oh, lord!

CARPENTER: To talk about affairs of state is prohibited on pain of life imprisonment.

JETTER: Alas for our liberty!

CARPENTER: And no one, on pain of death, is to criticize government actions.

JETTER: Alas for our heads!

CARPENTER: And fathers, mothers, children, kinfolk, friends, and servants are encouraged, by the promise of large rewards, to disclose before an expressly appointed tribunal what passes in the privacy of our own houses.

JETTER: Let's go home.

CARPENTER: And those who obey are promised that they shall suffer no injury, either in person or property.

JETTER: How generous!—I felt ill at ease the moment the Duke entered the town. Since then it has seemed to me as though the sky were covered with black crepe, hanging so low that one must stoop down to avoid knocking one's head against it.

CARPENTER: And how do you like his soldiers? That's another kind of crabs from what we've been used to, right?

JETTER: It's nasty! You almost have a heart attack when you see a troop like that march down the street, as straight as a ruler, with a fixed gaze, in one single step, however many of them there may be; and when they stand sentinel, and you pass one of them, it seems as if he'd like to see right through you; and he looks so stiff and sullen that you imagine you see a drill sergeant at every corner. I don't like them at all. Our militia were happy fellows; they took liberties, stood with their legs apart, their hats over their ears; they lived and let live; these fellows are like machines with a devil inside them.

CARPENTER: If one of them shouted "Halt!" and leveled his musket, do you think anyone would just stand there?

JETTER: I'd fall dead on the spot.

CARPENTER: Let's go home!

JETTER: No good can come of this. Farewell.

(Enter Soest.)

SOEST: Friends! Neighbors!

CARPENTER: Hush! Let's go.

SOEST: Have you heard?

JETTER: Only too much!

SOEST: The Regent is gone.

JETTER: Then heaven help us.

CARPENTER: She still supported us.

SOEST: She left suddenly and secretly. She couldn't get along with the Duke; she has sent word to the nobles that she intends to return. No one believes it.

CARPENTER: May God forgive the nobles for letting this new lash be laid on our necks. They could have prevented it. Our privileges are gone.

JETTER: For heaven's sake not a word about privileges. I detect the smell of an execution day; the sun won't come out, the fogs are rank.

SOEST: Orange is gone too.

CARPENTER: Then we're totally deserted!

SOEST: Count Egmont is still here.

JETTER: Thank God! May all the saints give him the strength to do his utmost; he's the only one who can help.

(Enter Vansen.)

VANSEN: Have I finally found a few people who haven't crept out of sight?

JETTER: Do us a favor and pass on.

VANSEN: You're not civil.

JETTER: This is no time for compliments. Does your back itch again? Are your wounds all healed?

VANSEN: Ask a soldier about his wounds! If I had worried about blows, I would never have amounted to anything.

JETTER: Things may get more serious.

VANSEN: The rising storm makes you feel a miserable weakness in your limbs, it seems.

CARPENTER: Your limbs will soon be headed somewhere else, if you don't keep quiet.

VANSEN: Poor mice! The master of the house gets a new cat, and right away you despair! There's a small difference, but we shall carry on as we did before; just be quiet.

CARPENTER: You're an insolent good-for-nothing.

VANSEN: Thanks for nothing, you fool! Let the Duke be. The old tomcat looks as though he had swallowed devils, instead of mice, and now couldn't digest them. Let him be, I say; he must eat, drink, and sleep, like other men. I'm not afraid, if we only watch our opportunity. At first he'll make quick work of it; by and by he too will find it's more pleasant to live in the larder, among the sides of bacon, and to rest at night, than to trap a few solitary mice in the granary. Go on! I know our governors.

CARPENTER: What a fellow like that can get away with! If ever in my life I had said such a thing, I wouldn't consider myself safe for a moment.

VANSEN: Don't make yourselves uneasy! God in heaven doesn't trouble himself about you, poor worms, much less the Regent.

JETTER: Blasphemer!

VANSEN: I know some other people who'd be better off if they had a little tailor's blood in their veins instead of their heroism and high spirits.

CARPENTER: What do you mean by that?

VANSEN: Hm! I mean the Count.

JETTER: Egmont! What has he to fear?

VANSEN: I'm a poor devil, and I could live a whole year on what he loses in a single night; yet he'd do well to give me his income for a year, to have my head on his shoulders for a quarter of an hour.

JETTER: You think very well of yourself, but the hairs of Egmont's head are wiser than your brains.

VANSEN: That's what you say! But not brighter. The gentry are the most apt to deceive themselves. He shouldn't be so trusting.

JETTER: How his tongue wags! Such a gentleman!

VANSEN: Just because he's not a tailor.

JETTER: Loudmouth!

VANSEN: I only wish I could breathe your courage into his limbs for an hour, to make him uneasy and plague and torment him, till he had to leave town.

JETTER: What nonsense you talk; why he's as safe as a star in the heavens.

VANSEN: Have you ever seen one snuffed out? It's just gone!

CARPENTER: Who would want to do anything to him?

VANSEN: Will you interfere to stop it? Will you stir up an insurrection if he is arrested?

JETTER: Ah!

VANSEN: Will you risk your ribs for him?

SOEST: Eh!

VANSEN (*mimicking them*): Eh! Oh! Ah! Run your surprise through the whole alphabet. So it is, and so it will remain. Heaven help him!

JETTER: Confound your impudence. Can such a noble, upright man have anything to fear?

VANSEN: In this world the rogue has the advantage everywhere. In debtor's court he makes a fool of the judge; on the bench, he takes pleasure in convicting the accuser. I once had to copy out a protocol, where the commissioner was handsomely rewarded by the court, both with praise and with money, because through his cross-examination an honest devil they had it in for was made out to be a rogue.

CARPENTER: That's another downright lie. What can they want to cross-examine out of a man if he is innocent?

VANSEN: Oh you bird brain! When nothing can be worked out of a man by cross-examination, they work it into him. Honesty is rash and no doubt defiant as well. First they question away quietly enough, and the prisoner—proud of his innocence, as they call it—comes out with much that a sensible man would keep back. Then, from these answers the prosecutor proceeds to put new questions and watches to see where the slightest contradiction appears. There he fastens his line; and let the poor devil lose his self-possession, say too much here, or too little there, or, heaven knows from what whim or other, withhold some trifling circumstance, or at any moment give way to fear— then we're on the right track. And I assure you no beggar woman searches for rags among the rubbish with more care, than such a fabricator of rogues uses to patch together from trifling, crooked, disjointed, mad, misplaced, and suppressed information, acknowledged or denied, a straw and rag scarecrow, by means of which he may at least hang his victim in effigy. And the poor devil may thank heaven if he's able to see himself hanged.

JETTER: The fellow has a ready tongue.

CARPENTER: That may work well enough with flies. Wasps laugh at the web you spin.

VANSEN: That depends on the kind of spider you are. The tall Duke, now, has the exact look of your garden spider; not the large-bellied kind, they are less dangerous; but your long-legged, slim-bodied one that doesn't get fat on his diet, and who spins a fine thread, but one that's all the tougher.

JETTER: Egmont is knight of the Golden Fleece; who can lay a hand on him? He can be tried only by his peers, by the assembled knights of his order. Your own foul tongue and evil conscience delude you into this nonsense.

VANSEN: You think that I wish him ill? It's all right with me. He's a fine gentleman. Some good friends of mine, who would have been hanged otherwise, he once let off with a sound drubbing.

Now leave, leave! I advise you! I see another patrol over there, commencing their round. They don't look as if they'd be willing to fraternize with us over a drink. We must wait, and watch quietly. I have a couple of nieces and a bartender chum—After the soldiers have had their fun with them, if they're still not tamed, then they're real wolves.

The Palace of Culenberg.
Residence of the Duke of Alba.
(Silva and Gomez, meeting.)

SILVA: Have you carried out the Duke's commands?

GOMEZ: To the letter. All the day patrols have received orders to assemble at the appointed time, at the various points that I have indicated. Meanwhile, they march as usual through the town to maintain peace and quiet. Each is ignorant of the other; each imagines the order to refer to it only; thus in a moment the cordon can be formed, and all the avenues to the palace occupied. Do you know the reason for this order?

SILVA: I am accustomed to obey blindly; and who is easier to obey than the Duke, since the event always proves the wisdom of his orders?

GOMEZ: All right! All right! I'm not surprised that you've become as reserved and monosyllabic as the Duke, since you have to be around him all the time. It seems strange to me. I'm used to the Italian service, which is more relaxed. In loyalty and obedience I'm the same old soldier as ever; but I've got accustomed to gossip and discussion. You are all silent, and you never allow yourselves to have a good time. The Duke seems to me like a bronze tower without gates, with the garrison lodged in the wings of it. Not long ago at table I heard him say of a gay jovial fellow that he was like a bad tavern, with a brandy sign displayed to lure in idlers, vagabonds, and thieves.

SILVA: And hasn't he brought us here secretly and in silence?

GOMEZ: You can't say anything against that. Certainly, whoever witnessed the skill with which he led the troops here out of Italy, has really seen something. How he sidled, so to speak, through friend and foe; through the French, both royalists and heretics; through the Swiss and their Confederates; maintained the strictest discipline, and accomplished with ease and without the slightest hindrance a march that was considered so perilous!—We've seen and learned something.

SILVA: Here too! Isn't everything as still and quiet as though there had been no disturbance?

GOMEZ: Well, it was already pretty quiet when we arrived.

SILVA: The provinces have become much more tranquil; if anybody moves now, it's only to try to escape; and I think the Duke will speedily close every outlet they might have.

GOMEZ: This means he'll really win the favor of the King.

SILVA: And nothing is more expedient for us than to retain Alba's. Should the King come here, surely the Duke and anyone he recommends will not go without reward.

GOMEZ: Do you believe the King will come?

SILVA: So many preparations are being made that it seems highly likely.

GOMEZ: That doesn't convince me.

SILVA: Keep your thoughts to yourself, then. For if it should not be the King's intention to come, certainly it's at least his intention that people should think so.

(Enter Ferdinand, Alba's natural son.)

FERDINAND: Has my father not appeared yet?

SILVA: We're waiting for him.

FERDINAND: The princes will be here soon.

GOMEZ: Are they coming today?

FERDINAND: Orange and Egmont.

GOMEZ *(aside to Silva):* I'm beginning to get the idea.

SILVA: Well, then, keep it to yourself. *(Enter the Duke of Alba; as he advances the rest draw back.)*

ALBA: Gomez.

GOMEZ *(steps forward):* My lord.

ALBA: You have distributed the guards and given them their instructions?

GOMEZ: Most precisely. The day patrols—

ALBA: Enough. Wait in the gallery. Silva will tell you at what moment you are to draw them together, and occupy the avenues leading to the palace. The rest you know.

GOMEZ: I do, my lord. *(Exit.)*

ALBA: Silva!

SILVA: Here I am.

ALBA: All the qualities which I have hitherto prized in you: courage, resolve, unswerving execution—show them today.

SILVA: I thank you for the opportunity to show you that I'm the same man I ever was.

ALBA: The moment the princes enter my cabinet, arrest Egmont's private secretary without delay. You have made all preparations to arrest and hold the others who have been designated?

SILVA: Rely on us. Their fate, like a well-calculated eclipse, will overtake them with terrible certainty.

ALBA: Have you had them all closely watched?

SILVA: All. Egmont especially. He is the only one whose behavior since your arrival has not changed. The whole day from one horse to another; invites guests; is always merry and entertaining at table, plays at dice, shoots, and at night steals away to his mistress. The others, by contrast, have made an obvious pause in their mode of life; they remain at home; to judge from the fronts of their houses it looks as if there were a sick man inside.

ALBA: Quickly then, before they spite us by recovering.

SILVA: I shall trap them without fail. In obedience to your command we load them with obsequious honors. They are alarmed; to be politic they thank us, but anxiously; they feel that flight would be the most prudent course, yet none dares to take a step; they hesitate, can't work together, while the bond which unites them prevents their acting boldly as individuals. They are anxious to withdraw themselves from suspicion, and only render themselves more suspect. I already contemplate with joy the successful realization of your entire scheme.

ALBA: I rejoice only over something that has already happened, and not lightly over that; for there is always something left to make us think and worry. Fortune is capricious; she often ennobles the common, the worthless, while she dishonors well considered actions with an ignoble outcome. Stay until the princes arrive, then order Gomez to occupy the streets, and you go without delay to arrest Egmont's secretary and the others who have been designated. When this is done, return, and announce to my son that he may bring me the news in the council meeting.

SILVA: I hope I may appear in your presence this evening. *(Alba approaches his son, who has been standing in the gallery.)* I dare not say it even to myself, but my hope wavers. I fear it will not turn out as he anticipates. I see before me spirits, who, still and thoughtful, weigh in dark scales the fate of princes and of many thousands. Slowly the beam moves up and down; deeply the judges appear to ponder; at length one scale sinks, the other rises, breathed on by the caprice of destiny, and all is decided. *(Exit.)*

ALBA *(advancing with his son)*: How did you find the town?

FERDINAND: All is quiet again. I rode from street to street, as if for the pleasure of it. Your well-distributed patrols keep Fear on such a tight rein that she does not venture even to whisper. The town resembles a plain when the coming storm flashes in the distance. No bird, no beast is to be seen, unless it is stealing away to a place of shelter.

ALBA: Has nothing further occurred?

FERDINAND: Egmont, with a few others, rode into the market place; we exchanged greetings; he had an unbroken charger, which I told him I must indeed praise. "Let's hurry and break in our steeds," he called out to me, "we shall need them soon!" He said that he should see me again today; he is coming here, at your desire, to deliberate with you.

ALBA: He will see you again.

FERDINAND: Among all the knights I know here, he pleases me the best. I think we shall be friends.

ALBA: You are still too rash and incautious. I recognize in you the frivolity of your mother, which threw her unconditionally into my arms. Appearances have already lured you prematurely into many dangerous connections.

FERDINAND: You will find me submissive to your will.

ALBA: I pardon this frivolous kindness, this heedless gaiety, in consideration of your youthful blood. Only do not forget on what mission I am sent, and what part in it I would assign to you.

FERDINAND: Warn me, and criticize me unsparingly whenever you consider it necessary.

ALBA *(after a pause)*: My son!

FERDINAND: My father!

ALBA: The princes will be here soon, Orange and Egmont. It is not mistrust that now, for the first time, I disclose to you what is about to take place. They will not leave again.

FERDINAND: What do you propose to do?

ALBA: The decision has been made to arrest them.—You are astonished! Learn what you have to do; the reasons you shall know when all is accomplished. Time is too short now to explain them. With you alone I should like to deliberate on the weightiest, the most secret matters; a powerful bond holds us linked together; you are dear and precious to me; I would bestow everything on you. Not only the habit of obedience would I impress upon you; I desire also to implant in you the power to fathom meaning and intent, to command, to execute. To you I would bequeath a great inheritance, to the King a most useful servant; I would endow you with the noblest of my possessions, so that you may not be ashamed to appear among your brethren.

FERDINAND: How deeply I am indebted to you for this love, which you bestow on me alone, while a whole kingdom trembles before you.

ALBA: Now hear what is to be done. As soon as the princes have entered, every avenue to the palace will be guarded. Gomez has the order to do that. Silva will make haste to arrest Egmont's secretary, together with those whom we hold most in suspicion. You will see to the orderly disposition of the guards at the gates and in the courts. Above all, secure the adjoining apartment here with the most trustworthy soldiers; then wait in the gallery till Silva returns, and bring me some unimportant paper, as a signal that his mission has been carried out. Remain in the ante-chamber till Orange retires. Follow him. I will detain Egmont here as though I had something more to say to him. At the end of the gallery demand Orange's sword, summon the guards, promptly arrest our most dangerous man; I will seize Egmont here.

FERDINAND: I obey, my father—for the first time with a heavy and an anxious heart.

ALBA: I pardon you; this is the first great day of your life.

Enter Silva.

SILVA: A courier from Antwerp. Here is Orange's letter. He is not coming.

ALBA: Does the messenger say that?

SILVA: No, my own heart tells me.

ALBA: My evil genius speaks in you. (*After reading the letter, he makes a sign to the two, and they retire to the gallery. Alba remains alone at the front of the stage.)* He's not coming! Till the last moment he puts off declaring himself. He dares *not* to come! So then, the prudent man, contrary to all expectation, is for once prudent enough to lay aside his prudence. The hour moves on! Let the hand travel a short space over the dial, and a great work is done or lost—irrevocably lost; for it can never be retrieved, nor kept secret. I had weighed everything maturely, foreseen even this contingency, and firmly resolved what, in that case, was to be done; and now, when it must be done, I can scarcely keep the pros and cons from wavering once again through my spirit. Is it expedient to seize the others if *he* escapes me? Shall I delay and let Egmont elude my grasp, together with his friends and so many others who now and perhaps for today only, are in my hands? So destiny constrains even you, the unconstrainable? How long considered! How well prepared! How grand, how beautiful the plan! The hope, how close to its goal! And now, at the decisive moment, placed between two evils; as in a lottery you reach into the dark future; the chance you draw remains tightly rolled, unclear to you whether prize or blank! *(He becomes attentive, like one who hears a noise, and steps to the window.)* It is he! Egmont! Did your steed bear you here so lightly; did it not shy at the scent of blood, at the spirit with the naked sword who received you at the gate? Dismount! So now you have one foot in the grave! And now both! Aye, stroke him and for the last time pat his neck for the gallant service he has rendered you. And for me no choice is left. The delusion in which Egmont ventures here today cannot deliver him into my hands a second time! Listen! *(Ferdinand and Silva enter hurriedly.)* Obey my orders! I am not changing my decision. I shall detain Egmont here as best I can till you bring me word from Silva. Then remain close by. You too fate has robbed of the high honor of arresting with your own hand the King's greatest enemy.

(To Silva) Hurry! *(To Ferdinand)* Advance to meet him.
(Alba remains some moments alone, pacing the chamber in silence.)
(Enter Egmont.)

EGMONT: I come to learn the King's commands; to hear what service he demands from our loyalty, which remains eternally devoted to him.

ALBA: He desires above all to hear your counsel.

EGMONT: On what subject? Is Orange coming too? I thought I'd find him here.

ALBA: I regret that he fails to join us at this important hour. The King desires your counsel, your opinion as to how these states may once again be pacified. Indeed he trusts that you will cooperate vigorously with him in quelling these disturbances and establishing complete and permanent order in these provinces.

EGMONT: You should know better than I that everything is already sufficiently tranquil, indeed that it was still more tranquil before the appearance of fresh troops agitated the public mind and filled it again with anxiety and alarm.

ALBA: You seem to intimate that it would have been most advisable if the King had not placed me in a position to interrogate you.

EGMONT: Pardon! It is not for me to judge whether the King should have sent the army here, or whether the power of his royal presence alone would not have had greater effect. The army is here, the King is not. But we should be most ungrateful, most forgetful, were we to lose sight of what we owe to the Regent. Let us admit it! By her prudence and valor, by her judicious use of authority and force, of persuasion and finesse, she pacified the insurgents, and, to the astonishment of the world, succeeded, over the course of a few months, in bringing a rebellious people back to their duty.

ALBA: I do not deny it. The insurrection is quelled; everyone appears to be forced back within the bounds of obedience. But does it not depend upon each one's individual caprice alone to overstep these bounds? Who will keep people from another outburst? Where is the power capable of restraining them? Who will answer to us for their future loyalty and submission? Their own good will is the sole pledge we have.

EGMONT: And is not the good will of a people the surest, the noblest pledge? By heaven! When can a monarch find himself more secure than when they stand all for one and one for all? More secure against domestic foes and foreign?

ALBA: Surely you would not have us believe that such is now the case here?

EGMONT: Let the King proclaim a general pardon; let him calm the public mind; and soon you will see how loyalty and affection will return when confidence is restored.

ALBA: And everyone who has violated the majesty of the King, the sanctuaries of religion, would go back and forth, free and unchallenged! Would live as convenient examples for others that enormous crimes go unpunished.

EGMONT: And should not a crime of frenzy, of intoxication, rather be excused than cruelly punished? Especially when there is such certain hope, indeed assurance, that the evil will not recur? Has that not made sovereigns more secure? Are not those monarchs most praised by the world and by posterity, who can pardon, pity, overlook with scorn an offense against their dignity? Are they not precisely on that account likened to God, who is far too exalted to be touched by any blasphemy?

ALBA: And precisely for that reason the King should fight for the honor of God and of religion, and we for the respect due the King. What the supreme power disdains to avert, it is our duty to avenge. If I am to offer my counsel, no guilty person will live to rejoice unpunished.

EGMONT: Do you think that you will be able to reach them all? Do we not hear every day that fear is driving them here and there, driving them out of the country? The wealthiest will escape with their property, their children, and their friends; the poor will offer their industrious hands to our neighbors.

ALBA: They will if they cannot be prevented. It is on this account that the King asks counsel and aid from every prince, serious effort from every provincial governor, not merely a description of how things are or what might happen if everything were allowed to go as it is going. To contemplate a great evil, to flatter oneself with hope, to trust to time, to strike an occasional blow like the clown in a Shrovetide play, so as to make a noise, and appear to do something when one would like to do nothing—does that not make one suspect, as if one were contemplating with satisfaction a rebellion which one would not incite but would gladly encourage?

EGMONT (*about to burst out, restrains himself, and after a brief pause, speaks with composure*): Not every intention is obvious, and a man's intentions are often misconstrued. Isn't it widely rumored after all that the King's intent is not so much to govern the provinces according to uniform and clearly defined laws, to maintain the majesty of religion, and to give his people universal peace, as it is to subjugate them unconditionally, to rob them of their ancient rights, to make himself master of their possessions, to curtail the fair privileges of the nobles, for the sake of which alone they are ready to serve him with life and limb? Religion, they say, is merely a splendid tapestry, behind which every dangerous design may be contrived with the greater ease. On their knees, the people adore the sacred symbols worked into it, while behind lurks the fowler ready to ensnare them.

ALBA: Must I hear this from *you*?

EGMONT: Not my own sentiments! I only repeat what is loudly rumored, and uttered here and there, by rich and poor, by wise men and fools. The Netherlanders fear a double yoke, and who will guarantee their freedom?

ALBA: Freedom! A fair word, rightly understood. What freedom would they have? What is the freedom of the most free? To do right! And in that the King will not hinder them. No! No! They do not imagine themselves free unless they have the power to injure themselves and others. Would it not be better to abdicate rather than rule such a people? When the country is threatened by foreign invaders, a possibility which never occurs to the citizen occupied only with his immediate interests, and when the King asks their support, they fall into disagreement among themselves, and thus, as it were, conspire with the enemy. Far better that they be tightly curbed, that they be treated like children and like children be guided to their greatest good. Trust me, a people grows neither old nor wise, a people remains always childish.

EGMONT: How rarely does a king attain wisdom! And shouldn't the many confide their interests to the many rather than to the one? And not even to the one, but to the few courtiers of the one, men who have grown old under the eyes of their master. It seems that they have the exclusive privilege of growing wise.

ALBA: Perhaps for the very reason that they are not left to themselves.

EGMONT: And therefore would like to leave no one else to himself. Let them do what they like, however; I have replied to your questions, and I repeat, it won't, it cannot succeed! I know my countrymen. They are men worthy to tread God's earth; each complete in himself, a little king, steadfast, active, capable, loyal, attached to ancient customs. It is difficult to win their confidence, but it is easy to retain it. Firm and unbending! They may be pressed, but not suppressed.

ALBA *(who meanwhile has looked around several times):* Would you repeat what you have said, in the King's presence?

EGMONT: So much the worse, if his presence made me afraid to speak! So much the better for him, and for his people, if he inspired me with confidence, if he encouraged me to say even more.

ALBA: What is of benefit, I can listen to as well as he can.

EGMONT: I would say to him—"It is easy for the shepherd to drive before him a flock of sheep; the ox draws the plow without resisting; but if you would ride a noble steed, you must study his thoughts, you must ask nothing unreasonable from him, nor ask unreasonably." The citizen desires to retain his ancient constitution, to be governed by his own countrymen. And why? Because he knows how he will be ruled. Because with them he can hope for unselfish fairness, for sympathy with his fate.

ALBA: And should not the Regent have the power to alter this ancient tradition? Should not this constitute his finest privilege? What is permanent in this world? And shall the constitution of a state remain unchanged? Must not every relationship change in the course of time? And for this very reason must not an ancient constitution become the source of a thousand evils, because it is not adapted to the present condition of the people? I fear that these ancient rights are so agreeable just because they afford hiding places where the crafty and the powerful may creep, or where they may lie concealed, to the detriment of the people and of the whole.

EGMONT: And these arbitrary changes, these unlimited encroachments of the supreme power, are they not a portent that one person will do what is forbidden to thousands? He alone would be free so that he can gratify his every wish, carry out his every idea. And if we should give him our trust as a good and virtuous sovereign, will he answer to us for his successors? That none of them will rule without consideration, without forbearance! And who then would deliver us from absolute caprice, should he send us his servants, his closest advisers who, without knowledge of the country and its needs, would govern according to their own good pleasure, meet with no opposition, and know themselves exempt from all responsibility?

ALBA *(who has meanwhile looked around again):* There is nothing more natural than that a king should choose to rule on his own and that he should choose to entrust his authority to those who best understand him, who desire to understand him, and who will unconditionally execute his will.

EGMONT: And it is just as natural that the citizen should desire to be governed by someone born and reared in the same land, whose notions of right and wrong are in harmony with his own, and whom he can regard as his brother.

ALBA: And yet the nobility has shared rather unequally with these brethren of theirs.

EGMONT: That happened centuries ago and is now tolerated without jealousy. But should new men, whose presence is not needed, be sent to enrich themselves a second time, at the cost of the nation; should the people see themselves exposed to harsh, bold, unconstrained rapacity—that would cause a ferment that would not soon be dissipated.

ALBA: You speak words to me which I ought not to hear; I too am a foreigner.

EGMONT: That they are spoken to you shows that I do not mean you.

ALBA: Be that as it may, I would rather not hear them from you. The King sent me here in the hope that I should meet with the support of the nobles. The King wills, and will have his will. After profound deliberation, he has seen what is best for the welfare of the people; things cannot go on as heretofore. His intention is to limit their power for their own good; if necessary, to force upon them their own salvation, to sacrifice the more dangerous citizens, so that the rest may find peace and enjoy the blessings of a wise government. This is his decision; this I am ordered to announce to the nobles; and in his name I require from them advice: *how* it is to be done, not *what*—he has decided that.

EGMONT: Your words, unfortunately, justify the fears of the people, the general fear! So the King has decided what no sovereign ought to decide. In order to govern his subjects more easily, he would weaken, suppress, destroy the strength of his people, their spirit, and their image of themselves! He would violate the core of their individuality, doubtless with the view of making them happier. He would annihilate them, to make them into something, a different something. Oh, even if his purpose is good, this will subvert it. It is not the King whom we oppose—we only place ourselves in the way of the King, who is about to take the first unhappy step on a false path.

ALBA: Such being your sentiments it would seem a vain attempt for us to seek agreement. You think poorly of the King, and contemptuously of his counsellors if you imagine that all of this has not already been thought out, examined, weighed in the balance. I have no order to examine every pro and con a second time. From the people I demand obedience—and from you, their leaders and princes, I demand counsel and support, as pledges of this unconditional duty.

EGMONT: Demand our heads; then it's done once and for all. To a noble spirit it is a matter of indifference whether he bend his neck to such a yoke or lay it upon the block. I have spoken much to little purpose. I have agitated the air, but accomplished nothing else.

(Enter Ferdinand.)

FERDINAND: Pardon me for interrupting your conversation! Here is a letter, the bearer of which urgently demands an answer.

ALBA: Allow me to see what it contains. *(Steps aside.)*

FERDINAND *(to Egmont):* It's a noble steed your people have brought to take you away.

EGMONT: I have seen worse. I have had him some time; I'm thinking of giving him away. If you like him, perhaps we shall strike a bargain.

FERDINAND: All right, we'll see.

(Alba motions to his son, who retires to the background.)

EGMONT: Farewell! Dismiss me; for, by heaven, I don't know what more I can say.

ALBA: Fortunately for you, chance prevents your disclosing your sentiments further. You incautiously lay bare the recesses of your heart, and accuse yourself more harshly than any adversary could do out of malice.

EGMONT: This reproach doesn't disturb me. I know myself well enough; I know how I am devoted to the King—far more than many who, in his service, serve only themselves. I don't like to leave our argument without resolving it and setting it aside, and I only wish that the service of the King and the welfare of our country may soon unite us; another conference, the presence of the other princes who today are absent may perhaps, in a more propitious moment, accomplish what at present appears impossible. In this hope I take my leave.

ALBA (*who at the same time makes a sign to Ferdinand*): Halt, Egmont!—Your sword!—(*The center door opens and discloses the gallery, which is occupied by guards, who remain motionless.*)

EGMONT (*after a pause of astonishment*): This was the plan? For this you summoned me here? (*Grasping his sword as if to defend himself*) Am I then unarmed?

ALBA: It is the King's order. You are my prisoner. (*At the same time armed men enter from both sides.*)

EGMONT (*after a pause*): The King?—Orange! Orange! (*After a pause, surrendering his sword*) Take it! It has been used far oftener in defending the cause of my King than in protecting this breast.

(*He leaves by the center door, followed by the guard and Alba's son. Alba remains standing while the curtain falls.*)

Act 5

A street. Twilight.
(*Clara, Brackenburg, Citizens.*)

BRACKENBURG: Dearest, for heaven's sake, what are you planning to do?

CLARA: Come with me, Brackenburg! You don't understand the people; we are certain to rescue him. What can equal their love for him? I swear it, everyone feels in his heart the burning desire to save him, to avert danger from a life so precious, and to give back freedom to the freest one of all. All that's wanting is a voice to call them together. The memory of all they owe him is still fresh in their hearts and they know that his mighty arm alone shields them from destruction. For his sake, for their own sake, they must risk everything. And what do we risk? At most, our lives, which, if he dies, are not worth saving.

BRACKENBURG: Unhappy girl! You don't see the power that holds us chained with iron bands.

CLARA: It doesn't seem invincible to me. Let's not lose time in idle words. Here come some of our old, honest, brave citizens! Listen, friends! Neighbors! Listen! Hark!—Say, how is it with Egmont?

CARPENTER: What does the girl want? Tell her to be quiet.

CLARA: Come closer so we may speak softly till we're united and stronger. Not a moment to lose! The same insolent tyranny that dared to chain him is already drawing the dagger to murder him. Oh, my friends! My anxiety grows step-by-step with the twilight. I dread this night. Come! Let's separate; we'll run from quarter to quarter and call out the citizens. Let everyone lay hold of his ancient weapons. In the market place we meet again, and our gathering stream will carry everyone forward. Our enemies will see themselves surrounded, overwhelmed, compelled to yield. How can a handful of slaves resist us? And he will return among us, he will see himself rescued, and will for once be able to thank us, we who are already so deeply in his debt. Perhaps he will see—no *surely* he will see the dawn in the free heavens once again.

CARPENTER: What's wrong with you, girl?

CLARA: Can you misunderstand me? I'm talking of the Count! I'm talking of Egmont.

JETTER: Don't speak the name! It's deadly.

CLARA: Not speak the name? What do you mean? His name? Is there anyone who doesn't speak it, at every possible occasion? Is there anywhere it isn't written? I've read it often, every letter of it, in these stars. Not speak it? What do you mean? Friends! Good, kind neighbors; you're dreaming; stop and think. Don't look at me with those fixed and anxious eyes. Don't look from side to side with such timid glances. All I say to you is what everyone wishes. Who, in this fearful night, before he goes to his restless bed, will not bend his knee and fervently pray Heaven to give him back his life? Ask each other! Each one ask himself! And who is there that won't say with me, "Egmont's liberty—or death!"

JETTER: God help us! This is a sad business.

CLARA: Wait! Wait! Don't draw away at the sound of his name; you used to be so happy to push forward to meet him—when it was rumored that he was coming, when they cried, "Egmont's coming! He's coming from Ghent!"—and then the citizens who lived on the streets through which he would pass considered themselves lucky. And when you heard the sound of his horses, everyone threw aside his work, and a ray of hope and joy, like a sunbeam from his countenance, stole over your toilworn faces as you peered from every window. Then, as you stood in the doorways, you would lift up your children and point to him, "See, that's Egmont, the tallest and greatest of all. He's the one! He's the one to whom you'll look for better times than those your poor fathers have known." Don't let your children ask you at some future day, "Where is he? Where are the better times you promised us?"—And here we talk back and forth and do nothing—we betray him.

SOEST: Shame on you, Brackenburg! Don't let her run on like this; stop the mischief.

BRACKENBURG: Dear Clara! Let's go! What will your mother say?

CLARA: Do you think I'm a child, that I'm mad? Perhaps—. What good is "perhaps"? You can't hide this dreadful certainty from me, not with any hope you hold out. You must listen to me and you will. Because I see it: you're overwhelmed, and you can't find your true selves again, in your own hearts. Cast just one glance through the present peril into the past—the recent past. Turn your thoughts to the future. Could you live, will you, if he were to perish? With his last breath the last draft of freedom expires. What was he to you? For whose sake did he expose himself to the direst perils? His blood flowed, his wounds were healed for you alone. That mighty spirit that sustained all of you is now confined in a dungeon, while around him hover the terrors of treacherous assassination. Perhaps he thinks of you, perhaps he hopes in you—he who was accustomed only to give, only to fulfill.

CARPENTER: Come on, neighbor.

CLARA: I have neither the arms nor the strength of a man; but I have what all of you lack—courage and contempt of danger. Oh that my breath could kindle your souls! If only I could press you to my bosom and inspire you! Come! I'll march in your midst! As a defenseless banner, waving, leads on a gallant army of warriors, so shall my spirit hover like a flame over your ranks, while love and courage shall unite the scattered and wavering multitude into a terrible host.

JETTER: Take her away; I pity her. *(Exeunt Citizens)*

BRACKENBURG: Clara! Don't you see where we are?

CLARA: Where? Under the dome of heaven, which has so often seemed to arch more gloriously as noble Egmont passed beneath it. From these windows I have seen them look out, four or five heads one above the other; at these doors, bowing and scraping, the cowards have stood when he looked down on them! Oh, I loved them so when they honored him. Had he been a tyrant they might have turned away with indifference when he fell. But they loved him! Oh hands that used to reach for your caps, you now can't reach for your swords. And we, Brackenburg? Is it for us to chide them? These arms that have so often embraced him, what do they do for him now? Cunning has accomplished so much in the world. You know the paths and the pitfalls. You know the ancient castle. Nothing is impossible—give me a plan.

BRACKENBURG: How would it be if we went home?

CLARA: All right.

BRACKENBURG: There at the corner I see Alba's guard; let the voice of reason reach your heart! Do you think me a coward? Do you doubt that I would die for you? Here we are, both mad, I as well as you. Do you not recognize the impossible? If only you'd be calm! You're beside yourself.

CLARA: Beside myself! That's horrible. You, Brackenburg, you're beside yourself. When you hailed the hero, called him your friend, your hope, your defender, shouted *vivat* as he passed— then I stood in my corner, half opened the window, hid while I listened, and my heart beat higher than yours, all the rest of you. Now it beats higher again, higher than all the rest of you! In the hour of peril you hide, you deny him, and you don't sense that if he perishes, you are lost.

BRACKENBURG: Come home.

CLARA: Home?

BRACKENBURG: Stop and think! Look around you! These are the streets on which you used to walk only on the sabbath, when you walked modestly to church; where, out of exaggerated propriety, you were displeased if I joined you with a friendly greeting. And now you stand and speak and take action before the eyes of the whole world. Stop and think, remember, my love! How can this help us?

CLARA: Home! Yes, I remember. Come, Brackenburg, let's go home!—Do you know where my home is? *(Exeunt.)*

A Prison. Lighted by a lamp, a couch in the background.
(Egmont alone.)

Old friend! Ever faithful sleep, have you too forsaken me, like my other friends? How willingly you would descend upon my brow, when I was free, cooling my temples as if with a fair myrtle wreath of love! In the din of battle, on the waves of love, I rested in your arms, breathing lightly like a growing boy. When storms whistled through the leaves and boughs, when branches and tree-tops swayed and creaked, the inmost core of my heart remained unmoved. What makes you tremble now? What shakes your firm and steadfast mind? I feel it, it's the sound of the murderous axe, gnawing at my roots. Still I stand erect, but an inward shudder runs through me. Yes, it prevails, this treacherous power; it undermines the tall, firm trunk, and before the bark withers, your crown will fall crashing to the earth.

But you, you who have so often swept great worries from your brow as if they were soap bubbles, why can't you now drive away this foreboding that rises and falls a thousandfold within you? Since when has death come to you as a terrible thing—death, amid whose varying forms you used to live calmly, as with the other shapes and figures of this familiar earth? But it is not he, the sudden foe, whom the sound heart longs to meet in eager contention—it is the dungeon, emblem of the grave, revolting alike to the hero and the coward. How intolerable I used to feel it was, to be seated on my cushioned chair, when in solemn assembly the princes pondered in endless discussion questions which scarcely required deliberation, while between gloomy walls the rafters of the ceiling stifled and oppressed me. Then I would hurry off as soon as possible, and onto my horse quickly, with a deep breath, and away to the open fields, man's natural element, where, rising from the earth like vapor, every new blessing of nature crowds around us, and wafting from the wide heavens, all the boons of the planets envelop us; where, like the earthborn giant, we lifted ourselves aloft, invigorated by our mother's touch; where we feel in all our veins the whole of humanity and human desire; where the soul of the young hunter glows with the longing to overtake, to conquer, to capture, to use his power, to win, to possess; where the soldier, with rapid stride, brashly assumes his inborn right to dominion over the world; and, with terrible freedom, sweeps like a desolating hailstorm over meadow, field, and forest, knowing no boundaries traced by the hand of man.

You are but a shadow, a remembered dream of the happiness I so long possessed; where has treacherous fate taken you? Did she deny you the right to meet the rapid stroke of never-shunned death in the open face of day, in order to prepare for you a foretaste of the grave in its loathsome corruption? How revoltingly its foul breath rises toward me from these damp stones! Life grows numb and my foot shrinks from the couch as from the grave.

Oh cares, cares! You who begin the work of murder before its time—forbear! Since when has Egmont been alone, so utterly alone in the world? It is doubt that renders you helpless, not chance. The justice of the King, in which you trusted throughout your life, the friendship of the Regent, which was almost—you may as well admit it—almost love—have these suddenly vanished, like a splendid meteor of the night, leaving you alone on your gloomy path? Will not Orange, at the head of your friends, contrive some daring scheme? Will not the people assemble, and with gathering might, rescue their faithful friend?

Oh, walls that hold me fast, do not separate me from the well-intentioned zeal of so many kindly souls. And may the courage which spoke from my eyes and flowed forth over *them,* now return again from *their* hearts to mine. Oh yes! They gather in thousands! they come! they stand beside me! Their pious hope rises to heaven and implores a miracle. And if no angel descends for my deliverance, I see them reach for lance and sword. The gates are forced, the bolts are riven, the walls fall beneath their hands, and Egmont rises in joy to meet the freedom of the dawning day! How many familiar faces receive me with acclaim! Oh Clara! if you were a man, I should see you here the very first, and thank you for that which it is hard to owe even to a king: freedom!

Clara's house.
(*Clara.*)

CLARA (*enters from her room with a lamp and a glass of water; she places the glass on the table and steps to the window*): Brackenburg, is it you? What was that I heard? No one yet? No one! I'll set the lamp in the window, so that he may see that I'm still awake, that I'm still waiting for him. He promised me news. News? Horrible certainty!—Egmont condemned!—What tribunal has the right to summon him?—And they dare to condemn him!—Is it the King who condemns him or the Duke? And the Regent withdraws! Orange hesitates, as do all his friends!—Is this the world, of whose fickleness and treachery I have heard so much and experienced nothing? Is this the world?—Who could be so evil as to bear malice against one so dear? Could evil itself be powerful enough to destroy so suddenly the object of universal homage? Yet so it is—it is—Oh Egmont, I thought you safe before God and man, safe as in my arms! What was I to you? You called me yours, my whole life was devoted to your life. What am I now? In vain I stretch out my hand to the snares that hold you fast. You, helpless—and I, free!—Here is the key that unlocks my door. My going out and my coming in depend upon my own free will; yet, alas, I'm powerless to help you!—Oh bind me so that I may not go mad; hurl me into the deepest dungeon, so that I may dash my head against damp walls, whimper for freedom, and dream how I would hope to help him if fetters did not hold me bound, how I *would* help him—Now I am free, and in freedom lies the anguish of impotence.—Conscious of my own existence, unable to stir a limb to help him. Alas! Alas! Even this small portion of your being, your Clara, is like you a captive, and, separated from you, can only exert her last energies in the agonies of death.—I hear a stealthy step—a cough—Brackenburg,—it is he! Kind, unhappy man, your destiny remains ever the same; your love opens the door to you at night,—alas! to what a doleful meeting.

(*Enter Brackenburg.*)

CLARA: You come here pale and terrified! Brackenburg! What's the matter?

BRACKENBURG: I have sought you through perils and roundabout paths. The main streets are occupied by troops; I've stolen to you through lanes and byways!

CLARA: Tell me what's going on.

BRACKENBURG *(sitting down):* Oh Clara, let me weep. I had no love for him. He was the rich man who lured the poor man's only lamb to better pasture. I did not curse him; God made me loyal— and soft. My life streamed down from me in pain, and each day I hoped I would die.

CLARA: Forget that, Brackenburg! Forget yourself. Speak to me of him! Is it true? Is he condemned?

BRACKENBURG: He is! I know it for certain.

CLARA: And still lives?

BRACKENBURG: Yes, he still lives.

CLARA: How can you be sure of that? Tyranny murders its glorious victim in the night! His blood flows, hidden from every eye. The people, stunned and bewildered, lie in sleep, dream of deliverance, dream of the fulfillment of their impotent wishes, while, angry at us, his spirit abandons the world. He is no more! Don't deceive me; don't deceive yourself!

BRACKENBURG: No, he lives, that is certain. And the Spaniards, alas, are preparing a terrible spectacle for the people on whom they are about to trample, in order to crush forever, by violence, every heart that stirs for freedom.

CLARA: Go on! Calmly pronounce my death warrant also! Near and nearer I approach that blessed land; from those realms of peace I already feel the breath of consolation. Proceed!

BRACKENBURG: I could tell it from the guards, from casual words, dropped here and there, that in the marketplace they were secretly preparing some terrible spectacle. Through byways and familiar lanes I stole to my cousin's house, and from a back window, looked out on the marketplace. Torches waved here and there, in the hands of a wide circle of Spanish soldiers. I strained my eyes, unaccustomed to the night, and out of the darkness there arose before me a scaffold, dark, spacious, and lofty! The sight filled me with horror. Several persons were employed in covering with black cloth such portions of the woodwork as yet remained exposed. The steps were covered last, also with black; I saw it all. They seemed to be preparing for the celebration of some horrible sacrifice. A white crucifix that shone like silver through the night was raised at one side. I saw this, and saw the terrible certainty become more certain still. Scattered torches still swayed here and there; gradually they flickered and went out. Suddenly the hideous birth of night returned into its mother's womb.

CLARA: Still, Brackenburg! Be still now! Let this veil rest upon my soul. The specters have vanished; and you, gentle night, lend your mantle to the earth which boils up within; she will no longer endure the loathsome burden; shuddering, she rends her yawning chasms, and with a crash swallows the murderous scaffold. And that God, whom they have profaned, making Him a witness of their madness, sends down some angel from on high; at the hallowed touch of the messenger, bolts and bars fly back; he casts around our friend a gentle splendor, and leads him softly and silently through the night to freedom. And my path too leads secretly through the darkness to meet him.

BRACKENBURG *(detaining her):* My child, where?! What would you do?

CLARA: Softly, my friend, lest someone should wake! Lest we should awaken ourselves! Do you know this vial, Brackenburg? I took it from you once in jest, when, as often happened, you threatened, in your impatience, to end your days—And now my friend—

BRACKENBURG: In the name of all the saints!

CLARA: You cannot stop me. Death is my destiny! Do not begrudge me the quick and quiet death you had prepared for yourself. Give me your hand! At the moment when I open that dark portal through which there is no return, I may tell you, with this pressure of my hand, how much I have loved you, how deeply I have pitied you. My brother died young; I chose you to fill his place; your heart rebelled, you tormented yourself and me, demanding with ever-increasing fervor that which fate had not destined for you. Forgive me, and farewell! Let me call you brother! It is a name that embraces many names. Receive, with a true heart, the last fair flower of a departing spirit—take this kiss. Death unites all, Brackenburg—us too it will unite.

BRACKENBURG: Then let me die with you! Share it! Share it! There is enough to extinguish two lives.

CLARA: Stay! You must live, you can live. Support my mother, who, without you, would languish in poverty. Be to her what I can no longer be; live together, and weep for me. Weep for our fatherland, and for him who could alone have sustained it. The present generation will never be rid of this bitter woe; vengeance itself could not obliterate it. Poor souls, live on, through this gap in time. Today the world suddenly stands still, its course is arrested, and my pulse will beat for only a few minutes longer. Farewell!

BRACKENBURG: Oh, live with us, as we live only for you! In taking your own life you take ours too; live—and suffer. We will stand by you, inseparably, side by side, and Love, ever attentive, shall prepare for you the sweetest consolation in her living arms. Be ours! Ours! I dare not say, mine.

CLARA: Hush, Brackenburg! You don't realize what chord you touch. Where you see hope, I see only despair.

BRACKENBURG: Share hope with the living! Pause on the brink of the precipice, look down, and then look back on us.

CLARA: I have overcome; don't call me back to the struggle.

BRACKENBURG: You are in a daze; enveloped in night you seek the abyss. Not every light is yet extinguished; many days!—

CLARA: Alas for you! Alas! Alas! Cruelly you rend the curtain from before my eyes. Yes, the day will dawn! In vain drawing its misty shroud about it—must dawn against its will. The townsman gazes timidly from his window, night leaves behind a speck of black; he looks, and the scaffold looms horrible in the morning light. With new anguish the desecrated image of the Savior lifts its imploring eyes to the Father. The sun dares not appear, it does not want to mark the hero's hour of death. Slowly the hands go their rounds—one hour strikes after another—Stop! Stop! Now is the time! The intimation of morning frightens me into the grave. (*She goes to the window as if to look out, and secretly drinks.*)

BRACKENBURG: Clara! Clara!

CLARA (*goes to the table, and drinks water*): Here is what's left. I will not tempt you to follow me. Do as you will; farewell. Extinguish this lamp silently and without delay; I am going to rest. Steal quietly away, close the door after you. Be still! Don't wake my mother! Go save yourself, if you would not be taken for my murderer. (*Exit.*)

BRACKENBURG: She leaves me for the last time just as she has always done before. What human soul could conceive how cruelly she lacerates a loving heart. She leaves me standing here, leaves me to myself, and life and death are alike hateful to me. To die alone! Weep, you who love! There is no fate more harsh than mine. She shares the death potion with me and sends me away, away from my place beside her! She draws me after her, and thrusts me back into life! Oh, Egmont, how priceless the lot you have drawn! She goes before you! From her hand you will receive the victor's wreath. She will bring heaven itself to meet you. And shall I follow? Stand to the side again? Carry this inextinguishable jealousy even to those distant realms? Earth is no longer a place where I can stay, and hell and heaven offer equal torture. How welcome to the wretched the dread hand of annihilation! (*Exit.*)

(*The scene remains unchanged for some time; music sounds, indicating Clara's death; the lamp, which Brackenburg had forgotten to extinguish, flares up once or twice and then suddenly expires.*) The scene changes to

A prison.

(*Egmont lies sleeping on a couch. A rustling of keys is heard; the door opens; servants enter with torches; Ferdinand, Alba's son, and Silva follow, accompanied by armed men. Egmont starts from his sleep.*)

EGMONT: Who are you who rudely banish slumber from my eyes? What do these vague and insolent glances mean? Why this fearful procession? With what dream of horror do you come to delude my half-awakened soul?

SILVA: The Duke sends us to announce your sentence.

EGMONT: Do you also bring the headsman who is to execute it?

SILVA: Listen, and you will know what awaits you.

EGMONT: It is in keeping with your infamous proceedings. Conceived in night and executed in the night; thus would this impudent act of injustice conceal itself. Step boldly forth, you who bear the sword concealed beneath your mantle; here is my head, the freest that tyranny ever tore from the body.

SILVA: You are wrong! What righteous judges have decided, they will not conceal from the light of day.

EGMONT: Then their insolence exceeds all imagination and belief.

SILVA *(takes the sentence from an attendant, unfolds it, and reads):* "In the King's name, and by virtue of special authority assigned to us by his majesty, to judge all his subjects, of whatever rank, not excepting the knights of the Golden Fleece, we declare—"

EGMONT: Can the King transfer that authority?

SILVA: "We declare, after a strict and legal procedure of investigation, you, Henry, Count Egmont, Prince of Gaure, guilty of high treason, and pronounce your sentence:—That at early dawn you be led from this prison to the market place, and that there, in sight of the people, and as a warning to all traitors, you shall be brought by the sword from life into death. Given at Brussels *(date and year so indistinctly read as to be imperfectly heard by the audience)* Ferdinand, Duke of Alba, president of the tribunal of twelve."

Now you know your fate. Only a brief time remains for you to resign yourself to it, to arrange your affairs, and to take leave of your friends.

> *(Exit Silva, with his followers; Ferdinand remains with*
> *two torchbearers. The stage is dimly lighted.)*

EGMONT *(stands for a time, buried in thought, and without looking around allows Silva to retire. He imagines himself alone, and on raising his eyes sees Alba's son):* You stand here? You're staying? Would you increase my amazement, my horror, by remaining here? Would you carry to your father the welcome news that you have seen me in unmanly despair? Go, tell him, tell him that he deceives neither the world nor me. At first it will be whispered cautiously behind his back, then spoken more and more loudly, and when, at some future day, that man of vaunting ambition descends from his proud eminence, a thousand voices will proclaim—that it was not the welfare of the state, nor the honor of the King, nor the tranquillity of the provinces that brought him here. For his own selfish ends he, the warrior, has counseled war, where the warrior counts. He has excited this monstrous insurrection so that he might be needed. And I fall, a victim to his mean hatred, his contemptible envy. Yes, I know it, and I can say it, the dying man, the mortally wounded man can say it: that conceited man envied me, he has long meditated and planned my ruin.

Even then, when we were still young, playing at dice together, and the stacks of gold passed rapidly from his side to mine, he would look on with affected composure, inwardly consumed with anger, more at my success than at his own loss. I remember his fiery glance, his treacherous pallor, when, at a public festival, we had a shooting match before thousands of people. He challenged me, and both nations stood by; Spaniards and Netherlanders wagered and watched. I beat him; his bullet missed, mine hit the mark, and the air was filled with loud shouts of joy from my friends. Now his shot hits me. Tell him that I know this, that I know him, that the world despises every trophy that a petty spirit erects for itself by surreptitious means. And you! If it be possible for a son to deviate from the habits of his father, practice shame before it's too late, by feeling shame for one whom you would like to revere with your whole heart.

FERDINAND: I listen without interrupting you! Your reproaches fall like blows of a club on a helm of steel. I feel the shock, but I am armed. You strike me, but you do not wound me; I am sensible only to the anguish that lacerates my heart. Alas for me! Alas! Have I lived to witness such a scene? Am I sent here to behold such a spectacle as this?

EGMONT: You break out in lamentation! What moves you, what distresses you? Is it late remorse at having lent yourself to this infamous conspiracy? You are so young, your appearance is so prepossessing. You were so friendly to me, so confiding! So long as I looked at you, I was reconciled with your father; and just as deceitful, more deceitful than he, you lured me into your net. You are the detestable one! Whoever trusts in *him*, does so at his own peril; but who could fear danger in trusting you? Go! Go! Don't rob me of the few moments left to me! Go, so that I may collect my thoughts, forget the world, and first of all you!

FERDINAND: What can I say? I stand here and I look at you, and I do not see you—I have no feeling of myself. Shall I ask to be pardoned? Shall I assure you that it was not till late, not till the last moment that I was made aware of my father's intentions? That I acted under duress, a passive instrument of his will? How does it matter what opinion you may have of me? You are lost; and I stand here an unhappy man, only to assure you of that and to lament your fate.

EGMONT: What strange voice, what unexpected consolation comes to me on my way to the grave? You, the son of my first, almost my only enemy, you pity me, you are not associated with my murderers? Speak! Tell me. What am I to take you for?

FERDINAND: Oh my cruel father! Yes, I recognize you in this command. You knew my heart, my disposition, which you so often censured as my inheritance from a tenderhearted mother. To mold me into your own likeness you sent me here. You compel me to see this man on the verge of the yawning grave, in the grasp of an arbitrary death, so that I may experience the profoundest anguish, so that I may be rendered callous to anyone's fate, so that I may become insensitive, no matter what happens to me.

EGMONT: I am amazed! Be calm! Stand, and speak like a man.

FERDINAND: Oh, I wish that I were a woman! So that people might say: what is it that moves you so, what agitates you? Tell me of a greater, a more monstrous crime, make me the witness of a deed more dire; I will thank you, I will say this was nothing.

EGMONT: You forget yourself. Consider where you are!

FERDINAND: Let this passion rage, let me give vent to my anguish. I will not seem composed when my whole being is convulsed. Must I see you here? You? It is horrible! You don't understand me! How should you understand me? Egmont! Egmont! (*Embraces him.*)

EGMONT: Explain this mystery to me.

FERDINAND: It is no mystery.

EGMONT: How can the fate of a stranger move you so deeply?

FERDINAND: Not a stranger! You are no stranger to me. It was your name that from my boyhood shone before me like a star in heaven. How often I listened for word of you, made inquiries. The hope of the boy is the youth; of the youth, the man. Thus you walked before me, always before me; I saw you there without envy and followed after you, step by step. I hoped finally to see you—I saw you, and my heart embraced you. I had destined you for myself, and when I saw you I made my choice of you anew. I hoped at last to be with you, to associate with you, to understand you, to—. Now it's all over, and I find you here!

EGMONT: My friend, if it can be any comfort to you, be assured that the moment we met my heart was drawn toward you. Now listen! Let us exchange a few quiet words. Is it the stern and settled purpose of your father to take my life?

FERDINAND: It is.

EGMONT: This sentence could not be a mere scarecrow then, designed to terrify me, to punish me through fear and intimidation, to humiliate me, and then to raise me up again by royal favor?

FERDINAND: No. Alas, no! At first I flattered myself with this delusive hope, and even then my heart was filled with pain and anguish to see you thus. Now it is real! It is certain! I am not in control of myself. Who will counsel me, who will help me to escape the inevitable?

EGMONT: Listen to me! If your heart is impelled so powerfully to save me, if you abhor the tyranny that holds me fettered, then deliver me! The moments are precious. You are the son of the all-powerful, and you have power yourself. Let us flee! I know the roads; the means of effecting our escape cannot be unknown to you. Only these walls, only a few short miles separate us from my friends. Loose these fetters, bring me to them; be ours. Surely the King will sometime thank you for saving me. Now he is taken by surprise, or perhaps he is completely uninformed. Your father takes the risk, and majesty, though horror-struck at the deed, must sanction what has been done. Oh, think of a way to freedom! Speak; nourish hope in a living soul.

FERDINAND: Stop! Oh stop! Every word deepens my despair. There is no way out here, no counsel, no escape. That tortures me, that lays hold of my heart, and tears it as if with talons. I have myself tightened the net; I know its firm unyielding knots; I know that every avenue is barred to courage and to stratagem. I feel that I too am fettered, like you, like all the rest. Do you think that I would give way to lamentation if I had not tried everything? I have thrown myself at his feet, I have spoken out, I have implored. He has sent me here in order to destroy in this one moment every remnant of joy and happiness within my heart.

EGMONT: And there is no deliverance?

FERDINAND: None.

EGMONT (*stamping his foot*): No deliverance!—Sweet life! Sweet, pleasant habit of being and doing! Must I part from you? So calmly part! Not in the tumult of battle, the din of arms, the excitement of the fray, do you grant me a hasty farewell; yours is no hurried leave; you do not shorten the moment of separation. Let me clasp your hand, gaze once more into your eyes, feel with keen emotion your beauty, your worth, then resolutely tear myself away, and say—depart!

FERDINAND: Must I stand by, and look on, not be able to save you or to stop you! What words suffice for lamentation! Whose heart would not break before such anguish?

EGMONT: Be calm!

FERDINAND: You can be calm, you can renounce; led on by necessity, you can take the hard step like a hero. What can I do? What ought I to do? You conquer yourself and us; you are the victor; I survive both myself and you. I have lost my light at the banquet, my banner in the turmoil of battle. The future lies before me, dark, desolate, perplexed.

EGMONT: Young friend, you whom by strange destiny I both win and lose at the same moment, you who feel for me, who suffer for me the agonies of death, look on me in these moments; you will not lose me. If my life was a mirror in which you loved to contemplate yourself, so also let my death be. People are not together only when they are in company together;—the distant, the departed, still live for us. I shall live for you, and for myself I have lived enough. I have enjoyed each day; each day I have been quick to perform my duty as my conscience revealed it to me. Now my life ends, as it might have ended, long, long, ago, on the sands of Gravelines. I shall cease to live; but I have lived. Live that way yourself, my friend, lead a cheerful and a joyous life, and do not fear death.

FERDINAND: You should have saved yourself for us. You could have saved yourself. You are the cause of your own death. Often I have listened when intelligent men talked about you; foes and friends, they would argue for a long time as to your merits, but on one point they finally agreed: none ventured to deny, everyone admitted that you were treading a dangerous path. How often I have wished I could warn you! Had you no friends?

EGMONT: I was warned.

FERDINAND: And when I found all these allegations, point for point, in the indictment, together with your answers—good enough to excuse you but not weighty enough to relieve you of culpability.

EGMONT: No more of this. Man imagines that he directs his life, that he governs his actions—and his inner being is drawn irresistibly toward his fate. Let us not dwell upon it; these reflections I can dismiss with ease—not so my apprehensions for these provinces; yet they too will be cared for. If my blood can flow for many, can bring peace to my people, it will flow willingly. Alas! This will not be. Yet it ill becomes a man to brood when the power to act is no longer his. If you can restrain or guide the fatal power of your father, do so. But who can?—Farewell!

FERDINAND: I cannot go.

EGMONT: Let me urgently commend my followers to your care! I have worthy men in my service; let them not be dispersed, let them not become destitute! How is it with Richard, my secretary?

FERDINAND: He has gone before you. They have beheaded him, as an accomplice in high treason.

EGMONT: Poor soul!—One more thing and then farewell; I can not go on. However powerfully the spirit may be stirred, nature at length irresistibly asserts her rights; and as a child enveloped in a serpent's folds enjoys refreshing slumber, so the weary man lays himself down to rest before the gates of death and sleeps soundly, as though a distant journey lay before him.—One thing more—I know a certain girl; you will not despise her because she was mine. Now that I can commend her to your care, I shall die in peace. You are a noble soul; a woman who finds such a man is sure to find a protector. Is my old Adolphus still living? Is he free?

FERDINAND: The lively old man who always attended you on horseback?

EGMONT: The same.

FERDINAND: He is alive, he is free.

EGMONT: He knows where she lives; let him guide you, and reward him to his dying day for having shown you the way to this treasure—Farewell!

FERDINAND: I cannot go.

EGMONT (*urging him toward the door*): Farewell!

FERDINAND: Oh let me stay a moment!

EGMONT: No leave-taking, my friend.

(*He accompanies Ferdinand to the door, and then tears himself away; Ferdinand, overwhelmed, hastily retires*)

(*Egmont alone.*)

EGMONT: Ah, you cruel man! You did not think to render me this service through your son. He has been the means of relieving me from care and sorrow, from fear and every anxious thought. Gently, yet urgently, nature claims her final tribute. It is past!— It is decided! And all that kept me wakeful on my bed, in the suspense of last night, now with inconquerable certainty lulls my senses to repose.

(He seats himself upon the couch; music.)

Sweet sleep! Like the purest happiness you come most willingly when uninvited, unsought. You loosen the knots of serious thinking, mingle all images of joy and of sorrow; unimpeded, the cycle of inner harmonies flows on, and wrapped in fond delusion, we sink down and cease to be.

(He falls asleep; music accompanies his slumber. The wall behind his couch appears to open and discloses a brilliant apparition. Freedom, in celestial garb, surrounded by an aureole, rests on a cloud. Her features are those of Clara; she bends down toward the sleeping hero. Her countenance expresses compassion, she seems to lament his fate. Soon she recovers her composure and with a gesture of encouragement exhibits the symbols of freedom, the bundle of arrows, with the staff and the cap. She bids him be of good cheer, and signifying to him that his death will secure freedom for the provinces, she hails him as a conqueror, and extends to him a laurel wreath. As she nears his head, bearing the wreath, Egmont moves like someone stirring in his sleep, in such a way that he lies with his face turned upward toward her. She holds the wreath suspended over his head; martial music with drums and pipes is heard in the distance; at the first soft sound the vision disappears. The music grows louder. Egmont awakes. The prison is dimly illumined by the dawn.—His first motion is to lift his hand to his head; he stands up and looks around, his hand still upraised.)

The wreath has vanished! Beautiful vision, the light of day has frightened you away! Yes, it was they, they were united, the two sweetest joys of my heart. Divine Freedom borrowed the form of my beloved; the lovely girl arrayed herself in the celestial garb of her friend. In a solemn moment they appeared united, with aspect more earnest than tender. With bloodstained feet the vision approached me, the waving folds of the hem of her robe were flecked with blood. It was my blood, and the blood of many noble hearts. No! It was not shed in vain! Forward! Brave people! The goddess of victory leads you on! And as the sea breaks through your dikes, just so tear down the wall of tyranny, and sweep it away, drowning, from the land which it usurps. *(Drums, closer now.)*

Hark! Hark! How often this sound has summoned me to stride freely to the field of battle and of victory! How bravely did my gallant comrades walk the dangerous path of fame! And now, from this dungeon I too shall go forth, to meet an honorable death; I die for freedom, the freedom for which I lived and fought, and for which, in my suffering, I now sacrifice myself.

(The background is occupied by Spanish soldiers wearing halberts.)

Yes, go ahead and gather them together! Close your ranks, you do not frighten me. I am accustomed to stand at the forefront of spears, against spears, and surrounded by the threat of death, to feel, with even greater zest, the energy of life.

(Drums.)

The enemy closes around you on every side! Swords are flashing; more courage, friends! You have your parents, your wives, your children behind you! *(Pointing to the guard.)*

And these are impelled by the hollow word of their commander, not by their own spirit. Protect your possessions! And to save that which is most dear to you, fall happily, in accord with the example I give you.

(Drums. As he advances toward the guards and to the door in the background, the curtain falls. The music joins in, and the play closes with a symphony of victory.)

Translated by Anna Swanwick;
adapted by Frank G. Ryder

IPHIGENIA IN TAURIS

CAST OF CHARACTERS

Iphigenia, daughter of Agamemnon, priestess in Tauris
Thoas, king of Tauris
Orestes, brother of Iphigenia
Pylades, his friend
Arcas, in the service of Thoas

Act 1

Scene 1

(Iphigenia.)

Out into shadows cast by treetops swaying
Over this ancient, sacred, leafy grove
I walk, as in the goddess's quiet temple,
With awe and apprehension even now,
As if it were the first time—and my spirit
Will not grow accustomed to this place.
These many years a higher will has kept me
Hidden here, a will to which I bend.
But I am still what I was then: a stranger.
For, oh, the sea parts me from those I love,
And so I spend long days beside the shore,
Sending forth my soul in quest of Greece.
The crashing waves bring back to me, in answer
To my sighs, nothing but muffled sounds.
Pity the one who leads a lonely life
Far from parents, brothers, sisters. Grief
Consumes the happiness that seemed so close
His lips could touch it. His thoughts keep drifting back
To the halls of his father's house, where the sun
First opened up to him the heavens, where
Children, born together, in their games
Drew close and closer the gentle bonds that joined them.
I have no quarrel with the gods, and yet
A woman's lot is much to be lamented.
Men are the masters still, at home, at war;
Far from home they need no help from others.

They have the joy of wealth, the wreath of victory.
The death decreed them is an honored death.
What narrow limits bind a woman's fortune!
Her duty, yes, her solace to obey
Even a brutish husband; sadder still
If hostile fate should drive her far from home.
So Thoas keeps me here, a noble man,
In solemn, holy bonds—of slavery;
And I in shame confess that I serve you
With mute resentment, Goddess, even you,
My rescuer. By every right my life
Should be devoted freely to your service.
Indeed I always placed my hope in you
And do so still, Diana, you who took me,
Forsaken daughter of our greatest king,
Into your gentle, holy arms. And now,
Daughter of Zeus, if you have guided home
In fame and honor to his fatherland,
From Troy's demolished walls, that highborn man
Whose heart you tried, claiming from him his daughter,
Godlike Agamemnon, who delivered
To your altar the dearest thing he had—
If you have kept his wife and children safe,
Electra and his son, his finest treasures:
Then give me back at last to my own people,
Saving me, as you once saved me from death,
From my life here as well, a second death.

Scene 2

(Iphigenia, Arcas.)

ARCAS: The King has sent me here to offer greetings—
Salutations to Diana's priestess.
This is the day when Tauris thanks its goddess
For new and marvelous victories. Ahead
Of King and army I have hurried here
To tell you: He is coming; it is near.
IPHIGENIA: We're ready to receive them both with honor.

Our goddess too will look with gracious eyes
On welcome sacrifice from Thoas's hand.
ARCAS: I wish that, looking in our priestess's eyes—
  Your eyes, high virgin, whom we love and honor—
  I'd see in them a clearer, brighter light,
  Good omen for us all! But grief still clouds
  Mysteriously the center of your being.
  We've hoped for years in vain that you would open
  Your heart to us with words of trust and friendship.
  But ever since you've been here, since I've known you,
  This look of yours has always made me shudder.
  Your soul still lies, as if in iron chains,
  Bound in the deepest recess of your bosom.
IPHIGENIA: As befitting one cast out and orphaned.
ARCAS: You think yourself an orphan here, an outcast?
IPHIGENIA: Can alien ground become one's fatherland?
ARCAS: Your fatherland is alien to you now.
IPHIGENIA: And that is why my wounded heart won't heal.
  When I was young, my spirit barely forming
  Ties to father, mother, sister, brother,
  When we, in graceful company, like shoots
  Sprung from the trunk of our ancestral tree,
  Strove skyward—then it was misfortune struck;
  An alien curse laid hold of me, tore me
  From those I loved, cut with an iron hand
  The dearest bond that joined us—lost and gone
  The best delights of youth, the flowering years,
  The earliest. Even rescued, still I felt
  No better than a shade; the freshening joy
  Of life will never bloom for me again.
ARCAS: If that is why you call yourself unhappy,
  I'd be right in calling you ungrateful.
IPHIGENIA: You've always had my thanks.
ARCAS: But not the pure kind,
  The thanks for which one does a generous deed,
  And not the happy look that shows one's host
  A life contented, an affectionate heart.
  When years ago a deep mysterious fate
  Brought you to this temple, Thoas came

To greet you as a gift sent by the gods,
With reverential awe and with affection.
These shores were kind to you and friendly, shores
That always filled the stranger's heart with terror,
For none before you ever reached our kingdom
Who did not fall, by ancient custom,
Sacrificed at Diana's holy steps.

IPHIGENIA: There's more to life than just the breath of freedom.
What life is this that I must waste in sadness
Within these holy precincts, like a shade
Circling 'round its own grave? Am I to call
My life a happy, self-fulfilling one,
When every day, hopelessly dreamed away,
Foreshadows those gray days on Lethe's shore,
Idled away in self-forgetfulness
By mournful companies of departed souls?
A useless life is an early death; and this,
A woman's fate, above all others mine.

ARCAS: This noble pride you take in self-reproach
I pardon, however much I pity you,
Because it robs your life of all enjoyment.
You've done nothing here since your arrival?
Our King—who cheered his melancholy temper?
The ancient, cruel custom which decreed
That every stranger bleed his life away
On Diana's altar—who held that at bay
From year to year, with soft persuasive words,
So often sending captives back again
To home and country, not to certain death?
Did not Diana, far from being angry
At loss of ancient bloody sacrifice,
Give ample hearing to your gentle prayer?
Does not Victory fly on joyful wings
Above our army—even soar ahead?
Does not each person feel his lot improved
Now that the King, who for so long has led us,
Wise and bravely, finds his pleasure too
In the grace of your presence, lightening
For us the duty to obey in silence?

You call it useless when your very nature
Sheds its healing force upon the thousands,
When you, god-given to our people, are
The everlasting source of their new joy,
And on death's inhospitable shore secure
The stranger's safety and his voyage home?

IPHIGENIA: The little done is quickly lost from sight
When one can see ahead what's left to do.

ARCAS: You'd praise one who demeans what he's accomplished?

IPHIGENIA: We censure those who measure out their deeds.

ARCAS: But also those so proud they scorn true worth,
And those so vain they set false worth too high.
Believe me—listen to the word of one
Devoted to you in good faith and trust:
When the King comes to talk with you today.
Don't make it hard for him to speak his mind.

IPHIGENIA: Your every word of kindness frightens me;
I've tried so hard to fend off his proposal.

ARCAS: Think what you're doing, think what's good for you.
Ever since his son was lost to him
The King has trusted few of those around him,
And those few not as once he used to do.
Jealously, in every noble's son
He sees his throne's successor, and he fears
A lonely helpless age, even perhaps
Bold rebellion and an early death.
Scythians set no store in eloquence,
Least of all the King. He's only used
To orders and to action, doesn't know
The art of bringing conversations 'round
From far off, slowly, subtly, to his purpose.
Don't make it hard for him by shy protesting
Nor by willed misunderstanding. Come!
Have the grace to go halfway to meet him.

IPHIGENIA: And hasten the very thing that threatens me?

ARCAS: You call the offer of his hand a threat?

IPHIGENIA: A threat more terrible than any other.

ARCAS: You could at least repay his love with trust!

IPHIGENIA: But only if he'll free my mind of fear.

ARCAS: Why do you tell him nothing of your background?
IPHIGENIA: Because—secrecy befits a priestess.
ARCAS: Nothing should be secret from the King;
    And though he's making no demands—he feels—
    And feels it deeply in his generous soul:
    You mean to hold yourself aloof from him.
IPHIGENIA: He grows impatient and displeased with me?
ARCAS: It almost seems so. He speaks little of you;
    Yet certain casual words of his persuade me
    That the wish to make you his has laid
    Firm hold upon his spirit. Do not leave him.
    Don't abandon him to his devices,
    Lest displeasure grow within his heart,
    Bringing you terror, and you think too late
    And with regret of my well-meant advice.
IPHIGENIA: What? Does the King propose to do a thing
    No worthy man who loves his name, whose heart
    Is bound by reverence for the heavenly gods,
    Should ever contemplate? Would he take me
    By sheer force from my altar to his bed?
    If so, then I shall call on all the gods,
    But on Diana first, the resolute,
    And she will grant her priestess sure protection,
    Virgin goddess to a mortal virgin.
ARCAS: Be calm! No new and violent surge of blood
    Will drive the King into the rash commission
    Of such a young man's deed. His way of thinking
    Makes me fear another harsh decision,
    Which he will execute without reserve,
    Because his soul is firm, not to be moved.
    Therefore I beg you: give him trust, be grateful,
    If you can give him nothing more than that.
IPHIGENIA: Tell me, tell me what else it is you know!
ARCAS: Learn it from him. The King, I see, is coming.
    You hold him in respect, and your own heart
    Bids you address him in a friendly fashion,
    Trustingly. A woman's kindly word
    Can lead a good man far.

(Exit.)

IPHIGENIA *(alone):*   I do not see
How I can take this loyal man's advice,
Yet I would gladly follow duty's course
And give the King good words for his good deeds.
I hope for strength to tell so great a lord
What pleases him and still to speak the truth.

Scene 3

(Iphigenia, Thoas.)

IPHIGENIA: The goddess bless you with the wealth of kings,
Give you fame and glory, victory,
Abundant riches, prospering of your house,
The full reward of every pious wish,
That you, with all the cares of ruling others,
Surpass all others in your rare good fortune!
THOAS: My people's praise would be enough for me.
What I have gained, others enjoy much more
Than I. He is the happiest, whether
King or man of low estate, to whom
Fate ordains the prospering of his line.
You understood and shared my bitter pain
When I lost my son, the last and best
Of all, cut from my side by enemy swords.
So long as thought of vengeance fed my spirit
I did not feel the emptiness of my house.
Now I am back, my satisfaction gained,
Their kingdom destroyed, my son avenged,
I have nothing left at home to please me.
The look of glad obedience I was used
To seeing in the eyes of everyone
Is clouded now by care and discontent,
Everyone wondering what the future holds,
Following the childless king because he must.
And so today I seek the temple where
I've often come with prayer for victory,
With thanks for victory. In my heart I bear
A long-held wish, one not strange to you,

And no surprise. I hope to take you home,
A blessing to my people and to me,
Leading you, a bride, into my house.
IPHIGENIA: You offer far too much to one you know
So little, Sire. Before you stands, shamefaced,
A fugitive, seeking nothing on this shore
Beyond the peace and safety you have given.
THOAS: Hiding as you do behind the secret
Of your descent, from me as from the lowliest—
Nowhere on earth would that be right and proper.
These shores strike fear in strangers' hearts; the law
Ordains, necessity commands. But you,
Enjoying every sacred privilege, well
Received as guest of ours, living each day
According to your will and inclination—
From you I hoped to have the trust a host
May rightfully expect for his allegiance.
IPHIGENIA: If I concealed from you my parents' names,
My lineage, Sire, I did so in confusion,
Not distrust. For if perhaps you knew
Who stood before you, knew what cursed creature
You were feeding and protecting, horror
Might seize your great heart with a rare dismay.
And then instead of offering me the place
Beside your throne you'd cast me prematurely
From your kingdom, plunging me perhaps—
Before such time as I am meant to go
In happiness back home, my wandering ended—
Into the misery everywhere awaiting
The aimless exile, banished from his people,
To touch him with the cold and alien hand
Of fear.
THOAS: Whatever the gods intend for you,
Or what they plan for you and for your house,
While you have lived among us and enjoyed
The privileges assigned a sacred guest
I've had no lack of blessings from on high.
It may not be so easy to convince me
That, harboring you, I harbor mortal guilt.

IPHIGENIA: You're blest by the good you do, not by your guest.
THOAS: Service rendered the wicked brings no blessing.
  So end your silence, end your long refusal.
  It's not the bidding of an unjust man.
  Our own goddess placed you in my hands.
  She held you sacred: I have done the same.
  So let her omen be my future law:
  If hope of going home exists for you,
  Then I'll declare you free of all demands.
  But if it be your way is blocked forever,
  If your line is banished, or by some
  Calamitous blow of evil blotted out,
  Then you are mine—and by more laws than one.
  Speak frankly, and you know I'll keep my word.
IPHIGENIA: My tongue, full of reluctance, frees itself
  Of ancient bonds, now at last revealing
  A secret long concealed in silence. For,
  Once confided, it leaves without return
  Its certain dwelling deep in the heart, hurts
  Or helps, however gods above may will.
  Hear me! My race is the race of Tantalus.
THOAS: That is a mighty name you speak so calmly.
  Do you call *him* your ancestor—him
  The world knows as a man once highly favored
  By the gods, that same Tantalus whom Jupiter
  Summoned to his council hall and table,
  Whose conversation, full of ancient wisdom,
  Weaving many threads of meaning, pleased
  The gods themselves like words of oracles?
IPHIGENIA: He is the one; but gods should never walk
  With men as they may do with their own kind.
  The race of mortals is far too weak to keep
  From dizziness at unaccustomed heights.
  Ignoble he was not, and no betrayer;
  Too great to be a slave, and as companion
  Of the great Thunderer, only a man.
  Human, too, his crime; the gods in judgment
  Strict, and poets sing: Excessive pride
  And breach of trust hurled him from Zeus's table

Down to the ancient shame of Tartarus;
And all his race, alas, incurred their hatred.
THOAS: Was their guilt ancestral or their own?
IPHIGENIA: Broad chest, the Titan's bone and brawn, oh yes,
These passed in certain heritage to sons
And grandsons, but the god had also forged
A band of brazen metal 'round their brows.
Good sense and moderation, patience, wisdom
He hid from their withdrawn and sullen gaze.
All wishes, all desires turned to fury,
And their fury raged about them, boundless.
First Pelops, man of violent will, beloved
Son of Tantalus, through treachery
And murder gained the fairest woman's hand:
Oenomaeus's daughter Hippodamia.
She bears, in answer to her husband's wishes,
Two sons: Thyestes, Atreus. Jealously
They watch their father's love for his firstborn:
Another son, sprung from another bed.
Hate binds them. The pair in stealth and secret
Dare their first deed: fratricide. Their father
Thinks Hippodamia to be the murderer,
In unrelenting rage demands that she
Return his son to him. She disembowels
    Herself.
THOAS: No more to say? Go on, keep talking!
Do not regret your trust in me. Speak!
IPHIGENIA: Lucky the one who can recall his forebears
Gladly, can tell his listeners pleasant tales
Of deeds and greatness, see in quiet joy
The last link forged in this fair chain:
Himself—herself! For no house breeds at once
Demigod or monster. No, instead,
A chain of evil beings or of good
At last brings forth true horror or true joy
For all the world. After their father's death
Atreus and Thyestes rule the city,
Jointly in command; but not for long
Could such harmony last. Thyestes soon

Dishonors Atreus' bed and is in vengeance
Cast from the kingdom by his brother. But
Thyestes long before, plotting evil,
Had foully stolen one of his brother's sons;
In secret, ever ingratiating, raised him
As his own. He fills his heart with rage
And vengeance, sends him to the royal city
To murder, in his uncle, his own father.
The boy's intent is soon unmasked. The King
Puts cruel sentence on the assassin, thinking
He kills his brother's son. Too late he learns
Who it is that in his reeling sight
Dies this tortured death. To purge the cry
For vengeance from his heart he plots in silence
An unexampled deed. Seemingly calm,
Indifferent, reconciled, he lures his brother,
Along with both his sons, back to his kingdom,
Lays hand upon the boys, slaughters the two
Of them and sets the vile, most dreadful dish
Before the father at their first repast.
Then—as Thyestes, sated with his meal
Of flesh and blood, is seized by melancholy,
Asks about his boys and even thinks
He hears their steps and voices at the door—
Atreus, lips twisted in a smile,
Throws him the head and feet of his murdered sons.
You turn your face in horror, Sire. Just so
Did the sun turn its countenance away,
From its eternal course divert its chariot.
These are the forebears of your priestess, Sire,
And much of their most wretched destiny,
Much work of minds confused still lies concealed
Beneath the heavy wings of night, and we
Are left to peer into a sickening twilight.
THOAS: So leave them hidden! Let there be an end
Of horrors! Tell now by what miracle
You came to spring from such a savage line.
IPHIGENIA: Atreus's eldest son was Agamemnon.
He is my father. Yes, I still maintain

That since my childhood years I've always seen
In him the model of a perfect man.
Clytemnestra bore me, first reward
Of his love, then Electra. Now he ruled
Serene as King; the house of Tantalus
Was granted what it long had lacked: peace.
And yet my parents' joy fell short; they had
No son. Hardly was this desire fulfilled—
Orestes growing up the favored child,
Between two sisters, and our house secure—
When soon we had to face renewed disaster.
Word of war has reached you, war which ranges
All the power of Greece's rulers 'round
The walls of Troy, in vengeance for a woman
Of surpassing beauty, kidnapped. Whether
They have taken the city, reached the goal
Of their revenge, I have not heard. My father
Led the Grecian army. There in Aulis
They waited for a favoring wind in vain.
Diana, angered at their noble leader,
Held him back in all his hurry, claimed
Through Calchas's lips the King's own eldest daughter.
They lured me with my mother to their camp.
They dragged me to the altar, pledged my life
In homage to the goddess. This appeased her.
She did not want my blood, but in a cloud
She hid and rescued me, and in this temple
I first found myself returned from death.
I am Iphigenia; it is I,
Grandchild of Atreus, Agamemnon's daughter,
Chattel of the goddess, with whom you speak.

THOAS: I give no more preferment, no more trust
   To the king's daughter than I do the stranger.
   I repeat my first proposal: Come,
   Follow me, and share in what I have.

IPHIGENIA: How dare I take a step like that, my lord?
   Has not the goddess, she who rescued me,
   Sole right to this, my consecrated life?
   She chose for me the place of sanctuary,

She keeps me for a father whom she punished
Enough in the mere semblance of the deed—
To be, perhaps, the joy of his old age.
Perhaps the happy time of my return
Is near; if I ignored her way, her plan,
Tied myself here against her will—what then?
I prayed for some clear sign if I should stay.

THOAS: You have the sign: your very presence here.
Don't go in desperate search for such evasions.
Much talk is of no use when one refuses;
The other person only hears the No.

IPHIGENIA: These aren't just words, intended to delude.
I have revealed my deepest heart to you.
And surely you yourself can tell what longing,
What sense of fear draws me to find my father,
My mother, sister, brother once again,
In hope that through the ancient halls, where mourning
Still from time to time whispers my name,
Joy such as attends the newly born
May wreathe, column to column, fairest garlands.
Oh, could you have your ships escort me there!
You'd give to me and everyone new life.

THOAS: Go back then! Do what your heart tells you to.
Do not listen to the voice of reason
Or good advice. Act just like a woman!
Yield to impulse, let it take the reins,
Lay hold of you and drag you this way, that way.
If some flame of desire burns in their hearts
No sacred bond will keep them from the traitor
Luring them from a father's or a husband's
Tried and true and ever-faithful arms.
And even if the sudden flame is silent
In their hearts, they stand, for all its truth
And force, unmoved by golden-tongued Persuasion.

IPHIGENIA: Recall, my lord, your noble word of promise.
Is this the answer to my trust? You seemed
Prepared, whatever I said, to hear me out.

THOAS: But not for things unhoped for, not for that.
It's what I should expect, though. After all,

I knew that I was dealing with a woman.
IPHIGENIA: My lord, do not discredit our poor sex.
  A woman's weapons, true, may not be splendid
  Like a man's, but they are not ignoble.
  Believe me, I am better here than you,
  In knowing, more than you, what makes you happy.
  Not understanding me and not yourself,
  You think that closer ties would bring us joy.
  Full of heart and full of good intentions,
  You keep insisting that I acquiesce.
  But here and now I thank the gods that they
  Gave me the strength and firmness not to enter
  This alliance they do not approve.
THOAS: No god says that. It's your own heart that speaks.
IPHIGENIA: It's only through our hearts they speak to us.
THOAS: And have I not a right to listen too?
IPHIGENIA: A sounding storm drowns out their gentle voices.
THOAS: You mean that only priestesses can hear them?
IPHIGENIA: The ruler, most of all, must heed their words.
THOAS: Your sacred office and your heritage
  Of place at Zeus's table brings you nearer
  The gods than any earth-born savage.
IPHIGENIA: So now
  I pay the price of trust you forced from me!
THOAS: I'm only human; we had better stop.
  Here is my final word: Be her priestess,
  The goddess's, as she has chosen you.
  But may Diana pardon me for having,
  Despite my sense of wrong, my self-reproach,
  Withheld from her the ancient sacrifice.
  No stranger pays our shores a happy visit;
  In past he always faced a certain death.
  Only you, with kindness which I fancied
  At times to be a tender daughter's love,
  At times the still affection of a bride—
  Only you held me enchained in bonds
  Of magic, so that I forgot my duty.
  You had lulled my senses into sleep;
  I failed to hear the muttering of my people;

Louder now they call down on my head
The guilt for my own son's too early death.
No longer will I check for sake of you
The people's urgent cry for sacrifice.
IPHIGENIA: I never asked you this for my own sake.
He mistakes the gods of heaven who
Believes they thirst for blood. He just imputes
To them his own most cruel instincts. Did not
My goddess save me even from her priest?
She welcomed more my service than my death.
THOAS: We have no license to subject these sacred
Rites to nimble reasoning and so
Interpret them and bend them to our purpose.
Go and do your duty. I'll do mine.
We've found two strangers hiding in the caves
Along the shore; they bring no good to me
Or to my country. They are in my hands;
Let your goddess take them in renewal
Of sacrifice—just, long-withheld, the first.
I'll send them here; you know the ritual.

Scene 4

(Iphigenia alone.)

Goddess of gracious rescue, you offer
Clouds to envelop innocent victims,
Out of the arms of brazen fate
Bearing them over the sea, on winds,
Over the farthest reaches of earth,
Anywhere it suits you to bear them.
Wisdom is yours, and future vision;
Past is not past for you and gone.
Those who are yours rest safe in your gaze,
Just as your light, the life of the night,
Rests and holds sway over the earth.
Oh, preserve my hands from this blood,
Never the bringer of blessing or peace!
For the shade of the casual victim

Waits for the mournful, unwilling murderer's
Moments of weakness, to fill them with terror.
For the immortals love the kindly
Far-flung generations of mankind,
Gladly prolong the fleeting life span
Given to mortals, gladly afford us
Glimpses of their own infinite heavens,
For our delight and our shared contemplation,
Which for a time they generously grant us.

Act 2

Scene 1

(Orestes, Pylades.)

ORESTES: The path we travel is the path of death.
  With every step my spirit grows more calm.
  I begged Apollo to remove the horrid
  Escort of the Furies from my side,
  And he in turn, with a god's hope-inspiring
  Words of unmistakable meaning, seemed
  To promise help and rescue in the temple
  Where his beloved sister reigns in Tauris.
  And now it's all come true: all this suffering
  Is meant to end forever with my life.
  How easy it is for me, heart oppressed
  By a god's hand, mind and sense benumbed,
  To yield my claim upon the sun's fair light.
  And if the sons of Atreus' sons aren't meant
  To end their lives in battle, victory-crowned,
  If, like my forebears, like my father, I
  Am meant to die a wretched death as bloody
  Beast of sacrifice, well, so be it!
  Better the altar than the den of shame
  Where kinfolk turned assassin set their snares.
  Leave me in peace till then, you deities
  Of Underworld, who track me down like dogs

Unleashed upon the spoor of blood that drips
From every step and marks the path I take.
Leave me; I'll join you down there soon enough.
The light of day won't see you, won't see me.
The fair green carpet of the earth is not
A playground meant for phantoms. There below
I'll seek you out, when one fate holds us all
Alike confined in pale eternal night.
You alone, my Pylades, blameless comrade
Of my guilt and of my banishment,
You I hate to take into that land
Of tears so soon. It is your life or death
Alone that still can bring me hope or fear.

PYLADES: I'm not as ready yet as you, Orestes,
  To go down into that domain of shadows.
  My scheme is still that these bewildering paths
  Which seem to lead into black night shall be
  The way by which I lift us back to life.
  I don't think death; I listen and plot to see
  Whether the gods will not afford us wisdom,
  The ways and means of fortunate escape.
  Fear it or not, death can never be
  Postponed. When the priestess lifts her hand
  To cut our locks of hair in consecration
  I shall be thinking still of one thing only:
  Escape for you and me. Lift up your heart
  From this despairing state. Your loss of faith
  Hastens danger. Apollo prophesied:
  Solace, help, and hope of rescue wait,
  Even for one like you, in his sister's temple!
  The gods do not speak words of double meaning
  As burdened men in desperation think.

ORESTES: Life's dark pall lay on my tender years,
  Cast by my mother's hand upon my head,
  So early. Thus as I grew up, my father's
  Image, my unspoken gaze became,
  For her and for her lover, bitter chiding.
  How often when my sister Electra sat
  Quiet by the fire in the deep hall

I'd nestle up to her, in my affliction,
And on her lap, as she wept bitter tears,
I'd stare at her with wide eyes. Then she'd talk
And talk about our honored father. How
I longed to see him, be with him. By turns
I wished myself in Troy, him with us here.
Then came the day—

PYLADES: Oh, let that moment be
The talk of hell's own spirits in the night.
Let memories of happy times renew
Our strength to run with courage the hero's course.
The gods have need of many able men
To serve their will on this broad earth. They must
Be counting on you still—or they'd have sent you
With your father, to escort him when
He made his unwilled journey down to Orcus.

ORESTES: I wish I'd held his robe tight in my hand
And followed him.

PYLADES: So those who kept you safe
Watched over me, for what I might have been,
Had you not lived, I cannot bear to think,
Since I have never lived nor wished to live
Other than with and for you, since my childhood.

ORESTES: Do not recall to me those happy days
When your house gave me room to live in freedom.
Your noble father, wise and loving, nurtured
The tender plant I was, half-frozen dead,
And you, a friend of never-failing humor,
Danced every day about me, full of life,
A light and many-colored butterfly
About a dark flower, playing the light
Of your own pleasure into my dark spirit,
Till, troubles all forgotten, I with you,
In haste of youth, dreamed and reeled in transport.

PYLADES: My life began when I began to love you.

ORESTES: Say: "My troubles." That would be the truth.
This is the frightening thing about my fate,
That I, like some disease-infected exile,
Bear secret hurt and death within my heart;

That, where I find a place of perfect health,
Soon the radiant faces all about me
Show the painful trace of lingering death.
PYLADES: I'd be the first to die this death, Orestes,
If indeed your breath were mortal poison.
Am I not still as full of joy, of courage?
And love and laughter are the wings that bear
Great deeds aloft.
ORESTES: Great deeds? Yes, I remember
Times when they were all we saw before us,
When together we would often chase
Our game through hills and valleys and, with time,
Equals in chest and fist to our high forebears,
Dared to hope with club and sword to track
And hunt the monster and the brigand down;
And so at nightfall, leaning back-to-back,
We'd sit in silence by the great broad sea,
The play of waves reaching to our feet,
The world lying before us, wide and open,
And often you or I would reach to draw
Our swords, and future deeds shone down like stars
Unnumbered 'round about us from the night.
PYLADES: There is no limit to the work our spirit
Urges on us. We wish each deed done now,
And great as only time and change will make it
When poets' lips have spread it magnified,
Through lands and generations, years on end.
The sound of what our fathers did is good
When young men resting in the quiet shade
Of evening drink it in with sound of harps;
Yet what we do is as it was for them:
Fraught with trouble, a thing of bits and pieces.
So we chase after that which flees before us,
Pay no attention to the road we follow,
Scarcely see beside us footprints left
By forebears, traces of their earthly life.
We hurry after them, after their shadows,
Which, far in the distance, godlike, crown
The mountain heads and ride on golden clouds.

I've no regard for one who sees himself
The way the world may sometime magnify him,
But you, young man, should thank the gods above
That they have done so much through you, so soon.

ORESTES: When they vouchsafe a man the chance to take
Pleasure in what he does, to save his house
From harm, to build his realm, secure its bounds,
And ancient enemies are slain or flee,
Then's the time for thanks, for then some god
Has given him life's first and last delight.
Me—I am their chosen slaughterer,
The murderer of my mother whom I honored
Still; and, shameful vengeance for a deed
Of shame, they signal thus my ruin. Trust me,
I know they've taken aim at Tantalus' house,
And I, last of the line, am not to die
In innocence or honor.

PYLADES: The gods do not
Avenge the father's misdeed through his son.
Good or bad, each person does his deed,
Takes with him his reward. What we inherit
Is our parents' blessing, not their curse.

ORESTES: It hardly seems their blessing brings us here.

PYLADES: At least it is the high will of the gods.

ORESTES: Then it's their will, as well, that ruins us.

PYLADES: Do what they command and wait the outcome.
You have a sister to return to Apollo.
When the two together dwell at Delphi,
Honored by a people nobly minded,
Then that highborn pair will grant their grace
To you for what you did and save you from
The Furies' hands. You see: not one of them
Has dared set foot within this sacred grove.

ORESTES: At least in that case I can die in peace.

PYLADES: I'm of a different mind; not without skill
I've linked what's been so far with what's to come
And quietly have analyzed the whole.
Perhaps within the councils of the gods
The great work's under way already. Diana

Longs to leave this rude barbarian shore
And all its bloody human sacrifice.
We were destined for the glorious deed,
We are charged to do it, and—strange to say—
Our capture brings us to the very gates.

ORESTES: How rare a skill you show, to weave one fabric
From the gods' designs and your desires.

PYLADES: What good is all man's wit unless it hears
And heeds the will of those who rule above?
Some god has summoned to this weighty deed
The noble man of great transgressions, charging
Him to end what seems to us unending.
The hero wins, and in his penance serves
The gods and all the world that honors him.

ORESTES: If I am destined so to live and act,
Then let some god take from my burdened brow
The madness driving me upon the slippery,
Mother-blood-bespattered path that leads me
Among the Dead. Let him in mercy dry
The spring that bubbles up at me, out from
My mother's wounds, to sully me forever.

PYLADES: Be more patient. You make bad matters worse
And take upon yourself the Furies' office.
Let me do the thinking. Keep your peace.
The final act will need concerted effort.
Then I'll call on you; the two of us
Will move with cautious boldness to fulfillment.

ORESTES: I hear Odysseus talking.

PYLADES: Don't belittle!
Every man must choose his special hero,
Whose path he follows as he works his way
Upward to Olympus. Let me confess:
Cunning and wit seem no disgrace to me,
For one who's pledged to bold, decisive action.

ORESTES: I respect the man who's brave and honest.

PYLADES: That's why I did not ask advice of you.
One step's been taken. I have talked our guards
Into revealing much. Already I know
A foreign, godlike woman holds in check

That bloody law of theirs, bringing the gods
As offerings a heart of purity,
Incense, and prayer. They bestow high praise
On her, her kindness; they believe she comes
From the race of the Amazons, and fled
In order to escape some great misfortune.

ORESTES: It seems her luminous realm has lost its power
At my approach, a criminal pursued,
Enveloped by his curse as by broad night.
The pious thirst for blood frees from its chains
The ancient ritual, to bring us ruin.
The King's own savage mind secures our death.
No woman will save us if he is angered.

PYLADES: We're lucky it's a woman. For a man,
Even the best, accustoms heart and mind
To acts of cruelty and in the end
Makes a rule of what he finds abhorrent,
Turns harsh from habit, hard to recognize!
A woman, though, holds to a single thought
Once she conceives it; more to be relied on,
Whether it be for good or bad.—Quiet!
Here she comes; leave us alone. I can't
Reveal our names to her at once, nor fully
Confide to her our fate. You go ahead;
Before she talks with you we'll meet again.

Scene 2

(Iphigenia, Pylades.)

IPHIGENIA: Your home and where you come from, stranger, tell
    me.
I have the feeling I should more compare you
To a Greek than to a Scythian.
                    (She removes his chains.)
The freedom that I give is dangerous.
May the gods avert what threatens you!

PYLADES: Sweet voice! Most welcome sound, my mother tongue

Heard in a foreign land. And I, a prisoner,
See before my eyes, once again,
A new and welcome vision: the blue hills
Of my ancestral harbor. Let my joy
Assure you that I also am a Greek.
For one brief moment I forgot how much
I need you and I turned my inner eye
To that incomparable picture in my mind.
Tell me, unless your lips are sealed by some
Unhappy fate, from which great clan of ours,
Or house, you count your godlike lineage.

IPHIGENIA: A priestess, chosen so by her own goddess,
And by her sanctified, addresses you.
Let that suffice. But tell me who you are
And what unhappy turn of destiny
Has carried you and your companion here.

PYLADES: Easy enough to tell you what misfortune,
Forcing itself on us, dogs our footsteps;
I wish you could as easily grant us,
Godlike lady, the happy glint of hope!
We are from Crete, Adrastes' sons, and I,
His youngest son, Cephalus by name.
And he's Laodamas, the eldest, scion
Of our house. Between us, wild, unruly,
Stood a middle son, even in games
Disrupting all the harmony and joy
Of youth. We calmly did our mother's bidding,
As long as Father's army fought at Troy;
But when he came back rich in loot of war
And not long after died, we brothers soon
Parted as rivals over wealth and rule.
I gave my preference to the eldest. He killed
His brother—this the blood-guilt which has brought
The Furies out, fierce in headlong pursuit.
Delphic Apollo, though, delivered us
In hope to this barbaric shore, with word
That in his sister's temple here we should
Await the blessing-laden hand of help.
We've been taken captive, brought here, handed

Over to you for sacrifice. You know this.

IPHIGENIA: Did Troy fall? Good man, give me this assurance!

PYLADES: In ruins. Oh give us surety of rescue!
Hasten on its way the help a god
Has promised us. Take pity on my brother!
Speak some kind, some gracious word to him,
I beg you earnestly; for joy and pain
And memory can all too quickly seize
Upon his inmost mind and lay it waste.
A fevered madness comes upon him then,
Delivering up his free and noble soul
Into the Furies' hands, to be their prey.

IPHIGENIA: However great your suffering, I implore you!
Forget it till you've set my mind at rest.

PYLADES: The same high city that for ten long years
Resisted all the martial force of Greece
Lies now in rubble, not to rise again.
Yet many graves of many of our finest
Compels our thoughts to that barbarian shore.
Achilles lies there with his handsome friend.

IPHIGENIA: So, men of godlike form, you too are dust.

PYLADES: Nor will Palamedes see the light
Of day and home, nor Telamonian Ajax.

IPHIGENIA: (He has not said my father's name nor mentioned
Him among the slain. Then he's alive,
And I shall see him. O dear heart, keep hoping!)

PYLADES: And yet this death of thousands, bittersweet,
At enemy hands, remains a blessing still.
Those who returned did not return to triumph
But to wild terrors and a miserable end
Decreed by some aroused and angry god.
Are you beyond the sound of human voice?
Within its farthest reach it bears report
Of unexampled deeds that have been done.
I see the woe which fills Mycenae's hall
With never-ending sighs is still a thing
Of which you have no knowledge. Clytemnestra,
With Aegisthus' help, entrapped her husband
And, on the day of his return, killed him!

You hold this kingly house in high esteem,
I see that, for your breast in vain rebels
Against the unexpected, monstrous word.
Are you the daughter of a friend? Are you
Of neighboring birth in that same city then?
Do not conceal the truth nor blame me for it,
For being first to bring the ghastly news.

IPHIGENIA: Go on, say how this awful deed was done!

PYLADES: The day of his arrival, when the King,
Stepping from his bath refreshed and calm,
Requested from his lady's hand his robe,
That fatal woman cast a woven web
Of many folds, artfully entangling,
About his shoulders and his noble head,
And as he vainly sought to free himself,
As from a net—then it was Aegisthus,
Traitor, struck the blow; and, thus enshrouded,
Down among the dead went that great prince.

IPHIGENIA: And what was the conspirator's reward?

PYLADES: A kingdom and a bed, both long since his.

IPHIGENIA: So evil passion bred the shameful deed?

PYLADES: And deep impulses of long-standing vengeance.

IPHIGENIA: How then had the King offended her?

PYLADES: With so grave a deed that, if excuse
Exists at all for murder, would excuse it.
He lured her out to Aulis and, once there,
Since some god had loosed tempestuous winds
To halt the movement of the Grecian force,
Brought their eldest daughter, Iphigenia,
Before Diana's altar, and she fell,
A bloody sacrifice, to serve the Greeks.
This, they say, implanted such revulsion
Deep within her heart that she accepted
Aegisthus' suit and went herself to meet
Her husband with the embracing nets of ruin.

IPHIGENIA (*hiding her face*):
That is enough: You will see me again.

PYLADES (*alone*):
The royal family's fate has, it would seem,

Moved her deeply. Whoever she may be
She surely knew the King. She is herself
Of noble house and was to our great good
Sold into exile here. Now steady, heart;
Let us set course, wisely and confident,
Toward the star of hope whose light shines on us.

Act 3

Scene 1

(Iphigenia, Orestes.)

IPHIGENIA: Poor man, I come to loose the bonds that bind you,
As token of a far more painful fate.
The freedom which this sanctuary grants
Is, like the last bright glimpse of life that comes
In mortal illness, harbinger of death.
I cannot yet—and must not—tell myself
That you are lost. My hand anointing you
For sacrifice would be a murderer's hand.
How could I? While I am Diana's priestess
No one, no matter who, shall touch you. Yet
If I refuse to carry out the duty
Demanded of me by the irate King,
He'll choose one of the virgins serving me
To take my place and then the only help
That I can give will be my ardent prayers.
Good countryman! The merest slave whose feet
Have barely touched the hearth of family gods
Is a welcome sight in foreign lands.
How shall I greet you then with joy and blessing
Great enough, when you bring me the image
Of heroes I was taught to honor as
A child, and comfort so beguilingly
My heart of hearts with sweet renewal of hope.
ORESTES: Do you conceal your name and lineage

By clever purpose? Or may I be told
Who stands before me like some heavenly being?
IPHIGENIA: You'll soon know who I am. But now tell me
   What your brother only half revealed:
   The end of those who, coming back from Troy,
   Were met upon the thresholds of their houses,
   Silent, by harsh and unexpected fate.
   They brought me to these shores when I was young,
   It's true, but I remember well the shyness
   With which I looked in wide-eyed trepidation
   Upon those heroes. When they marched to war
   It was as if Olympus, opening up,
   Sent down on terror-stricken Ilium
   The very forms of glorious ages past,
   And Agamemnon still outshone them all.
   Tell me then: he fell, entering his house,
   Betrayed by his own wife and by Aegisthus?
ORESTES: You've told it all.
IPHIGENIA: Alas for you, Mycenae,
   In your misery. Thus the sons of Tantalus,
   Sow curse on curse with full, unbridled hand,
   Shaking their ravaged heads like weeds, strewing
   Seeds a thousandfold about themselves,
   Begetting, for their children's children, murderers
   Close of kin, and rage for rage unending!
   Tell me what it was your brother said—
   The sudden darkness of my fear obscured it:
   How the last son of that great house, fair child,
   Is sometime destined to become his father's
   Avenger, how Orestes fled the day
   Of blood—or did a similar fate enfold him
   In the nets of dark Avernus? Was he
   Saved? Is he alive? Is Electra?
ORESTES: Both are living.
IPHIGENIA: Golden sun, grant me
   Your fairest rays; lay them in thanks before
   Jove's throne, for I have nothing, and am mute.
ORESTES: Are you connected to this royal line
   By hospitality—or closer bonds,

As your sweet show of joy leads me to think?
If so, rein in your heart and hold it fast.
A sudden plunge back into pain is more
Than any happy soul can bear. I see
That all you know is Agamemnon's death.
IPHIGENIA: Is that not news enough for me to hear?
ORESTES: What you know is only half the horror.
IPHIGENIA: What's left to fear? Orestes lives! Electra!
ORESTES: Have you no fear for Clytemnestra then?
IPHIGENIA: No hope, no fear can ever rescue her.
ORESTES: She too departed from the land of hope.
IPHIGENIA: Shedding her own blood in remorse and rage?
ORESTES: No, but still she died by her own blood.
IPHIGENIA: Speak more clearly. Do not leave me longer
  Puzzling. Somber wings of Doubt now beat
  A thousandfold about my anxious head.
ORESTES: Then it is true: the gods have chosen me
  The herald of a deed that I would gladly
  Leave hidden in the dull and soundless realms
  Of night. But your sweet lips constrain me now
  To speak, against my will, and they may ask
  For painful things as well and shall receive them.
  The day her father fell Electra hid
  Her brother, thus to save him. Strophius,
  The King's own brother-in-law, gladly took him,
  Educated him with his own son,
  Named Pylades, who bound the new arrival
  To himself with the fair bonds of friendship.
  As they grew up, there grew within their souls
  Burning desire to see the great King's death
  Avenged. Unannounced, in foreign garb,
  They reach Mycenae as if bearing with them
  Mournful tidings of Orestes' death,
  And his remains; then, welcomed by the Queen,
  Enter the house. Orestes meets Electra,
  Reveals to her his true identity;
  She fans the flames of vengeance in him, flames
  That in a mother's sacred presence had
  Subsided, all but dying—leads him then

In silence to the place his father fell,
Where, old and faint, a lingering trace of blood,
Shed in a wicked act, had left its stain
On well-scrubbed floors, in dim, portentous lines,
And with a tongue of fire she painted in
Each feature of so infamous a deed,
Her wretched life, spent in servitude,
The arrogance of fortunate betrayers,
And the perils facing both of them
From such a mother, turned stepmother. Then
She forced into his hand the ancient dagger,
Long a terror stalking Tantalus' house.
And Clytemnestra fell by her son's hand.

IPHIGENIA: Immortals, you who live the crystal days
In happiness, on clouds ever-renewed,
Is this why you have left me all these years
Apart from human beings, so much in
Your company, assigning me a task
For children—tending the flames of holy fire!—
And, like those flames, drawing my soul in constant
Shining faith up to your dwelling places,
Only that I might feel, later, more deeply,
The horror of my family? Give me word
Of him, most sad! Tell me about Orestes.

ORESTES: I wish that I could tell you he was dead!
There rose like reek up from the bloody corpse
His mother's ghost,
Crying out to Night's primeval daughters,

> "Don't let the mother-murderer go!
> Hunt down the killer, your sacred prey."

They strain to hear. Their hollow eyes look around
With all the lust of eagles. In the blackness
Of their caves they stir, and from the corners
Silently crawl their boon companions, Doubt
And Remorse; there rises up before them,
From Acheron, a haze of mist within
Whose circling clouds the poor transgressor's head
Is swirled and tossed about in never-ending

Contemplation of his deed. And they,
With right of utter ruin, walk again
The fair ground of the gods' seed-scattered earth,
Long since forbidden them by ancient curse.
Their rapid steps pursue the fugitive.
Granting him respite only for new terror.

IPHIGENIA: Unhappy man, you share the selfsame fate.
You feel what he, the fugitive, must suffer.

ORESTES: What's that you say? You think—. What selfsame fate?

IPHIGENIA: Like him, you bear the guilt of fratricide.
Your younger brother has already told me.

ORESTES: I can't endure that someone of great soul,
Like you, should be misguided by false words.
A web of lies is fit to be the snare
That strangers set before the feet of strangers,
Cunning and used to stratagems. Between us
Let there be truth!
I am Orestes! These guilt-ridden eyes
Sink downward toward the grave, in search of death—
And welcome to it in whatever form!
Whoever you may be, I wish you rescue,
For my friend, too; I wish it not for me.
You seem to live here much against your will—
Figure some way to flee, and leave me here.
Let life depart, my body plunge from cliffs,
Into the sea my blood go reeking down
To bring its curse on this barbarian shore!
Go, both of you, back home to lovely Greece
And there begin a new life lived in friendship.
(He leaves.)

IPHIGENIA: Goddess of hope fulfilled, fairest daughter
Of our greatest father, you descend
To me at last; your image stands before me,
Awesome, my eyes must strain to reach your hands,
Which, filled with fruit and wreaths of blessing, bring
The treasures of Olympus down to earth.
Just as we know a king by his abundant
Giving—for what to thousands would be riches,
To him must seem but little—so we know

Our gods by gifts long treasured up, long
And wisely held in readiness for giving.
For you alone can tell what's good for us,
And view the far-flung kingdoms of the future,
While every evening's veil of stars and mist
Conceals the prospect from us. Undisturbed,
You listen to our childlike voices urging
Haste. And yet your hands will never pick
The golden fruits of heaven before their time.
And woe to the impatient, who'd lay hand
On them, eating themselves to death on bitter
Fruit. Oh, do not let this long-awaited,
Scarce-imagined happiness slip by me,
Insubstantial, like the shadow of
A friend departed—and three times more painful.

ORESTES *(returning):*
Pray to the gods for you and Pylades,
But do not name my name with yours. Make common
Cause with him and you will still not save
The criminal, only share his curse, his peril.

IPHIGENIA: My fate is one with yours, close-knit together.

ORESTES: Not so! Alone and unescorted let me
Join the dead. Shroud him in your own robes
And veils, you'll still not hide the guilty man
From the sight of the Ever-Watchful Ones.
Even your presence, Heaven-born, will only
Turn them aside; it will not drive them off
For good. Their impious, brazen feet may not
Touch this sanctuary's forest floor,
Yet from a distance here and there I hear
Their hideous laughter. Wolves will gather thus
Around a tree to which a traveler
Has tried to flee. They've set up camp out there,
To rest. And if I leave this grove they'll come
Scrambling up from every side, shaking
Their serpent heads, causing great clouds of dust
To whirl about, driving their prey before them.

IPHIGENIA: Orestes, can you hear a friendly word?

ORESTES: Save it for a good friend of the gods.

IPHIGENIA: But they are showing you the light of new hope.
ORESTES: Through smoke and mist I see the pallid glow
  Of Acheron, lighting my way to hell.
IPHIGENIA: Have you one sister only—Electra?
ORESTES: One I knew. The eldest, by the kindness
  Of her destiny, which seemed to us
  So dread, escaped the misery of our house,
  But just in time. Please, ask no more! Don't join
  The Erinyes! In lust for cruelty
  They blow away the ashes covering
  My soul; they will not let the final embers
  Of the fire that ravages our house
  Die down in me. Are flames of torment then
  To burn forever on my soul, by purpose
  Fanned to life and fed with hell's own sulfur?
IPHIGENIA: I come to place sweet incense on the flame.
  Let the pure breath of love, like a soft breeze,
  Cool the fire that glows within your heart!
  Can you not hear my words, dear Orestes?
  Have your guardian gods of terror so
  Dried up the very blood that filled your veins?
  Does magic, as if from the head of awful
  Gorgon, stalk your limbs, leaving them stone?
  Oh, if the voice of mother's blood once shed
  Can call in somber tones, far down to hell,
  Shall not an innocent sister's word of blessing
  Call, from Olympus, gods of help and rescue?
ORESTES: The voice! The voice! Would you have me destroyed?
  Is there some vengeful goddess hidden in you?
  Who are you, that, hearing you speak, I feel
  Such turmoil in my very depths of being?
IPHIGENIA: Your deepest heart tells you the truth: I am
  Iphigenia! Look at me, Orestes.
  I am alive!
ORESTES: You!
IPHIGENIA: Brother!
ORESTES: Leave me! Go!
  I warn you: do not touch my head, my hair!
  Inextinguishable fire leaps from me,

As from Creusa's wedding gown. Leave me!
I am no good. Like Hercules I want
To die: death in disgrace, closed off, alone.
IPHIGENIA: You will not perish. Would that I could hear
  Just one untroubled word from you. Dissolve
  My doubts and let me be assured as well
  Of happiness, long and devoutly prayed for.
  Fortune's wheel of joy and pain turns 'round
  Inside my soul. A shudder drives me from
  A stranger, but my inmost being draws me
  To a brother, irresistibly.
ORESTES: What is this? Bacchus' temple? Is the priestess
  Seized by uncontrollable, holy madness?
IPHIGENIA: Hear me! Look at me! See how my heart,
  After so long a time, opens at last
  To the delight of greeting with a kiss
  The dearest thing the world still holds for me,
  Of taking you into my arms, so long
  Outspread but only to the empty winds.
  Oh let me, let me! The eternal springs
  That well up from Parnassus are no brighter,
  Dashing from rock to rock on their way down
  To golden valleys, than the joy that flows
  In waves from my heart, holding me embraced,
  A blessed sea. Orestes! Brother!
ORESTES: Lovely
  Nymph, I do not trust you and your flattery.
  Those who serve Diana must be stern;
  She sees to that. And she'll avenge a temple
  Desecrated. Take your hand away!
  If you would save a young man with your love,
  Holding out the tender prospect of
  Sweet happiness, turn your mind to my friend,
  The better man. He's somewhere over there,
  Roaming the rocky paths. Go and find him,
  Guide him—and leave me alone.
IPHIGENIA: Be calm,
  My brother! Recognize me; you have found me.
  Don't condemn as thoughtless, guilty passion

Heaven's pure joy that fills a sister's heart.
Gods, lift the madness from his staring eyes,
Let not the moment of our greatest joy
Become a threefold misery. She's here,
Your long-lost sister, snatched up from the altar
By Diana, rescued, brought to this,
Her sanctuary. And you, taken captive,
Marked for sacrificial death, discover
The priestess of the temple is your sister.

ORESTES: Unhappy woman! Let the sun of this day
See the final horrors of our house!
Is not Electra here, so that she too
May perish with us, not prolong her life
For harsher fate and suffering? So be it,
Priestess. On to the altar; I shall follow.
Fratricide is a time-honored custom
In our ancient line. And Gods above,
My thanks that you've resolved to cut me down,
Childless. And you, priestess, take my advice:
Don't love the sun, don't love the stars too much.
Come! Follow me below to the dark kingdom!
Begotten in a pool of sulfur, dragons,
Battling kin and spawn, devour each other;
Like them, this rabid line destroys itself.
Come down with me, come childless down and guiltless.
You look at me with eyes of pity. Stop it!
Glances like that were Clytemnestra's way
Of seeking access to her son's heart. Still
His arm, drawn back, swung forward, struck her breast.
His mother fell.—Come forth, you sullen ghost!
Close your circle, Furies, step up now.
Attend this welcome spectacle, the last
And most abominable of your devising.
Her dagger is not sharpened by revenge
And hate; a loving sister finds herself
Forced to the deed. Don't weep. It's not your fault.
Since my first youth there's nothing I have loved
As much as I could love you, Sister. Yes,
Let the steel flash, do not hold back. Tear

This ribcage open, clear the way and let
The streams that boil and surge there find release.
(He sinks down, exhausted.)
IPHIGENIA: I cannot bear this happiness and misery
By myself. Where are you, Pylades?
Where shall I find your helping hand, dear man?
(She leaves, looking for him.)

Scene 2

(Orestes, alone.)

ORESTES *(waking from his stupor, drawing himself up):*
One more drink! From Lethe's quiet waters
Pass me the final, cool, refreshing cup!
How soon, the rage of life purged from my heart,
My spirit flowing softly, unresisting,
To the springs of sweet oblivion,
I'll join you, shadows, in eternal night.
In charity permit the harried son
Of earth to share the balm of your repose.
But I hear whispers in the branches, noises
Rustling in the darkness. What is this?
They come, curious to see who's joined them now;
This company in splendor gathered, like
The glad reunion of a princely house,
Who are they? Old and young, women and men,
Walking in peace; godlike, of like appearance,
These moving figures seem. That's who they are!
Ancestors of my line! Thyestes strolling,
Immersed in friendly talk with Atreus; 'round them
All their boys, running back and forth
In play. Is discord at an end among you,
Revenge extinguished like the light of sun?
Then I am welcome too, and I may join
Your solemn train of festive celebrants.

Ancestors, all hail! Orestes greets you,
Last male descendant of your line.

The seed you sowed he harvested.
Burdened with guilt he descended here;
But here no burden is hard to bear.
Take him, oh take him into your circle!
I honor you, Atreus; you too, Thyestes;
All of us here are freed of hostility.
Show me my father, whom I saw only
Once in my life. Is it you, Father?
And Mother, walking with you in friendship?
If Clytemnestra may give you her hand,
Orestes then may go to her, too,
And say to her: Here is your son!
The son of both of you! Offer him welcome!
On earth, in our house, a salutation
Served always as the password to murder.
Joy, in the ancient line of Tantalus,
Lies on the other side of night.
You bid me welcome and you accept me.
Show me the way to the old patriarch!
Where is the ancient one? I want to see him,
Beloved man and deeply honored,
Who sat with the gods and offered them counsel.
You seem to hesitate, turning away.
What's wrong? The godlike man, is he still
In pain? Alas, those almighty beings
Have fettered his heroic breast,
In cruel torment, with brazen chains.

Scene 3

(Orestes, Iphigenia, Pylades.)

ORESTES: The two of you, down here already?
I'm glad for you, Sister. Electra's missing!
May some kind god with tender arrows
Send her, the last one, down to us soon.
I'm sorry for you, poor friend. But come
With me to the throne of Pluto, there,

As his new guests, to salute our host.

IPHIGENIA: Sibling gods, who bring to human beings,
Across the broad sky, the fair light of day
And night, and cannot shine on souls departed,
Rescue the two of us, brother and sister!
Diana, you love your dear brother more
Than anything that earth and heaven offer;
You turn your virgin countenance, in silent
Longing, toward his everlasting light.
Let my beloved one, long lost, late found,
Not wander raving in the dark of madness.
And if what you intended when you brought me
Safely here is now fulfilled, and if
You'd grant your blessed help to me through him,
To him through me, release him from his bonds,
His curse, lest precious time for rescue fade.

PYLADES: Look, do you know us, and this sacred grove,
This light that does not shine upon the dead?
And do you feel the hand of friend and sister
Holding you tight and still alive? Touch
Us hard! We are not empty shades. Mark well
What I say; hear my words; and pull yourself
Together! Every moment counts. Return
For all of us hangs by a slender thread
Spun, so it seems, by some benevolent Fate.

ORESTES *(to Iphigenia)*:
Oh, let me for the first time, free in heart,
Feel pure happiness in your embrace!
You gods, who walk the skies with flaming power
And, walking, swallow up great, heavy clouds,
And grant the earth your solemn gift of rain,
Long supplicated, pouring down in torrents,
With voice of thunder and with roar of winds,
But soon dissolve men's dread presentiment
In blessings, and transform their awed amazement
Into joyful looks and thankful words,
When in the drops from newly freshened leaves
The new sun gleams a thousand times reflected,

And Iris, friendly, gay in colors, parts,
With gentle hand, gray veils of lingering cloud:
Oh, in my sister's arms, at my friend's side,
Let me with perfect gratitude enjoy
And keep forever what you grant to me!
The curse has loosed its grip, my heart tells me.
Now the Eumenides are leaving, bound
For Tartarus, I hear them, slamming closed
The brazen gates behind them with a distant
Thunder. The earth exhales a bracing fragrance,
Bidding me, here on its wide expanse,
Pursue the joy of life and noble deeds.

PYLADES: Don't waste the time we have. It's limited.
The wind that fills our sails should be the one
That brings our full joy to Olympus. Come!
What's needed now is thought and quick decision.

Act 4

Scene 1

(Iphigenia.)

If the gods have in mind,
For one of us mortals,
Endless confusion;
If they design for us
Shattering transitions
From pleasure to pain
And from pain to pleasure,
Then they also prepare—
Perhaps near our city,
Perhaps on a far distant shore—
Someone to help us
In the hour of our need,
An imperturbable friend.

Gods, grant your blessing to our Pylades
In everything that he may undertake,
He will be the young man's arm in battle,
The eyes of the old man, bright in debate.
His soul is calm; it keeps inviolate
The inexhaustible treasury of peace,
From its depths extending aid and wisdom
To the driven outcast. As for me,
He's torn me from my brother, whom I gazed at
Over and over, still amazed, unable
To claim as mine such happiness, not freeing
Him from my embracing arms, nor feeling
The nearness of the danger that surrounds us.
Down by the sea, to carry out their plan,
They've gone now, where the ship with their companions,
Hidden in a cove, awaits the signal.
They've put words in my mouth, words of cunning,
Taught me my answers to the summoning King,
When his demand for sacrifice becomes
More urgent. Yes, alas, it's clear that I
Must let myself be guided like a child.
I've never learned the practice of deceiving,
Of tricking someone out of something. Lies!
Oh, wretched lies! They do not free the heart
As any word spoken in truth can do.
They bring no solace to us, only fear
To those who forge them secretly, come back
Like arrows sped from bows, turned by a god,
Striking the marksman. Thus, worry on worry
Trembles in my heart. Perhaps my brother
Will be fiercely set upon by Furies,
There on the sands of that unhallowed shore—
Perhaps discovered, with his friend? I think
I hear armed men approaching. Yes! Here comes
The herald from the King; his step is hurried.
My heart is pounding; darkness clouds my soul,
As I see face-to-face the very man
Whom I am meant to welcome with a lie.

Scene 2

(Iphigenia, Arcas.)

ARCAS: Prepare the sacrifice, and hurry, Priestess,
   The King is ready and the people wait.
IPHIGENIA: I would obey my duty and your order,
   Except that obstacles, quite unforeseen,
   Have come between me and their full performance.
ARCAS: What's happened to obstruct the royal order?
IPHIGENIA: Chance events, of which we are not master.
ARCAS: Say what it is! I must inform him quickly;
   Because his firm decree was death for both.
IPHIGENIA: The gods have not decreed it yet. The guilt
   Of blood lies on the older of the two.
   The blood he shed was closely kin to his.
   The Furies follow him wherever he goes.
   Yes, inside the very temple building
   The sickness seized him, and the holy place
   Was desecrated by his presence. Now
   I must be off to the sea with my handmaidens
   To bathe the goddess' image in fresh waters,
   Performing holy rites of consecration.
   So let no one disturb our still procession.
ARCAS: I'll tell the King of this new obstacle
   Without delay. But see that you don't start
   Your sacred work before he gives permission.
IPHIGENIA: That's for the priestess only to decide.
ARCAS: The King should know of such a special case.
IPHIGENIA: His orders or opinions make no difference.
ARCAS: The great are often asked, for mere politeness.
IPHIGENIA: Don't force me into what I should refuse.
ARCAS: Don't refuse what's good and useful both.
IPHIGENIA: Promise no delay, and I'll agree.
ARCAS: I'll take the news to camp, and be there quickly
   And back here with his answer quickly too.
   I wish I could bring him another message
   Which would resolve all things that now confuse us;
   But you've ignored a loyal man's advice.

IPHIGENIA: Everything I could, I did, and gladly.
ARCAS: You still can change your attitude in time.
IPHIGENIA: That is something quite beyond our power.
ARCAS: You call impossible what costs you effort.
IPHIGENIA: You call it possible from wishful thinking.
ARCAS: You mean to risk all this so calmly then?
IPHIGENIA: I've placed it all in the hands of the gods.
ARCAS: They generally save us humans humanly.
IPHIGENIA: One gesture of the gods determines all.
ARCAS: I tell you this: the whole is in your hands.
  The King's indignant state of mind alone
  Condemns these strangers to their bitter death.
  The army here has long since lost its taste
  For cruel sacrifice and bloody ritual.
  Yes, more than one of us, himself cast up
  By hostile fate on some strange shore, could see
  How godlike any friendly human face
  Appears to someone driven, lost and wandering,
  Along the borders of a foreign land.
  Oh, don't deny us what is in your power!
  It won't be hard to end what you have started;
  Because nowhere does grace, in human form
  Descending from the heavens, build itself
  A realm more swiftly than where, dull and savage,
  A new people, full of life, vitality,
  And courage, left to itself and anxious doubt,
  Shoulders the heavy burden of human life.
IPHIGENIA: You must not try to break my spirit, which
  You cannot bend to make it suit your will.
ARCAS: While there is time, we'll spare no pains, nor stop
  Repeating any kind word we have said.
IPHIGENIA: You're causing trouble for yourself and pain
  For me, and both in vain. So leave me now.
ARCAS: I call upon that pain to help us out;
  The pain is friendly and its counsel good.
IPHIGENIA: It holds my spirit in a mighty grip
  And yet it does not lessen my aversion.
ARCAS: Does a generous spirit feel aversion
  Toward kindness offered by a noble man?

IPHIGENIA: Yes, if that noble man unfairly aims
  At winning not my gratitude but me.
ARCAS: Those who feel no stirring of emotion
  Never lack for words to make excuses.
  I'll go and tell the Prince what's happened here.
  I wish that you'd go over in your mind
  And soul how nobly he's behaved toward you,
  From your arrival to this very day.

Scene 3

(Iphigenia alone.)

I find my heart within me suddenly
Turned quite around by what this man has said—
And most inopportunely. I am frightened.
As rapid waters of the rising tide
Flood over rocks that lie in sands along
The shore, just so a flood of joy had swept
Over my inner being. In my arms
I held the impossible. It seemed to me
As if a cloud once more descended gently
To enclose me and to lift me up
From earth and cradle me in that same slumber
Which my kindly goddess laid about
My temples when her arms reached out to rescue
Me and save my life. Finding my brother,
My heart with stunning force laid claim to him.
I listened only to his friend's advice.
Only to save them did my soul press forward.
And as the sailor gladly turns his back
Upon the cliffs of some deserted island,
Tauris lay behind me. Now the voice
Of loyal Arcas reawakens me,
Reminding me that I leave human beings
Here as well; and the deceit becomes
Doubly hateful. Oh, be calm, my soul!
Have you begun to waver and to doubt?
You have to leave the solid ground that is

Your loneliness. On ship again, you'll feel
The waves possess and rock you; world and self
Will fade from sight in gloom and dull foreboding.

Scene 4

(Phylades, Iphigenia.)

PYLADES: Where is she? Let me in a few words quickly
  Tell her all the good news of our rescue.
IPHIGENIA: Here—and filled with concern and expectation
  By the sure hope and comfort that you promise.
PYLADES: Your brother's cured! We walked along the sands,
  The rocky ground of this unhallowed shore,
  Deep in happy conversation, left
  The grove behind us, never noticing.
  Glorious, ever more glorious,
  The lovely flame of youth glowed round his head,
  His locks. His great eyes, opened wide, were bright
  With courage, hope. His liberated heart
  Gave itself wholly to the joy and pleasure
  Of rescuing you, his rescuer, and me.
IPHIGENIA: I offer you my blessings—and my hope
  That lips which spoke good things never have
  To voice the sounds of suffering and lament.
PYLADES: I've more to tell. Happiness has a way
  Of coming, like a prince, with fair escort.
  We've found all our companions too. They'd hidden
  Their ship inside a rocky cove and they
  Were sitting sadly there, in expectation.
  They saw your brother and they all rose up
  With shouts of joy, asking urgently
  That we advance the hour of our departure.
  Every hand longed for the tiller. Whispers
  Of breezes even rose on fair wings off
  The land—we felt it, all of us at once.
  So let us hurry. Lead me to the temple;
  Admit me to the sanctuary; let me

In worship touch the object of our hopes.
Alone I'm strong enough to carry off
The goddess' statue on my well-trained shoulders,
And how I long for such a welcome burden!
(As he speaks these last words he walks toward the temple with-
out noticing that Iphigenia has not followed him; at last he turns
around.)
You stand there, hesitating. Tell me—you say
Nothing—you seem confused. Does some new evil
Threaten our good fortune? Tell me this:
Did you have them give the King the message,
The artful words that we agreed upon?
IPHIGENIA: I did, dear man, but you'll have cause to blame me.
Seeing you is my silent reprimand.
The King's own herald came and I told him
The very words that you put in my mouth.
He seemed amazed and urgently demanded
That word of this unusual rite be first
Reported to the King for his decision,
And now I am awaiting his return.
PYLADES: Ye gods! Now danger's back again, to hover
About our heads. You might have had the foresight
To cloak yourself in priestly privilege.
IPHIGENIA: Never have I used it as a cloak.
PYLADES: Then you, the soul of purity, will ruin
Yourself and us. Why didn't I foresee
This possibility? I could have taught you
How to evade this order too.
IPHIGENIA: Rebuke
No one but me. The fault is mine, I know it.
How else could I have treated such a man,
Who in good faith and reason asked of me
What my heart must admit was his by right?
PYLADES: Danger closes in on us, but still
Let's not be timid or, in too great haste
And little prudence, give ourselves away.
Wait calmly for the messenger's return.
And then stand firm, no matter what he says.
Such rites of consecration are the province

Of priestesses to order, not of kings.
Should he demand to see the stranger, heavy
With the burden of his madness, then
Refuse, as if to say you held us both
Securely in your temple. This will give us
Breathing space, time to retrieve the holy
Treasure from this crude, unworthy people,
And flee. Apollo sends us excellent omens;
Before, in piety, we meet his terms,
In his divinity he meets his promise:
Orestes free and cured! Oh, favoring winds,
Take us across, with our companion freed,
To the god's home, the rocky island. Then,
On to Mycenae, so that it may live,
And from the ashes of the darkened hearth
The family gods may rise again, rejoicing,
And flames of beautiful fire rim with light
Their dwelling place. Your hand shall scatter incense
First, from golden vessels. You shall bring
Over that threshold life and new well-being;
You'll absolve the curse and wreathe your loved ones
Gloriously with the fresh blooms of life.
IPHIGENIA: When I hear what you say, dear man, my spirit,
Like the flower turning toward the sun,
Is touched by the bright sunlight of your words,
And turns again toward sweet encouragement.
How precious is the presence of a friend,
His words of certainty, whose heavenly power
The lonely person lacks and, lacking, sinks back
Listless. Locked in the heart, thoughts and decisions
Ripen slowly; having someone near,
Who cares, will bring them swiftly to fruition.
PYLADES: Farewell! I'll hurry to our friends and quickly
Set their minds at rest; they wait in eager
Expectation. Then I'll come back here,
Hide in the rocks and bushes, waiting for
Your sign—What's in your mind? Your brow, once clear,
Is suddenly overcast with quiet sorrow.
IPHIGENIA: Forgive me! Much as light clouds pass before

The sun, slight cares and trepidations pass
Before my soul.

PYLADES: You must not be afraid.
A close and treacherous alliance binds
Together fear and danger. They are comrades.

IPHIGENIA: I'd call it noble, this concern that warns me
Not to rob or foully to betray
The King, who's come to be my second father.

PYLADES: You flee the man who'd be your brother's butcherer.

IPHIGENIA: The same one who has always showed me kindness.

PYLADES: Sheer need compels; that's not ingratitude.

IPHIGENIA: Yes, it is! Need's only an excuse.

PYLADES: For you it surely is, in sight of gods
And men.

IPHIGENIA: But my own heart's not satisfied.

PYLADES: Making too strict demands is hidden pride.

IPHIGENIA: I do not analyze, I simply feel it.

PYLADES: If you feel rightly, you'll respect yourself.

IPHIGENIA: The heart is only happy when it's blameless.

PYLADES: You've kept yourself protected in your temple.
Life has taught us to be less severe
With ourselves and others; you'll learn too.
This human race is of such wondrous, strange
Design, so closely linked and interwoven
That no one, within himself or with others,
Can remain pure and uncomplicated.
Nor are we called upon to judge ourselves.
To walk one's way and heed the way one walks
Is any human being's first, best duty.
One seldom fathoms rightly what one's done,
And almost never fathoms what one's doing.

IPHIGENIA: You've virtually convinced me you are right.

PYLADES: When there's no choice, who needs convincing? Only
One way remains to save us: brother, friend,
And you. Are we in doubt whether to take it?

IPHIGENIA: Grant me my hesitation! You yourself
Would not unthinkingly so hurt someone
To whom you felt obliged for kindness done you.

PYLADES: If we're destroyed, harsher reproach will lie

Ahead for you and, in its train, despair.
It's clear to see: You are not used to loss,
If, to escape great evil, you won't make
The sacrifice of one untruthful word.

IPHIGENIA: I wish the heart within me were a man's heart,
That, when it cherishes some bold resolve,
Closes itself to any other voice.

PYLADES: Refusal is in vain; Necessity
Commands with iron hand; and her stern bidding
Is a law supreme, to which the gods
Even must submit. She rules in silence,
Sister of eternal Fate, uncounseled.
The burden she lays on you, bear; and do
What she commands. You know the rest. Soon
I shall return, and from your sacred hand
Receive the final seal of our fair rescue.

Scene 5

(Iphigenia alone.)

And I must follow. For I see my loved ones
In dire danger. Oh, but my own fate
Makes me more and more afraid. Alas,
Then, am I not to rescue that still hope
I raised and cherished in this solitude?
Shall this curse endure forever? Shall
This race never be lifted up again,
Newly blessed? Everything must ebb.
Fortune's finest gifts, life's fairest powers
All fade at last; why not, too, this curse?
Have I then hoped in vain, protected here,
Cut off from my family's destiny,
Hoped sometime, pure in hand and heart, to bring
Atonement to my sorely tainted home?
No sooner do I find a brother cured
From violent evil, wondrously and swiftly,
In my arms; no sooner comes a ship,
Long prayed for, guiding me to port in my

Ancestral world, than harsh necessity
With iron hand lays on me double wrongs:
To steal the sacred image given me
In trust and reverence, and betray the man
To whom I owe my life and destiny.
I pray that in the end profound aversion
Will not take root and grow within my heart,
Nor the deep-seated hatred of the Titans,
And of the ancient gods, for you Olympians
Seize with vulture claws my tender breast.
Save me, and save your image in my soul!
The ancient song is ringing in my ears—
        I had forgotten it, forgot it gladly—
The Parcae's song, the one they sang in horror
When Tantalus fell from his golden chair.
They suffered with their noble friend; their hearts
Were savage in their breasts, fearsome their song.
When we were young—my brother, sister, I—
Our nurse sang it to us. I knew it well.

                Let men of all races
                Learn fear of the gods!
                They hold their dominion
                In undying hands
                And they can employ it
                However they choose.
                And those they exalt
                Have doubly to fear them.
                On cliffs and on clouds
                Their seats are arranged
                At tables of gold.

                If discord arises
                The guest will be hurtled
                In scorn and disgrace
                To nocturnal depths
                And wait there in vain,
                Imprisoned in darkness,
                For judgment and justice.

But they—they remain,
Still endlessly feasting,
At tables of gold.
They stride from their mountain
To mountains beyond;
From clefts in the deep
Comes, stifled, the breathing
Of Titans immured,
Like odor from altars,
A vapor of cloud.

The mighty ones turn
The eye of their favor
From whole generations,
Refusing to see in
His children the same
Still, eloquent features
They loved in their father.

The song of the Parcae!
In caves of the night
The old one, the exile,
Hears what they are singing,
And listening sees
His sons and his grandsons,
And shakes his head.

Act 5

Scene 1

(Thoas, Arcas.)

ARCAS: I must admit I'm puzzled and don't know
Which way I should direct my own suspicions.
Are the prisoners, in secret, plotting
Their escape? Or is perhaps the priestess
Helping them to do so? Rumor spreads:

They say the ship that brought them here may still
Be hidden somewhere in a nearby cove.
That fellow's madness, and these holy rites,
The pretext for the long delay—both speak
More loudly for suspicion and for caution.
THOAS: See to it that the priestess comes here—fast!
Then go and search the shoreline—and be sharp!—
Between the foothills and the goddess's grove;
But spare the inner sanctuary; set
A careful ambush, seize them when and where
You find them, take them captive—you know how!

Scene 2

(Thoas alone.)

Awful turns of anger grip my heart
First against her, whom I had so revered,
Then toward myself, for training her to treason
Through my consideration, through my kindness.
People adapt themselves to slavery well,
And quickly learn obedience, if one takes
Their freedom from them wholly. Had she fallen
Into the cruel hands of my forefathers—
If, despite their holy wrath, they'd spared her—
She'd have been well pleased to save herself
Alone; acknowledging her fate with thanks,
She'd shed this alien blood upon the altar.
Giving to necessity
The name of duty. Now my kindness
Tempts her heart to nourish bold desires.
I hoped to link her life with mine—in vain.
And now she dreams of shaping her own fate.
She won my heart through flattery and now,
When I resist, she tries to get her way
By guile and cunning, and she takes my kindness
As her vested right, her property.

Scene 3

(Iphigenia, Thoas.)

IPHIGENIA: You summoned me? What brings you here to us?

THOAS: You've stopped the sacrifice. Tell me why!

IPHIGENIA: I told it all to Arcas—very clearly.

THOAS: I'd like some further word from you.

IPHIGENIA: The goddess
   Is giving you the time to reconsider.

THOAS: A time which seems most opportune for you.

IPHIGENIA: You should not come here if your heart is hardened
   To this cruel decision. Any king
   Who's bent on inhumanity will find
   Minions enough, who for his grace and pay
   Rush to take half the curse for what is done,
   While he preserves his own untainted presence.
   In overhanging dark clouds he devised
   Death; his messengers meantime bring flaming
   Ruin down upon the poor man's head,
   But he floats calmly on his lofty heights,
   A god unreachable, borne on the storm wind.

THOAS: A wild song echoes from these holy lips.

IPHIGENIA: Priestess, no! But Agamemnon's daughter!
   You honored once an unknown woman's word
   And now you give curt orders to a princess?
   No! Since I was young I've learned obedience,
   First to my parents, then to a divinity,
   And in obeying I have always felt
   My soul supremely free. But to comply
   With harsh instructions, laid down by a man,
   I've never learned, not then, nor here and now.

THOAS: It is not I—an ancient law commands you.

IPHIGENIA: We're always grasping eagerly at laws
   When they can serve our passions as a weapon.
   I listen to another, older law,
   Bidding me resist you: the commandment
   Which says that every stranger's life is sacred.

THOAS: You seem to hold these prisoners very close

At heart; in sympathy and agitation
You forget the first command of wisdom:
Not to provoke the one who wields the power.

IPHIGENIA: Whether I speak or keep my peace, you'll always
Know what's in my heart and ever will be.
Does not the memory of a similar fate
Open a cloistered heart to sympathy?
Then how much more so mine! I see myself
In them. I too have trembled at the altar
Kneeling, I felt the ritual embrace
Of early death. The knife was drawn and ready
To cut the living breast and pierce the heart.
My inmost self reeled dizzily, in terror.
My eyes went black and I—found myself saved.
What gods in mercy grant us, are not we
Obliged to pass to those less fortunate?
You know this, you know me—and you would force me?

THOAS: Obey the call of duty, not the sovereign.

IPHIGENIA: Enough! Don't try to sanctify oppression
That revels in the weakness of a woman.
I'm born as free as any man. If you
Stood face-to-face with Agamemnon's son
And were to make unwarranted demands,
He would have a sword, an arm to guard
The rights and interests of his heart. Words
Are all I have, but it behooves a man
Of honor to respect a woman's word.

THOAS: And so I do—more than a brother's sword.

IPHIGENIA: The luck of battle turns and turns again,
And no wise warrior underestimates
His foe. Even the weak have not been left
By Nature unprotected from abuse
And cruelty. She gave them joy in cunning,
Taught them tricks—outflank, delay, evade!—
And if they play them, those with power deserve it.

THOAS: Precautions can be taken against cunning.

IPHIGENIA: The pure in heart will neither need nor use it.

THOAS: Be careful! Don't pass sentence on yourself.

IPHIGENIA: If only you could see how my heart fights

For courage to ward off the first assault
Of evil fate that's bent on conquering me.
Do I then stand defenseless here before you?
The sweet request, the lovely olive-branch,
More powerful in a woman's hand than sword
And arms, you turn aside. What can I do
Now to defend myself, my inner self?
Shall I cry to the goddess for a miracle?
Is there no strength in the depths of my soul?

THOAS: The fate of these two strangers seems to cause you
Immoderate concern. Who are they, tell me,
That you take up their cause with so much spirit?

IPHIGENIA: They are—they seem—I think that they are Greeks.

THOAS: So, countrymen? No doubt they have renewed
In you the happy prospect of return?

IPHIGENIA *(after a brief silence)*:
Who has the right to unexampled action?
Men alone? They clutch the impossible
To great heroic hearts. Only they?
What is greatness? What inspires with awe
The souls of bards, in ever-echoing songs,
Other than what the bravest undertake
With scant hope of success? He who, alone,
At nighttime stalks the hostile army, seizes,
Like a fire raging unexpected,
The sleeping and the waking both; at last,
Pressed hard by enemy horsemen now aroused
To hot pursuit, still returns with booty—
Praise him! But him alone? Only him,
Who, scorning ways of safety, boldly roams
His lonely path through mountains and through forests,
Trying to sweep a region clean of brigands?
Is nothing left for us? Must gentle women
Forfeit their inborn right, turn savagely
On savages, like Amazons, and steal
From you the right of force by sword, with blood
Avenging their suppression? Now my heart
Rises and falls with a bold undertaking.
I shall not escape severe reproach,

Nor deep misfortune either, should I fail.
Still, I leave it in your hands, and if
You truly are as you are praised, then show it,
Gods, by your support, and glorify
Through me the truth. Yes, Sire, hear what I say:
A secret chain of guile is being forged.
You'll ask about the prisoners in vain;
Both are gone; they're off to find their friends
Waiting ɟlong the seashore with their ship.
The older, who was struck here by the evil
Curse, which now has left him—is Orestes,
My brother; and the other, his confidant,
And friend since youth, by name of Pylades.
Apollo sent them to this shore from Delphi
With divine command to steal the image
Of Diana and restore to him
A sister lost; and in return he promised
This hunted prey of Furies, bearer of
The guilt of mother's blood, his liberation.
So now I have delivered up to you
Two survivors of the house of Tantalus.
Destroy us—if you can.

THOAS: You think the Scythian,
Coarse son of a barbarian tribe, will hear
The voice of truth and true humanity
That Atreus did not—he, the Greek?

IPHIGENIA: It's heard
By anyone, born under any sky,
If through his heart the springs of life flow pure
And unimpeded. What do you intend
For me, deep in the silence of your soul?
If ruin for us all, then kill me first.
For now I know, when there is no more rescue
For us, the awful danger into which
I've placed the ones I love, in overhasty
Purpose. Now, alas!—now I shall see them
Bound and tied before me. How am I
To look at him and say good-bye—my brother,
Whom I murder? Never can I gaze

Again into those eyes I love so much.
THOAS: The traitors, then, have told their artful lies,
    Have cast this web about the head of someone
    Long secluded, all too quick and eager
    To believe her wishes.
IPHIGENIA: No, Sire, no!
    I'm not immune to guile; but they are true
    And loyal. Should you prove them otherwise,
    Let both of them face death, and banish me,
    Condemned in punishment for my own folly,
    To some rocky island's wretched shore.
    But if this man is my beloved brother,
    Long prayed for, free us; let your friendship grace
    Brother and sister, as it did the sister.
    My father died by the guilt of his wife;
    And she by her son's hand. The final hope
    Of Atreus' line must rest on him alone.
    So let me, pure in heart and pure in hand,
    Cross the sea and purge our house of guilt.
    I know you'll keep your word: You swore if ever
    Chance of return to kin and home were granted
    Me, to let me go; and now it has been.
    A king does not say yes from awkwardness,
    As commoners do, to rid himself awhile
    Of his petitioner, nor promise something,
    Hoping the need will not arise to do it.
    He feels the measure of his greatness only
    When he can gladden those who ask his favor.
THOAS: Angrily, as fire battles water,
    And hissing, seeks to overcome its foe,
    So the fury in my heart contends
    Against your words.
IPHIGENIA: Let mercy blaze and shine
    Upon me like the holy light of silent
    Sacrificial flames, all wreathed about
    In songs of praise, in gratitude and joy.
THOAS: How many times that voice has calmed my spirit.
IPHIGENIA: Oh, give me as a sign of peace your hand.
THOAS: You ask for much in very little time.

IPHIGENIA: But doing good needs no deliberation.
THOAS: A lot! For good can also lead to evil.
IPHIGENIA: Doubt is what turns good things into bad.
  Don't hesitate—grant what you feel is right.

Scene 4

(Orestes, others as before.)

ORESTES *(back turned to the audience):*
  Double your strength! Fight harder! Hold them back!
  Only a few more moments. Don't yield ground
  To numbers. Give us cover down to the ship,
  Me and my sister.
                (To Iphigenia; not having noticed the King.)
                        Come, we've been betrayed.
  There's little time or room for flight. Be quick!
                        (Sees the King.)
THOAS *(reaching for his sword):*
  While I am present here, no man draws sword
  From sheath and goes unpunished.
IPHIGENIA: Don't defile
  The goddess' dwelling place with rage and murder.
  Call on your forces, order truce. Hear what
  A priestess—what a sister says!
ORESTES: Tell me,
  Who is this threatening us?
IPHIGENIA: Honor in him
  The King who came to be my second father.
  Forgive me, Brother. My heart, like a child's,
  Has placed our fate entirely in his hands.
  I have confessed to him your whole design,
  And saved my soul from stain of treachery.
ORESTES: And will he grant us our return in peace?
IPHIGENIA: Your flashing sword forbids my answering you.
ORESTES *(sheathing his sword):*
  Then speak! You see, I listen to your words.

Scene 5

(The above; Pylades, and soon thereafter, Arcas,
both with drawn swords.)

PYLADES: No more delay! Our men have summoned up
Their last resources. They are giving way,
Pushed slowly backward toward the sea! But here!
What conference of princes do I see?
We're in the honored presence of the King.
ARCAS: Calmly, my King—for so it most befits you—
You face your enemy. Their affront will soon
Be punished. Those that fight for them retreat,
Many are dead. Their ship is ours. A word
From you and it will be in flames.
THOAS: Go to
My troops. Order an end to fighting. No one
Harms the foe as long as we are talking!
                    (Arcas leaves.)
ORESTES: I too accept. My true friend, go, collect
All our remaining force. Calmly await
Whatever end the gods may grant our actions.

Scene 6

(Iphigenia, Thoas, Orestes.)

IPHIGENIA: Free me from my concern, before you start
To talk together. I fear grave discord
If you, oh King, refuse to hear the gentle
Voice of justice—if you, my brother, fail
To hold in check the rash impulse of youth.
THOAS: I shall restrain my anger, as is proper
For the older man. Answer me! How—
How can you prove that you are Agamemnon's
Son, the brother of this woman?
ORESTES: Here is
The sword with which he killed the mighty men
Of Troy. I took it from his murderer, begging

The gods to give to me the courage, arm,
And fortune of the mighty king, and grant
To me a better death than his. Choose one
Among the finest nobles of your army,
Set me against the best you have. Wherever
Earth bears heroes as its sons, no stranger
Ever is denied this one request.

THOAS: That privilege was, by ancient custom here,
Never allowed the foreigner.

ORESTES: Then begin
The newer custom now, with you and me.
Whole nations emulate their rulers' noble
Deeds, confirming them as sacred law.
And let me fight not only for our freedom;
Let me, the stranger, fight for other strangers.
If I should fall, their sentence then is passed
With mine; but if good fortune should permit
That I prevail, let no man ever set foot
On this shore without a ready hand,
A look of love to meet him, and let each
Depart again, restored and confident.

THOAS: Young man, I find you not unworthy of
The ancestors from whom you boast descent.
My retinue abounds in men of courage,
Noble men; but even at my age
I face the enemy myself. I'm ready
Now to risk with you the luck of battle.

IPHIGENIA: Not that! There is no need for such a proof
By bloodshed, Sire. Take your hand from your sword.
Think of me and of my destiny.
Swift battle grants a man immortal life:
Should he fall quickly, songs of bards will praise him.
But of the tears, of the unending tears
Of his survivors, of his wife abandoned,
Posterity takes no count; no poet tells
The weeping of a thousand days and nights,
When a soul in silence yearns to summon
Back the suddenly departed friend,
In vain, and wastes away. An anxious feeling

Warned me instantly: No thief's deceit
Should ever snatch me from the safe protection
Of my sanctuary and betray me
Into servitude. I questioned them
With care, inquired into every point
Of fact, demanded evidence. Now my heart
Is sure. See here on his right hand the birthmark,
As of three stars, which showed itself the very
Day that he was born, and which the priest
Interpreted to mean momentous deeds
This hand would do. And then I am persuaded
Doubly by the scar that cuts across
His eyebrow here. While he was just a child,
Electra, after her quick, careless fashion
Let him fall from her arms; he struck his head
Against a tripod. It is he! Or need I
Cite the likeness he bears to his father,
The exultation deep within my heart,
As further witnesses of my assurance?
THOAS: And even if your words resolved all doubt—
If I should tame the anger in my heart—
Weapons would still have to decide between us.
I see no chance of peaceful resolution.
They came, as you yourself admit, to steal
The sacred image of the goddess from me.
Do you think I can view this calmly? Greeks
Have often turned their lusting eyes upon
The distant treasures of barbarian peoples:
The Golden Fleece, horses, and lovely daughters;
But force and cunning did not always get them
Safely home with all the wealth they seized.
ORESTES: The statue, Sire, shall not divide us. Now
We recognize the error which a god
Cast like a veil about our heads when he
Ordered us on our journey home. I begged him
For advice, for freedom from the Furies'
Constant escort; and he spoke these words:
"Bring back to Greece the sister who against
Her will must stay on Tauris' shores, within

The temple, and the curse will be absolved."
This we took to mean Apollo's sister—
It was you he meant. The rigid bonds
Are loosed; and you, our sacred one, restored
To kin and home; I, touched by your hand,
Am cured. For in your arms the evil force
Seized me with all its talons—for the last time—
Shaking the marrow of my bones with terror.
Then it fled as serpents flee to caves.
Now, thanks to you, my pleasure in the light
Of day has been renewed. The goddess's plan
Reveals itself to me, splendid and fair.
She bore you off, your family's guardian, like
A sacred image, to which by divine
Decree a city's changeless fate is linked,
Mysteriously; preserved you in a sacred
Stillness, to be a blessing to your brother,
To all your kin. When every hope of rescue
On this wide earth seemed lost, you give us back
Everything. Let your soul turn to thoughts
Of peace, oh King. Do not prevent her now
From carrying out the rites of consecration
In our paternal house, from leading me
Once more to halls now purged of guilt, from placing
On my head the ancient crown. Repay
The blessing she bestowed on you: Let me
Enjoy the rights most dear to me. Thus
Shall power and cunning, highest boast of men,
Be shamed by truth, the truth of her great soul;
And purest, childlike trust placed in a man
Of honor be accorded due reward.

IPHIGENIA: Think of the promises you gave, and let
Your heart be moved by what these loyal, honest
Lips have spoken. Look at us! Not often
Will you have the chance to act so nobly.

THOAS: Then go!

IPHIGENIA: Not so, my King! Without a blessing,
In hostility?—I will not part
From you that way. Don't banish us! Let friendship,

Let hospitality be the link between us.
Then we shall not forever be cut off
And driven far apart. Dear to me
And valued, as my father was, so are
You now; my soul will always bear this mark
Upon it. Should the humblest of your people
Ever touch my ears with the accents of
Your speech, that tone of voice I know so well,
If in the poorest man I see again
Your way of dress, I'll greet him like a god.
I shall myself prepare a bed for him,
Invite him to be seated by the fire,
And ask of you alone and of your fate.
Oh, may the gods give you the well-deserved
Reward of your good deeds and generous ways,
Farewell! Oh, look at us; and in return
Grant to me a kindly word of parting.
For then the wind will swell the sails more gently,
And from our eyes as we take leave the tears
Will flow less painfully. Farewell! Give me
In pledge of lasting friendship your right hand.
THOAS: Farewell!

Translated by Frank G. Ryder

TORQUATO TASSO

CAST OF CHARACTERS

Alfonso II, Duke of Ferrara
Leonore of Este, sister of the Duke, Princess
Leonore* Sanvitale, Countess of Scandiano
Torquato Tasso
Antonio Montecatino, Secretary of State

The scene is the palace of Belriguardo, a country retreat.

---

*Instead of "Leonore" Goethe occasionally uses "Eleonore" or "Lenore."

Act 1

Scene 1

A garden spot adorned with busts of the epic poets: downstage right, Virgil; downstage left, Ariosto.
                    (The Princess; Leonore.)

PRINCESS: You look at me and smile, Eleonore,
   And look back at yourself and smile again.
   What is the matter? Tell me as your friend.
   You seem bemused and yet you seem quite pleased.
LEONORE: Yes, my Princess, it pleases me to see
   Us both decked out in rural fashion here.
   We seem like truly happy shepherdesses,
   And we are busy, too, happy like them—
   We're making wreaths. And this one, bright with flowers,
   Keeps growing more and more beneath my hand.
   With loftier mind and nobler heart you've chosen
   As your own the slender, fragile laurel.
PRINCESS: The branches I have woven, deep in thought,
   Have found a worthy place already. Here,
   In gratitude, I crown the head of Virgil.
                    (She crowns the bust of Virgil.)
LEONORE: Then I will set my own full, joyous wreath
   On Master Lodovico's lofty brow—
                    (She crowns the bust of Ariosto.)
   That he, whose happy fancies never fade,
   May have at once his share of this new springtime.
PRINCESS: My brother favors us, bringing us here
   To spend this season in the countryside.
   We can be by ourselves for hours on end,
   Dreaming back to the golden age of poets.

I love it here at Belriguardo. Here
I spent so many happy days of childhood.
And this new greenness and this sun bring back
To me the feeling of that bygone time.

LEONORE: Oh yes, we find ourselves in a new world!
The shade of these eternally green trees
Already brings us joy, these fountains with
Their murmuring already lift our spirits.
Young branches sway upon the morning wind.
The flowers in the beds gaze up at us
In friendly fashion, with their childlike eyes.
With confidence the gardener unroofs
The hothouse for the oranges and lemons,
The blue sky over us is in repose,
And on the far horizon there the snow
Of distant mountains melts to fragrant mist.

PRINCESS: The springtime would be very welcome to me
If it did not deprive me of my friend.

LEONORE: O no, my Princess, in these precious moments
Do not remind me how soon I must leave.

PRINCESS: Whatever you are losing, you will find
Again, and doubly, in that mighty city.

LEONORE: My duty summons me, love summons me
Back to my husband, who has been so long
Without me. I bring him his son, who's grown
So fast this year, in body and in mind,
And I will share in his paternal joy.
Florence is vast and splendid, but the worth
Of all of its accumulated treasure
Can never match the jewels of Ferrara.
That city is a city made by its people;
Ferrara gained its greatness through its princes.

PRINCESS: Or rather through good human beings, who
By chance met here and, happily, joined forces.

LEONORE: What chance has gathered chance may soon disperse.
A noble mind draws other noble minds
And can retain them firmly, as you do.
Around you and your brother gather men
Of high intelligence, worthy of you,

And you are worthy of your great forefathers.
Freedom of thought and the fair light of learning
Were first enkindled here, in joy, while elsewhere
Barbarism still enclosed the world
In gloomy darkness. I was still a child
When my ears rang with names like Hercules
Of Este, like Hippolytus of Este,
My father praised Ferrara generously,
As much as Rome and Florence. Often then
I yearned to go there; and now here I am.
Here Petrarch was received, here he was fostered,
And Ariosto found his models here.
No great name can be named by Italy
Which this house has not named among its guests.
And to be host to a genius has its own
Reward: Give him a gift and he will leave
A finer one behind for you. The place
Where once a good man has set foot is sacred.
After a hundred years his words and actions
Will echo forth among our children's children.

PRINCESS: Yes, if their feelings are as strong as yours.
    I often envy you that happy fortune.

LEONORE: Which you enjoy serenely, purely, as
    Few others do. My full heart forces me
    To say straight off whatever I feel strongly;
    You feel it better, feel it deeply, and—
    Say nothing. Brief appearances do not
    Bedazzle you, sharp wit does not beguile you,
    And flattery glides vainly past your ear.
    Your mind stands firm, and faultless your good taste,
    Your judgment's true, your sympathy is great
    With greatness, which you know as your own self.

PRINCESS: You should not cloak this lofty flattery
    Beneath the borrowed robes of intimate friendship.

LEONORE: A true and proper friendship! It alone
    Can know the total compass of your worth.
    Let me give opportunity and fortune
    Their share as well in your accomplishment;
    You have it, all the same, and such you are.

And all the world reveres you and your sister:
First of the greatest women of your time.
PRINCESS: That, Leonore, can move me but little
When I consider just how small one is,
And what one is, one owes to other people.
My knowledge of the ancient tongues, of all
Our finest heritage, I owe my mother;
Yet neither daughter ever was her equal
In learning or in excellence of judgment;
If either one of us should be compared
With her, Lucretia surely has that right.
Also, I can assure you I have never
Taken as right of rank or as possession
What Nature or what fortune granted me.
When clever men discuss things I'm delighted
That I can understand what they are saying.
Whether it be their judgment of a man
Of ancient times, the worth of what he did,
Whether the topic be some branch of learning
Which by extension through experience
Will profit human beings and uplift them—
Wherever noble men's discourse may lead,
I gladly follow, for I do so with ease.
I like to hear disputes of clever men,
When speakers' lips with elegance play upon
The forces which so amicably and yet
So fearsomely inspire the human breast;
Or when the princely eagerness for fame,
For more extensive lands and power forms
The thinker's theme, and when the clever talents
Of such a clever man, deftly deployed,
Instead of duping us, give us instruction.
LEONORE: And then, after such serious entertainment
Our ear and inner senses take delight
In the repose afforded by the rhymes
Of poets who with gracious tones inspire
Feelings of utmost beauty in our souls.
Your lofty mind encompasses vast realms,
While I like best to dwell upon the island

Of poetry amid the laurel groves.
PRINCESS: In this fair land the myrtle tends to grow—
    Or so they would assure me—more than all
    The other trees. And though there are a lot
    Of muses, one is not so apt to seek
    Among them for a friend and boon companion
    As one may be to hope that one might meet
    A poet, though he seems to avoid and flee us,
    Seems to be seeking something we don't know
    And which perhaps he does not know himself.
    How nice, then, it would be if meeting us
    Some lucky hour he were suddenly
    Elated to discover in us the treasure
    He long had sought through all the world in vain.
LEONORE: I must admit your jest is well deserved.
    I grant that it strikes home, but not too deeply.
    I honor every man and his true worth
    And I am being only just to Tasso.
    His vision scarcely dwells upon this earth,
    His ear perceives the harmony of Nature;
    What history provides, what this life gives,
    His heart at once absorbs and makes his own.
    His spirit gathers what was widely scattered,
    His feelings, too, give life to lifeless things.
    And what seemed base to us he may ennoble,
    While what we treasure turns, for him, to nothing.
    Within this private magic circle walks
    This most remarkable man and draws us on
    To walk with him, to join and share with him.
    Approaching us, it seems, yet staying far,
    He seems to look at us, while ghostly spirits,
    Strangely, may stand before him in our stead.
PRINCESS: You have described with truth and tact the poet
    Who hovers in the realm of his sweet dreams.
    I feel, however, that reality
    Attracts him strongly too, and holds him fast.
    Those lovely songs which we from time to time
    Discover fastened to our trees and which,
    Like golden apples, make a fragrant, new

Hesperia, surely you must recognize
Them all as gracious fruits of a true love.
LEONORE: I too take pleasure in those lovely pages.
　With his far-ranging mind he glorifies
　In all his many rhymes one single image.
　At times he lifts it up in shining glory
　To the starry sky, bows down before the image
　As angels would, above the clouds, adoring;
　Then through quiet meadows, he pursues it,
　Entwining every flower in his garland.
　If his adored one leaves, he consecrates
　The path that her fair foot has softly taken.
　Concealed in thickets like the nightingale,
　He fills the grove and air with the harmonies
　Of his laments, poured from his lovesick heart.
　His charming grief, the blissful melancholy
　Entices every ear, all hearts must follow—
PRINCESS: And if he were to name his subject, then
　He'd call it by the name of Leonore.
LEONORE: That is your name as much as it is mine.
　I would resent it if it were another.
　I am delighted that he can conceal
　His feeling for you in that double meaning.
　I'm pleased that he remembers me as well
　With the sweet gentle echo of that name.
　There is no question here of any love
　That seeks to be the master of its object,
　Exclusively possess it, jealously
　Deny the very sight of it to others.
　When in rapt contemplation he expands
　Upon your merits he may also take
　Some pleasure too in my own lesser person.
　He does not love us—pardon my so speaking!
　From all the spheres he conjures what he loves
　Down into the one name which we both bear
　And he communicates his feelings to us;
　We seem to love the man, and we love only
　In him the highest things that we can love.
PRINCESS: You have gone very deeply, Leonore,

Into this science, and you tell me things,
Things which scarcely more than touch my ear
And hardly pass from there into my soul.
LEONORE: Student of Plato? You? And not to grasp
What a mere novice dares to prattle of?
Unless of course I've erred too seriously.
And yet I am not wholly wrong, I know.
In this sweet School, love won't be seen
The way he used to be, a mere spoiled child;
For now he is the youth who wed with Psyche
And one who in the council of the gods
Has his own seat and voice. He does not storm
Wantonly back and forth from breast to breast.
Nor straightaway lay hold on form and beauty
With sweet misjudgment, and he does not pay
For sudden rapture with disgust and loathing.
PRINCESS: Here comes my brother. Let us not betray
The turn that once again our words have taken,
Or we shall have his jesting to endure,
Just as our costume met his mockery.

Scene 2

(Enter Alfonso.)

ALFONSO: I have been looking everywhere for Tasso
And do not find him—even here with you.
Can you not give me any news of him?
PRINCESS: I saw him little yesterday, and not
At all today.
ALFONSO: It is his longtime failing
To seek seclusion more than company.
If I forgive his shunning motley crowds
Of people and preferring to commune
In quiet freedom with his spirit, still
I can't approve the way that he avoids
The very circle which his friends have formed.
LEONORE: If I am not mistaken, sire, soon
You will transform your blame to joyful praise.

I saw him from afar today; he had
A book and tablet, wrote, and paced, and wrote.
A word he spoke in passing yesterday
Announced, I thought, the finish of his work.
He only needs to make a few improvements
And then at last repay with worthy tribute
Your favor which has meant so much to him.

ALFONSO: He shall be welcome if and when he brings it,
Shall be acquitted for a good long time.
Much as I sympathize with all his labor
Much as the great work pleases me and must
Please me in many ways, nevertheless
My own impatience is increasing too.
He cannot finish, cannot reach an end;
He keeps on changing, slowly moves ahead,
Stops once again, giving the lie to hope.
One hates to see postponed to some far time
A pleasure one had thought so near at hand.

PRINCESS: I praise the modesty, the care he shows
In moving step-by-step toward his goal.
Only by favor of the Muses will
So many lines close rank in perfect union.
And his soul cherishes this impulse only:
His poem must be rounded to a whole.
He will not simply heap up tale on tale
To entertain delightfully and then,
Like empty words, delude and fade away.
Leave him alone, my brother. Time is not
The measure of the greatness of a work.
If future worlds are meant to share the pleasure,
The artist's world and time must sacrifice.

ALFONSO: Let us, dear sister, work together here,
As we have often done to our advantage.
If I am overzealous, you be gentle;
And if you are too gentle, I will press.
Perhaps then we shall see him suddenly
Reaching the goal we long have wished for him.
And then our fatherland and all the world
Will marvel what a work has been accomplished.

I shall have my own share in the renown,
And he will be inducted into life.
A noble man can't let one narrow circle
Shape his whole character. His fatherland,
The world at large, must have effect on him.
He must learn to endure both praise and blame.
He must be forced to know himself and others.
Seclusion will no longer cradle him
In praise. Foes *will* not and friends *must* not spare him.
The youth will then exert his strength in conflict,
Feel what he is, and soon feel like a man.

LEONORE: Then, sire, you'll still do everything for him,
Just as you have already done so much.
A talent forms itself in solitude,
A character amid the stream of life.
O may he form his spirit like his art,
On your instruction, may he cease to shun
The company of men, may his suspicion
Not be transformed at last to fear and hatred!

ALFONSO: But only those who don't know people fear them
And one who shuns them never truly knows them,
Such is his case, and so by gradual stages
A free mind comes to be confused and prisoned.
And so he's often vastly more concerned
About my favor than he ought to be.
He feels mistrust for many who, I know,
Are not his enemies. And if by chance
A letter goes astray, or should a servant
Transfer from his own service to some other,
If there's a paper he can't get his hands on,
Immediately he thinks design, betrayal,
And malice undermine his destiny.

PRINCESS: Dear brother, let us not forget: no man
Can stand aside and truly see himself.
And if a friend, upon a walk with us,
Injured his foot, we'd surely choose to walk
More slowly and extend our hand to him
Gladly and willingly.

ALFONSO: Better by far

If we could cure him, try without delay
Some treatment on advice of trusted doctors,
Then in good spirits follow the fresh path
Of a new life with someone fully healed.
Dear ladies, still I hope I never must
Assume the onus of the cruel surgeon.
I do whatever I can do to inspire
His heart with confidence, a sense of safety.
Often in company of many persons
I give him unmistakable signs of favor.
If he submits complaints, I have them seen to,
As I did recently when he suspected
His room was burglarized. If nothing's found
I show him calmly how I see the matter.
And since one must use every means, I practice
Patience with Tasso, for he does deserve it.
And you, I know, both willingly support me.
I have now brought you to the country and
Myself return this evening to the city.
There will be time to see Antonio briefly;
He comes from Rome to fetch me. We have much
To settle and discuss. Decisions must
Be made and many letters must be written.
All this compels me to return to the city.
PRINCESS: Will you allow us to accompany you?
ALFONSO: Remain in Belriguardo, and together
  Go over to Consandoli. Enjoy
  The lovely days entirely at your leisure.
PRINCESS: You cannot stay with us? You can't conduct
  Your business here as well as in the city?
LEONORE: You take Antonio away from us
  Just when he'd have so much to tell of Rome?
ALFONSO: It can't be done, my children. But as soon
  As possible I shall return with him,
  And he'll tell you his stories, while you help me
  Give due reward to him who once again
  Extends himself so greatly in my service.
  And then, once we have finished our discussions—
  Then let the busy crowds arrive, so that

Our gardens may be gay, and that I too—
It's only fair—should find a beauty glad
To see me, should I seek her, in the cool
Of night.
LEONORE: As friends we'll look the other way.
ALFONSO: But you know that I do not press advantage.
PRINCESS *(looking offstage)*:
It's Tasso. I have watched him for some time now.
His pace is slow. At times he stops completely,
As if in indecision, then he heads
For us again, but faster—and once more
He stops.
ALFONSO: If he is thinking and composing,
Do not disturb his dreams, but let him walk.
LEONORE: No, he has seen us, he is coming here.

Scene 3

(Enter Tasso with a book bound in parchment.)

TASSO: I'm coming—slowly—to present my work,
And still I hesitate to give it to you.
I know too well it still remains unfinished.
Though it might seem to have attained completion.
But though I was concerned lest I present it
To you unfinished, other new concerns
Compel me now: I should not like to seem
Too anxious—nor ungrateful. As a man
May say no more than "Here I am," and friends
Be glad, accepting him for what he is,
So I can only say: "Receive it now!"
                    (He presents the volume.)
ALFONSO: You quite surprise me with your gift and make
This lovely day a festival for me.
And so at last I hold it in my hands
And call it in a certain sense my own!
I long have wished you might make up your mind
And finally tell me: "Here! It is enough."
TASSO: If you are satisfied, then it is finished;

For it belongs to you in every sense.
If I considered all the effort spent,
If I looked at the tracings of my pen,
Then I might well declare: "This work is mine."
But if I look more closely at what gives
This poem its dignity and inner worth,
I see that I have this from you alone.
If kindly Nature by a generous whim
Gave me the lovely gift of poetry,
By cruel whim Fortune rejected me,
Casting me off with ruthless savagery,
And if the fair world drew the youngster's gaze,
Raptly, with all the fullness of its splendor,
The youthful mind was early overcast
By loving parents' undeserved privation.
If lips were ever parted then to sing
It was a mournful song that came from them,
And I accompanied with muted tones
My father's sorrow and my mother's pain
And it was you alone who raised me up
Out of a narrow life to lovely freedom,
Who lifted every care from off my head
And gave me liberty so that my soul
Was able to unfold in valiant song.
Whatever praise my work may now obtain
I owe to you, for it belongs to you.
ALFONSO: Twice now you merit every praise; you honor,
  With modesty, yourself as well as us.
TASSO: Could I but say what I acutely feel,
  That what I bring I have from you alone!
  The youth of no achievements—could he draw
  This poem from himself? The shrewd command
  Of swift-paced war—did he invent all that?
  The art of weapons mightily displayed
  By every hero on the day appointed,
  The captain's wisdom, bravery of knights,
  How vigilance and cunning are subdued,
  O did you not inspire all that in me,
  My wise and valiant Prince, as if you were

My Genius, who could take delight in making
His high, his unattainably high being
Thus manifest through a mere mortal man?
PRINCESS: And now enjoy the work, which gladdens us.
ALFONSO: Rejoice in every good man's approbation.
LEONORE: Rejoice now in your universal fame.
TASSO: This single moment is enough for me.
Thinking and writing, I had only you
In mind; to please you was my greatest wish,
To entertain you was my highest goal.
One who can't see his world's made up of friends
Doesn't deserve to gain the world's attention.
Here is my fatherland, here is the circle
Within whose bounds my soul is pleased to move.
I pay attention here, mark every word;
Learning speaks here, experience, taste. I see
My world and my posterity before me.
The masses make an artist shy and troubled;
But only those who are like you, who feel
And understand, shall judge and grant reward!
ALFONSO: If we're your world and your posterity
It is not right that we should merely *take*.
The splendid symbol that rewards a poet,
Which even heroes, who have need of him,
Behold upon his head, yet feel no envy,
I see here twined about your forebear's brow.
                    (*pointing to the bust of Virgil.*)
Was it some genius or coincidence
That wove and brought it? Not for nothing do
We see it here. For I hear Virgil say:
"Why honor ye the dead? They had their joy
And their reward while they were still alive.
Now if you so admire and reverence us,
Then give unto the living their due share.
My marble image has been crowned enough:
These boughs are green and they belong to life."
(*Alfonso beckons to his sister; she takes the wreath from the bust
        of Virgil and approaches Tasso. He falls back.*)
LEONORE: Refusing? See whose hand presents the wreath,

The beautiful, imperishable wreath!

TASSO: O let me hesitate! I do not see
How I can ever live beyond this hour.

ALFONSO: Live in enjoyment of the fine possession
Which for the initial moment frightens you.

PRINCESS *(as she holds the wreath aloft):*
You grant me the unwonted pleasure, Tasso,
Of telling you my thoughts without a word.

TASSO: Kneeling I take upon my poor weak head,
From your dear hands, the weight of this fair burden.
*(He kneels; the Princess places
the wreath upon him.)*

LEONORE *(applauding):*
Long live the poet for the first time crowned!
O how the wreath befits the modest man!
(Tasso stands up.)

ALFONSO: It is no more than token of the crown
That shall adorn you on the Capitol.

PRINCESS: And louder voices will acclaim you there;
Here the soft lips of friendship pay you tribute.

TASSO: O take it off my head again, take it
Away! It scorches every lock of hair,
And like a ray of sunlight striking hot,
Too hot upon my head, it burns the power
Of thought from my poor brain. A fever heat
Excites my blood. Forgive me! It's too much!

LEONORE: Say rather that these boughs serve to protect
The head of him who has to walk the burning
Regions of worldly fame, and cool his brow.

TASSO: I am not worthy of the cooling winds
Which should blow only 'cross the brows of heroes.
Raise up the wreath, ye gods, transfigure it
Among the clouds so that it floats on high
And higher, out of reach! so that my life
May be eternal progress toward that goal!

ALFONSO: When one acquires early, one learns early
To cherish all the good things of this life.
Enjoying early, one will not by choice
In this life do without what once he had,

And once possessing, one must be well-armed.
TASSO: And someone who would be well-armed must feel
  Within his heart a strength that never fails him.
  It fails me even now! In my good fortune
  It leaves me now, the innate strength that bade me
  Steadfastly meet misfortune and with pride
  Confront injustice. Has my present joy,
  Has the enchantment of the moment caused
  The very marrow in my limbs to melt?
  My knees give way beneath me! O Princess,
  You see me once again bowed down before you.
  Hear, then, my plea and take the wreath away
  So that, as though awakened from a dream
  Of beauty, I may feel a life new-quickened.
PRINCESS: If you can quietly and humbly bear
  The talent which the gods have given you,
  Then learn to bear as well these laurel sprigs,
  The finest thing that we can give. For one
  Whose head has ever merited their touch
  Will find that they forever wreathe his brow.
TASSO: Then let me go away in shame. Within
  The deep grove let me hide my happiness,
  As formerly I hid my sorrows there.
  There I will walk alone, nothing I see
  Will call to mind my undeserved good fortune.
  Should the clear water of some fountain show me
  By chance a man in its pure mirror, resting
  In thought and oddly crowned in the reflection
  Of sky between the trees, between the rocks,
  Then it will seem as if I were beholding
  Elysium upon that magic surface
  Imaged, and I will ponder and inquire:
  Now who may this departed spirit be,
  This youth of ancient times? So fair in garlands?
  Who will reveal his name? His claim to merit?
  I'll wait a long, long time and think: If only
  Someone would come and someone else again
  To join him here in friendly conversation!
  If I could see the heroes and the poets

Of ancient times assembled by this fountain,
See them forever here inseparable,
Firmly united as they were in life.
Just as the magnet by its power joins
Things iron with things iron fast together,
So equal striving joins heroes and poets.
Homer forgot himself, his life was wholly
Consumed in contemplation of two men,
And Alexander in Elysium
Hastens to seek out Homer and Achilles.
I wish I could be present to behold them,
Greatest of spirits, now at last united!

LEONORE: Wake up! Awake! And do not make us feel
You have no understanding of the present.

TASSO: It is the present moment that exalts me.
I only seem distracted; I'm enraptured!

PRINCESS: When you converse with spirits I am glad
You talk so humanly with them. I like it.
                    (*A page steps up to the
                    Prince and quietly delivers something.*)

ALFONSO: He has arrived, just at the best of times.
Antonio!—Bring him here.—Ah, here he comes.

Scene 4

(*Enter Antonio.*)

Welcome! You favor us twice over, bringing
Good news and your own self.

PRINCESS: Our greetings to you!

ANTONIO: I almost dare not say what pleasure fills
My life again when I am in your presence.
Seeing you, I find everything again
That I have missed so long. You seem content
With what I've done and what I have accomplished,
And thus I am repaid for all my worries,
For many days dragged out in restless waiting,
And others wasted by intent. We have
Now what we want, there's no more disagreement.

LEONORE: You have my greetings too, though I resent
  Your coming back just when I have to leave.
ANTONIO: To keep my joy from being too complete
  You take the fairest part away at once!
TASSO: My greetings also! I too hope to enjoy
  The presence of a man of such experience.
ANTONIO: You'll find me open if you ever care
  To shift your gaze from your world into mine.
ALFONSO: Although you have informed me in your letters
  What you have done and how things fared with you,
  I still have many things to ask about
  And by what means the business was accomplished.
  Across that strange and wonderful terrain
  One's step must be well gauged if in the end
  It is to lead you to your own true purpose.
  Whoever views his ruler's interests purely
  Will have no easy time of it in Rome;
  For Rome takes everything but gives you nothing.
  Whoever goes there to get something will
  Get nothing, unless he in turn gives something,
  And he is lucky if he gets it then.
ANTONIO: It is not my demeanor or my skill
  That let me carry out your will, my Lord.
  What shrewd man would not find his master in
  The Vatican? No, many things concurred
  Which I could turn to our advantage. Gregory
  Respects and greets you and sends you his blessing.
  That aged man, the noblest on whose head
  A crown's weight ever lay, recalls with joy
  The time when he embraced you. Connoisseur
  Of men, he knows you well and values you
  Highly, and did a great deal for your sake.
ALFONSO: I'm grateful for his good opinion of me,
  Assuming it is honest. But you know
  That one who looks down from the Vatican
  Sees at his feet whole kingdoms, each of which
  Looks very tiny—let alone plain men
  And princes. Now confess: what helped you most?
ANTONIO: Good! If you wish: the Pope's own lofty mind.

For he sees small things small and great things great.
In order that he may control his world
He yields with friendly goodwill to his neighbors.
The strip of land that he surrenders to you—
He knows its worth, values as well your friendship.
There must be calm in Italy, he wants
To see friends close to home, keep peace along
His borders, so the might of Christendom,
Which he controls with power, may destroy
Turks on the one hand, heretics on the other.

PRINCESS: And do we know the men he favors more
   Than others, who in confidence approach him?

ANTONIO: Only experienced men possess his ear,
   And energetic ones his trust and favor.
   Since early manhood servant of the state,
   He now controls it. Over courts he saw
   And knew and often guided, years ago
   As Nuncio, he now exerts his influence.
   The whole world lies as clear before his gaze
   As does the special interest of his state.
   To see this man in action is to praise him
   And to rejoice when passing time reveals
   What secretly he worked for and accomplished.
   There is no finer sight in all the world
   Than to behold a Prince astutely ruling,
   Or see a realm where all obey with pride,
   Where each man thinks to serve himself alone
   Because he's only asked to do what's right.

LEONORE: How much I long sometime to see that world
      Close by!

ANTONIO: But surely to be active in it?
   For Leonore is not a mere onlooker.
   And would it not be nice, madame, my friend,
   If we could sometimes get our tender hands
   Into the mighty game—Is that not so?

LEONORE *(to Alfonso):*
   You want to tease me, but you won't succeed.

ALFONSO: I owe you a great deal from other days.

LEONORE: Today I will remain, then, in your debt.

Forgive me, and don't interrupt my questions.
               (to Antonio)
Has he done much to help his relatives?
ANTONIO: He has done neither less nor more than proper.
  A man of power who won't care for his own
  Will be condemned, and by his very people.
  With quiet moderation Gregory
  Knows how to help his relatives who serve
  The state as honest men, and thus fulfills
  With one concern two allied obligations.
TASSO: Do art and learning also profit from
  His patronage? And does he emulate
  The mighty sovereigns of ancient times?
ANTONIO: He honors learning where it helps to rule
  The state and teach the ways of other nations.
  Art he esteems as far as it adorns
  And glorifies his Rome, makes palaces
  And temples works of wonder on this earth.
  He has no tolerance for idleness.
  To count, a thing must serve and have its function.
ALFONSO: And do you think that we can finish off
  Our business soon? Might they not, here or there,
  Scatter our path with further obstacles?
ANTONIO: Unless I'm much mistaken this dispute
  Can be directly settled and forever,
  Just by your signature and a few letters.
ALFONSO: Then I will praise these days of my career
  As times of much advantage and good fortune.
  I see my boundaries enlarged and know
  They're safe for future times. This you've accomplished
  Without a clash of swords, for which you well
  Deserve a civic crown. And that our ladies
  Shall weave from freshest oak leaves on the fairest
  Of mornings and shall place it on your brow.
  And meanwhile Tasso has enriched me also:
  For he has won Jerusalem for us,
  Thus putting modern Christendom to shame,
  With courage, joy, and tireless industry
  Attaining a remote and lofty goal.

And for his efforts you behold him crowned.

ANTONIO: You solve a riddle for me. When I came here
I was surprised to see two persons crowned.

TASSO: And as your eyes behold my great good fortune,
I wish that with the same glance you could see
What deep embarrassment my spirit feels.

ANTONIO: I long have known Alfonso is immoderate
In his rewards; so you discover now
What all his subjects long ago discovered.

PRINCESS: Once you find out how much he has achieved
You'll see how fair we are and moderate.
We're but the first and silent witnesses
Of the applause the world will not deny him
And future years will grant him ten times over.

ANTONIO: Through you he can be certain of his fame.
Who would presume to doubt when you give praise?
But tell me who has set this wreath upon
The brow of Ariosto?

LEONORE: My hand did so.

ANTONIO: And wisely done! It decks him beautifully;
Laurel itself would not so well adorn him.
As Nature cloaks the inmost riches of
Her breast with garments green and many-colored,
He clothes all things that make a human being
Worthy of our respect and our affection
In the full flower and raiment of his fictions.
Contentment, wisdom, and experience,
And strength of mind, good taste, the pure awareness
Of the true good—all these appear to rest
In spirit yet in person too, at peace
Beneath some flower-bearing tree, enshrouded
In snowy covering of soft light blossoms,
Enwreathed with roses, whimsically encircled
With wanton magic of the Amoretti.
The spring of plenty bubbles close at hand—
We see its many-colored wondrous fishes.
The air is filled with rarities of fowl,
As copse and meadow are with unknown herds;
Roguishness lurks half-hidden in the green;

Wisdom from time to time out of a cloud
Of gold intones exalted maxims, while
Upon a well-tuned lute wild madness seems
To storm about, first one way, then another,
Yet hold the measure of a perfect rhythm.
Whoever dares to stand beside this man
Deserves the wreath for sheer audacity.
Forgive me if I seem myself possessed
And, like a man in ecstasy, can not
Take heed of time or place or what I speak;
For all these poets, all these wreaths, these ladies,
Lovely in finery I seldom see,
Transport me from myself to a strange land.
PRINCESS: A man who can so well appreciate
One merit will not fail to see the other.
Some day you shall point out in Tasso's songs
What we have felt but only you perceived.
ALFONSO: Antonio, come along! I have a lot
That I am eager still to ask about.
And then till set of sun your time shall be
The ladies' to command. So come! Farewell.
                    (Antonio follows the Prince;
                    Tasso, the ladies.)

Act 2

Scene 1

A room.
(The Princess; Tasso.)

TASSO: I follow you, my Princess, but my steps
Still waver, and within my soul rise thoughts
Without proportion or coherent order.
Seclusion seems to beckon me and whisper
Complaisantly: "Come and I will resolve
The newly risen doubts within your breast."
But if I even glance at you, or if

My listening ear hears one word from your lips,
I feel a new day dawn around me, all
The ties that hold me captive fall away.
Freely I will confess to you, the man
Who joined us unexpectedly awakened
Me from a lovely dream—not gently either.
His manner and his words affected me
In such a wondrous way that more than ever
I feel I am two things in one, again
In discord and confusion with myself.

PRINCESS: We can't expect that any friend of old,
    Having long led an alien life far from us,
    Should at the moment he returns to us
    Be found precisely as he was before.
    Yet in his inner self he has not changed;
    Just let us live with him for a few days—
    Now and again the strings will be retuned
    Until the welcome time when once again
    Fair harmony shall join them. If he comes
    To see more closely what you have achieved
    In all this time, then surely he will place you
    Beside the poet he now sets against you,
    Contrasting you with him, a towering giant.

TASSO: The praise of Ariosto from his lips,
    My Princess, rather was a source of pleasure
    Than cause to take offense. It's reassuring
    For us to hear praise lavished on a man
    Who stands before us as a mighty model.
    In quiet heart we then can tell ourselves:
    If you achieve a portion of his merit,
    A portion of his fame cannot escape you.
    No, what disturbs my heart within its depths,
    What even now fills my entire soul,
    Were those forms of that other world which circles,
    Alive, immensely vast, and never resting,
    Around one great, uniquely subtle man
    In orderly completion of the orbit
    Boldly assigned it by that demigod.
    I listened eagerly and heard with pleasure

The self-assured words of the experienced man.
Alas, the more I listened, more and more
I sank in my view of myself and feared
That I would vanish on the rocks like Echo,
And like some nonexistent thing be lost.
PRINCESS: And yet a while ago you felt and said,
Heroes and poets live for one another,
Heroes and poets seek each other out,
And neither need feel envy of the other?
The deed that merits song is splendid surely;
It's also fine to bring to future times,
Through songs of merit, rich displays of deeds.
Content yourself with gazing on the world's
Wild course, as from a shore, within the safety
Of one small state that grants you its protection.
TASSO: Was it not here that I first saw, amazed,
How splendidly a brave man is rewarded?
I came here as an inexperienced boy
In days when festivals one after another
Would make Ferrara seem the very center
Of worldly honor. O what a sight it was!
The spacious square where skill and valor were
To show themselves in glory was encircled
By such a throng as light of sun will scarcely
Shine on a second time. Here close together
Sat all the fairest ladies of our day,
The most important men as well. One's gaze
Ran through the noble crowd, amazed. We cried:
All these our fatherland has gathered here,
That one small land surrounded by the sea,
And all of them together constitute
The most illustrious court that ever sat
In judgment over honor, worth, and virtue.
Go through them one by one, you'll find nobody
Who needs to be embarrassed by his neighbor—
And then the barrier gates were all thrown open.
Then horses stamped and shields and helmets gleamed,
Then grooms thronged in, then trumpet fanfares rang,
And lances shattered with a splintering sound.

Helmets and shields rang loud with blows, and dust,
Swirling, enveloped for a moment both
The victor's glory and the loser's shame.
O let me draw a curtain over all
That far too brilliant spectacle so that
In this fair hour my own unworthiness
May not be too acutely clear to me.

PRINCESS: That noble company, those valiant deeds
   May have inspired you to toil and striving,
   But I, young friend, could at the same time serve
   As witness to the quiet creed of patience.
   Those festivals you praise, and which were praised
   To me both then and many years thereafter,
   And by a hundred tongues, I did not see.
   In solitude where even the last echo
   Of joy almost without a break could fade
   And die, it was my fate to bear much pain
   And many a melancholy thought as well.
   With wings outspread, Death's image hovered there
   Before my eyes and blocked the view that opens
   Onto the world that is forever new.
   Only by slow degrees did it withdraw
   And let me glimpse as if through veils, the many
   Hues of life, all pale but pleasant still.
   I saw the forms of living things stir gently
   Once more and for the first time left my sickroom,
   Supported by my ladies still. Then came
   Lucretia full of all the joy of life,
   Leading you by the hand. You were the first
   Whom I encountered, new and quite unknown,
   In that new life of mine. I had great hopes
   For you and me, and that same hope of ours
   Has not betrayed us yet, in all this time.

TASSO: And I, bewildered by the tumult of
   The surging throng, bedazzled with such splendor,
   And deeply moved by various emotions,
   Walked silently along beside your sister
   Through tranquil hallways of the palace, entering
   The room where shortly you appeared before us,

Supported by your ladies—What a moment
That was for me! Forgive me! Just as someone
Possessed by frenzy and delusion can,
Through very presence of a god with ease
And grace be healed, so by one glance exchanged
Between us I was cured of all my dreaming,
Of all my false desires and morbid fancies.
If in naïveté I'd let myself
Covet a thousand things at random once,
I now stepped back within myself for shame
And came to know what's really worth desiring.
Thus one may search the wide sands of the sea
In vain to find a pearl that lies enclosed
And hidden in the quiet of a shell.

PRINCESS: That was the start of a delightful time,
  And had my sister not gone to Urbino
  To be the Duke's betrothed, year after year
  Would have flown by in quiet happiness.
  But now alas we know too well: We miss
  That gracious lady's cheerful soul, her wealth
  Of wit, her heart so full of life and courage.

TASSO: I realize, and all too well, that since
  The day of her departure no one could
  Replace for you the pure delight you lost.
  How often it has wrenched my heart! How often
  I told the quiet grove my grief for you!
  "Alas!" I cried "Is it her sister's right
  Alone, her privilege, to mean so much
  To one so dear? No other heart deserves
  Her confidence?—No spirit quite attuned
  To hers? Have mind and wit been quite extinguished?
  Was this one woman, excellent as she was,
  All things in all?" O pardon me, my Princess!
  I often thought then of myself and wished
  I might mean something to you. Very little,
  Yet something, not with words, but with my deeds
  I wished to be so—show you by my life
  Just how my heart was pledged to you in secret.
  But I did not succeed, and far too often,

Mistakenly did things that caused you pain,
Outraged the man to whom you gave protection,
Confused unwisely what you wished resolved,
And always felt farther and farther off
At moments when I wanted to be closer.

PRINCESS: No, Tasso, I have never failed to see
Your true intent; I know how quick you are
To seek your own undoing. Where my sister
Could get along with anyone at all,
You scarcely have a friend you feel at ease with,
Not even after all these years.

TASSO: Rebuke me—
But tell me afterward, where is the man
Or woman I dare talk to from the heart,
And quite as freely, as I do with you?

PRINCESS: You ought to try confiding in my brother.

TASSO: He is my Prince!—But please do not believe
My heart is driven by the wild desire
For freedom. Man is not born to be free.
And for a noble mind no happiness
Is finer than to serve a Prince whom he
Reveres. He is my Lord; I understand
The total compass of that lofty word.
I must learn to be silent when he speaks,
And do as he commands, no matter how
Intensely heart and judgment contradict him.

PRINCESS: But with my brother that need never be.
And now we have Antonio back again,
You may be sure you'll have a wise new friend.

TASSO: So I had hoped; now I despair almost.
How much I would have learned from being with him,
How useful his advice in countless cases.
He has, I daresay, all I lack. Yet—though
All gods conjoined to bring gifts to his cradle,
Unfortunately the Graces stayed away,
And lacking gifts from those well-favored beings,
One may own much and may give much away,
Yet have no comfort in his heart for others.

PRINCESS: One may confide in him, and that is much.

You must not ask one man for everything,
And this man does what he has promised you.
Once he declares himself to be your friend,
He will provide whatever you may lack.
You two must be allied! I trust myself
To manage this good work before too long.
Only, do not resist, as is your habit.
Thus we have long had Leonore here,
Who is refined and lovely and with whom
It is not hard to get along, yet you've
Not been as close to her as she had hoped.

TASSO: I have obeyed you, otherwise I would
Have held aloof instead of drawing closer.
As amiable as she appears to be—
I don't know how it is—I rarely could
Be wholly frank with her, and even if
Her purpose may well be to please her friends,
One senses purpose and it makes one cross.

PRINCESS: We'll never find companionship this way,
Tasso; this path leads us astray, to roam
Through solitary groves and silent valleys,
Letting our spirit turn to self-indulgence
And strive increasingly to re-create
Within itself the golden age it finds
No longer present in the world outside—
However unsuccessful the attempt.

TASSO: Ah what a word my Princess utters there!
The golden age, where has it gone? The age
For which all hearts are filled with hopeless yearning!
When on the free earth human beings roamed
At pleasure, just like happy flocks and herds,
When a primeval tree on bright-hued meadow
Afforded shade for shepherdess and shepherd,
And new young shrubs entwined their tender branches
Around their longing love, in intimacy,
Where clear and still, on sand forever pure,
Gently the supple stream embraced its nymph,
Where in the grass the startled serpent vanished
Harmlessly, where the bold young faun, rebuked

At once by the courageous youth, took flight;
Where every bird in freedom of the air
And every beast through hill and valley roving
Told man: Whatever's pleasing is permitted.

PRINCESS: My friend, the golden age is doubtless past,
But good men will establish it anew.
And would you like to know the way I see it?
The golden age with which the poet often
Beguiles us, that same golden age existed,
It seems to me, as little then as now.
And if it did exist, it surely was
No more than what can once again be ours.
For kindred hearts still chance on one another
And share enjoyment of the lovely world.
But one word in your motto must be changed,
My friend: Whatever's proper is permitted.

TASSO: Ah, if a general court consisting solely
Of good and noble human beings would
Decide what things are proper and not have
Each man deem proper that which serves his purpose!
We see how all goes well for clever men
With power, and they permit themselves all things.

PRINCESS: If you would learn precisely what is proper,
Then do no more than ask of noble women.
It is above all others their concern
That everything that happens should be proper.
Propriety erects a wall around
The tender, easily offended sex.
Where rules morality, there they rule also,
Where impudence controls, they count for nothing.
And if you make inquiry of both sexes:
Men strive for freedom, women for decorum.

TASSO: You call us coarse, intractable, unfeeling?

PRINCESS: Not that. But distant gain is what you strive for,
And all your striving must be violent.
While you make bold to set eternal goals,
We only want to own one single thing,
One limited estate upon this earth,
And want it to endure for us, unchanging.

Of no man's heart can we be sure, no matter
How warmly it surrendered to us once.
Beauty, the only thing you seem to prize.
Is transitory. What remains has no
More charm, and what has no more charm, is dead.
If there were men who gauged a female heart
At its true value, who could realize
What blessed treasure of fidelity
And love a woman's breast can hold within it;
If memory of supremely happy hours
Would keep their living freshness in your souls;
If your gaze otherwise so penetrating,
Could also penetrate the veil that age
Or illness casts upon us; if possession,
Which is supposed to give tranquillity,
Did not cause you to covet others' wealth;
Why, then a fair day would have dawned for us,
Then we would celebrate our golden age.

TASSO: You tell me things which cause a mighty stirring
   Within my heart of fears half lulled asleep.

PRINCESS: What do you mean? Speak frankly with me, Tasso.

TASSO: I often hear it said, and recently
   Have heard it said again, and had the word
   Not come I'd still have guessed it: noble princes
   Sue for your hand! And what we must expect
   We fear; and we could utterly despair.
   For you will leave us, that is natural.
   How we will bear it, though, I do not know.

PRINCESS: You need have no fears for the present moment.
   I'd almost say: have no fears whatsoever.
   I'm happy being here and happy staying.
   I know of no engagement that would tempt me.
   And if you really want to keep me, show it
   In bonds of harmony, building for yourself
   A happy life, and through you, one for me.

TASSO: O teach me how to do the possible!
   To you are dedicated all my days.
   When my heart opens up to sing your praise
   To give you thanks, then only do I feel

The purest happiness that man can know;
What's most divine I learned through you alone.
Thus earthly gods from other humans are
Distinguished, just as high fate is distinguished
From all the counsel and the will of men,
Even the most astute. Many the things
They let pass by, noticed no more than wavelets
Rippling before their feet, where we see wave
On mighty wave; they do not hear the storm
That rages all around and overthrows us;
They barely hear our plea for help and let
The air be filled with sighs and lamentation,
Just as we treat a poor benighted child.
My goddess, you have often treated me
With patience; often like the sun your glance
Has dried away the dew upon my eyelids.

PRINCESS: It's only right that women should accord you
  Their fullest sympathy, because your poem
  Glorifies our sex in many ways.
  Gentle or brave, you have consistently
  Presented them as lovable and noble,
  And though Armida does appear as hateful,
  Her love and beauty reconcile us quickly.

TASSO: Whatever things reecho in my poem,
  I owe them all to one, to one alone.
  No fancied immaterial image hovers
  Before my brow, now dazzling as it nears
  My soul and now retreating. I have seen
  It with my very eyes, the archetype
  Of every virtue and of every beauty.
  What I have copied from it will endure:
  Heroic love of Tancred for Clorinda,
  Erminia's quiet faithfulness unnoticed,
  Sophronia's greatness and Olinda's pain,
  These are not shadows by illusion bred;
  I know they are eternal, for they *are*.
  And what has any better right to last
  For centuries, working its quiet magic,
  More than the secret of a noble love

Confided modestly to graceful verse?

PRINCESS: And shall I tell you one more point of merit
This poem has, in secret ways, acquired?
It lures us on and on; we listen and
We listen, and we think we understand;
And what we understand we cannot blame;
And thus this poem finally wins us over.

TASSO: O what a heaven you disclose for me,
Princess! Unless this splendor blinds my eyes,
I see eternal happiness, unhoped for,
Descending gloriously on golden rays.

PRINCESS: No further, Tasso! There are many things
Which we must seize upon with vehemence,
But others can be ours through self-restraint
Alone, and through renunciation. Such,
They say, is virtue; such, they say, is love,
Which is related to it. Mark this well.

(Exit.)

Scene 2

TASSO *(alone):*
Is it permissible to raise your eyes?
Do you dare look about? You are alone!
And did these columns hear what she has said?
And need you fear these silent witnesses
Of highest happiness? The sun is rising
On a new day in my existence, one
With which the past is not to be compared.
Descending from on high the goddess swiftly
Lifts up the mortal man. What new domains
Reveal themselves before my eyes, what kingdoms!
How richly are my ardent wishes met!
I dreamed that I was near to highest bliss,
And *this* is bliss surpassing any dream.
Let one who was born blind conceive of light
And colors as he may; a new day breaks:
It seems to him a new and different sense

Full of presentiment and courage, reeling,
Drunk with joy, I take this path. You give
Me much, giving as earth and heaven shower
Gifts on us lavishly and with full hands,
And in return ask only what a gift
Like this entitles you to ask of me.
I must renounce, I must show self-restraint,
And thus deserve your confidence in me.
What have I ever done that she could choose me?
What must I do now to be worthy of her?
I *am*—by virtue of her confidence.
Yes, Princess, to your words and in your sight
Let my soul be forever consecrated!
Ask anything you will, for I am yours!
Let her send me in search of toil and peril
And fame in foreign lands, or let her hand me
The golden lyre amid the tranquil grove,
Ordain me for repose and praise of her:
I'm hers; transforming me she shall possess me.
For *her* my heart has hoarded all its treasures.
Had some god given me a thousand times
My skills and arts I scarcely could express
Sufficiently my speechless adoration.
The painter's brush, the poet's lips, the sweetest
That on the early honey ever fed—
These I hoped for. No, henceforth Tasso shall
Not wander powerless, alone, and gloomy,
Among the trees, among his fellow beings!
He is no more alone, he is with *you*.
O if the noblest deed of all would only
Present itself here visibly to me,
Ringed round with grisly peril! I would cast
Myself upon it, gladly risk the life
I now have from her hands—I'd call upon
The finest human beings as my friends,
A noble company, at her command
And will, to do the impossible for her.
Rash man, why were your lips not sealed to hide
Your feelings until you were worthy—worthier—

To place yourself before her, at her feet?
That was your purpose and your wiser wish.
But be it so! Far better to receive
Such gifts unmerited, without conditions,
Than half and half to fancy that one might
Have had a right to ask. See the bright side!
What lies before you is so great, so vast;
The hopefulness of youth entices you
Once more into a bright and unknown future.
—Swell high, my heart!—Climate of happiness,
Accord your favor to this plant for once!
It strives toward heaven, and a thousand branches
Press forth from it, unfolding into blossoms.
May it bear fruit, and O may it bear joy!
And may a dear hand pluck the golden bounty
From all its fresh and richly laden boughs!

Scene 3

(Tasso, Antonio.)

Welcome to you, whom, as it were, I see
For the first time now. I've heard no man
So greatly heralded before. Hence, welcome!
I know you now and I know your full worth;
I offer heart and hand unhesitating
And hope for your part you will not disdain me.
ANTONIO: Fair gifts you offer me, and generously.
I recognize their value as I should,
Hence let me hesitate before I take them.
I do not know yet whether I in turn
Can offer you the same. I should not like
To seem too hasty nor to seem ungrateful;
Let me be prudent and concerned for both.
TASSO: Who will blame prudence? Every step in life
Reveals how indispensable it is.
But it is finer when the soul informs us
Where we've no need of narrow circumspection.
ANTONIO: On that score let each man ask his own heart,

For he must pay for his mistakes himself.

TASSO: So be it, then. I have performed my duty.
I have revered the Princess's command,
Who wants to see us friends, and have presented
Myself to you. For I could not hold back,
Antonio, but I'll not impose myself.
Time and acquaintance will perhaps bring you
To ask more warmly for the gift which you
Now coldly put aside and almost scorn.

ANTONIO: A self-restrained man often is termed cold
By those who think themselves more warm than others
Because a passing heat comes over them.

TASSO: You censure what I censure, what I shun.
I too am capable, young as I am,
Of ranking permanence ahead of fervor.

ANTONIO: Most wisely so! Be always of that mind.

TASSO: You are entitled to advise me and
To warn me, for you have experience
Standing beside you as a proven friend.
Yet be aware: A quiet heart does listen
To every day's and every hour's warning
And practices in secret all the virtues
Your strictness thinks to teach as something new.

ANTONIO: It's nice enough, no doubt, to be concerned
With one's own self, if that but serve a purpose.
No man can learn to know his inmost self
By introspection. Measuring on his own,
He finds himself too small, often, alas,
Too great. Man knows himself through man alone
And only life can teach him what he is.

TASSO: I hear you with approval and respect.

ANTONIO: Yet at these words I fear you're thinking something
Quite different from what I mean to say.

TASSO: We'll draw no closer to each other this way.
It makes no sense at all, it is not fair
To misjudge any man deliberately,
Whoever he may be. I did not need
The Princess' word, I knew you right away.
I realize you want what's good—and do it.

Your own fate leaves you wholly unconcerned,
You think of others, give support to others,
And on the restless currents of this life
You keep a steadfast heart. So I perceive you.
What would I be if I did not approach you,
If I were not ambitious to acquire
A portion of the treasure you keep secret?
I know you won't regret it if you open
Your heart to me, I know you'll be my friend
When once you know me, and I long have needed
Just such a friend. I feel my inexperience
And youth no cause for shame. About my head
The future's golden cloud still gently hovers.
O take me, noble man, into your heart,
Initiate me, rash and inexperienced,
Into the temperate usages of life.

ANTONIO: In space of one brief moment you demand
    What time alone and careful thought can grant.

TASSO: And yet in one brief moment love will grant
    What lengthy time and effort barely gains.
    I do not ask this of you, I demand it.
    I challenge you in the name of that virtue
    That vies in making allies of good men.
    And shall I name you one more name? The Princess—
    The Princess hopes for it, she wishes it—
    Eleonore—yes she wants to bring me
    To you and you to me. Let's meet her wishes!
    Let us together go before that goddess
    And offer her our service, our whole souls
    As one, to do the noblest things for her.
    Once more I say to you!—Here is my hand!
    Accept it! Don't step back, refuse no longer,
    O noble man, grant me the fairest joy
    Any good man can know: to yield his trust,
    Without reserve, to one who is his better.

ANTONIO: You go with all sails crowded. It would seem
    That you are used to winning, used to finding
    The road smooth everywhere, the gates wide open.
    I gladly grant you all you gain by merit,

Or by good luck; but I see far too clearly
How great a distance separates us still.
TASSO: In years, in tested merit, that may be;
In boldness and in will I yield to none.
ANTONIO: It is not will that conjures up great deeds.
And boldness sees the path as shorter than
It may be. He who gains his goal is crowned;
A worthy man will often lack a crown.
There are, however, wreaths of little weight
And wreaths of very different sorts. Sometimes
They're comfortably acquired while taking walks.
TASSO: What some god freely grants to one and sternly
Denies another, such a prize will not
Be every man's to gain at will and wish.
ANTONIO: Give Luck the credit over other gods
And I will listen, for his choice is blind.
TASSO: But Justice wears a blindfold too; her eyes
Are tightly closed in face of all delusion.
ANTONIO: A lucky man may well extol Good Luck,
For favors rendered, may impute to him
A hundred eyes, shrewd choice, and strict discernment,
Call it Minerva, call it what he will,
Mistake a generous gift for just reward,
Chance finery for jewels merited.
TASSO: You need not speak more plainly. That's enough!
I now see deep into your heart and know
You for a lifetime. Would that my Princess
Also knew you this way! Do not waste
The arrows of your eyes and of your tongue!
You aim them all in vain against the wreath,
The never-fading wreath upon my head.
Be big enough not to be envious—
That first, and then perhaps you may vie for it.
I deem it sacred, a supreme possession.
Show me the man who has achieved the thing
That I am striving for, show me the hero
Of whom I've only heard in stories told me;
Show me the poet who may be compared
With Homer and with Virgil, yes, and what

Goes further still, show me the man who ever
Deserved with triple merit that reward
And yet was three times more than I embarrassed
By that fair crown—then you will see me on
My knees before the god who so endowed me,
Nor would I rise until that god transferred
That mark of honor from my head to his.

ANTONIO: Till then, admittedly, you merit it.

TASSO: Appraise my worth: I will not shrink from that.
But I have not deserved contempt. The crown
My Prince has deemed me worthy of and which
My Princess' hand entwined for me shall not
Be cast in doubt by sneers from anyone!

ANTONIO: This haughty tone and sudden heat of yours
Ill suits you both with me, and in this place.

TASSO: What you permit yourself suits me as well.
Has truth perhaps been banished from this place?
Is the free mind imprisoned in this palace?
Must noble men endure oppression here?
Highness is here, I fancy, in its surest place,
The highness of the soul! May it not relish
The company of the leaders of this world?
It may and shall. We join a Prince's circle
By noble blood alone, ours from our fathers,
Why not by mind, largeness of which Nature
Gave not to every man, no more than she
Could give each man a noble lineage.
Smallness alone should feel uneasy here,
The envy which appears to its own shame,
Just as no dirty spiderweb may be
Allowed to cling upon these marble walls.

ANTONIO: It's you yourself who prove me right to spurn you!
So the presumptuous boy would force his way
Into the grown man's confidence and friendship?
With your ill-breeding still you think you're good?

TASSO: Far rather what you choose to term ill-bred
Than what I could not help but term ignoble.

ANTONIO: You still are young enough that proper training
Can teach you something of a better way.

TASSO: Not young enough to bow to idols; old
Enough to brave defiance with defiance.

ANTONIO: Where lip and lyre play decide the contest
You do come off the hero and the victor.

TASSO: It would be rash to boast about my fists,
For as yet they've done nothing, but I'd trust them.

ANTONIO: You trust forbearance, which has left you spoiled
Through all the brazen course of your good fortune.

TASSO: I am a man full-grown, I feel that now.
You are the last with whom I should have liked
To try the hazard of a test with weapons,
But you rake fire on top of fire until
My inmost marrow scorches and the painful
Lust for revenge seethes foaming in my breast.
So if you are the man you boast of, face me.

ANTONIO: You know as little who you are as where.

TASSO: No sanctuary bids us bear abuse.
You blaspheme and you desecrate this place,
Not I, who offered you my confidence,
Respect, and love, the finest offerings.
It is your spirit which defiles this paradise,
Your words that now defile this stainless room,
Not my heart's surge of passion which now rages,
Determined to avoid the slightest stain.

ANTONIO: What lofty spirit in a narrow chest!

TASSO: There's room enough to vent that bosom freely.

ANTONIO: The rabble also vent their hearts with words.

TASSO: If you're a nobleman as I am, show it.

ANTONIO: I am indeed but I know where I am.

TASSO: Come down, then, where our weapons may decide.

ANTONIO: You should not challenge, and I will not come.

TASSO: Such obstacles are welcome to a coward.

ANTONIO: The coward threatens only where he's safe.

TASSO: Safety like that I can forgo with pleasure.

ANTONIO: You compromise yourself; this place you cannot.

TASSO: The place forgive me for enduring this!
                    (*He draws his sword.*)
Now draw or follow, lest forevermore
I should despise you as I hate you now.

Scene 4

(Enter Alfonso.)

ALFONSO: You surprise me. What's this quarrel about?
ANTONIO: You see me standing calmly, O my Prince,
　Before a man who's in the grip of fury.
TASSO: I thank you as I'd thank a god for this:
　You check me with a single glance of warning.
ALFONSO: Tell me, Antonio; Tasso, you inform me:
　How did dissension get into my house?
　How did it seize upon you, carrying off
　Sane men in frenzy from the path of good
　Behavior and of laws? I am astonished.
TASSO: I do not think that you quite know us both.
　This man, renowned as sensible and upright,
　Behaved toward me maliciously and rudely
　Like an ignoble man, devoid of breeding.
　I had approached him trustfully, but he
　Thrust me away; I in persistent love
　Pressed on, and he, with growing bitterness,
　Did not rest once till he had turned to gall
　The purest drop of blood in me. Forgive me!
　You found me acting like a madman here.
　This man's to blame for any blame I earned.
　He was the one who rudely fanned the fire
　That seized me and offended me and him.
ANTONIO: His high poetic flight swept him away!
　Prince, you addressed me first; you asked me questions.
　May I now be allowed to speak as well,
　After this overhasty orator?
TASSO: O yes! Relate, relate it word for word!
　And if you can repeat before this judge,
　Each syllable and every look, just dare!
　Disgrace yourself again—a second time
　And testify against yourself! But I
　Will not deny one breath or pulsebeat of it.
ANTONIO: If you have any more to say, then say it.
　If not, be still and do not interrupt me.

Did I, my Prince, or did this hothead here
Begin the quarrel? Which of us was in
The wrong? That is an ample question, one
We must hold for the moment in abeyance.

TASSO: What's this? That's the first question, I should think,
Which one of us is right and which is wrong.

ANTONIO: Not just the way the mind, undisciplined,
May fancy it.

ALFONSO: Antonio!

ANTONIO: Gracious Lord,
I honor your behest, but keep him quiet.
Once I have spoken, he can talk again.
You will decide. Thus I will merely say:
I cannot argue with him, I can neither
Accuse him, nor defend myself, nor offer
Myself to give him satisfaction now.
For as he stands, he is not a free man.
A heavy law holds him in sway, one which
At best your favor can alleviate.
He made threats to me here, he challenged me,
He hardly hid his naked sword from you,
And had you, Lord, not intervened between us,
I too would stand here now as one disloyal,
Accessory to guilt, and shamed before you.

ALFONSO (*to Tasso*):
You have not acted well.

TASSO: My own heart, Lord,
Acquits me; yours will surely do the same.
Yes, it is true, I threatened and I challenged;
I drew. But you cannot imagine how,
With well-planned words, insidiously, his tongue
Gave me offense; how, sharp and swift, his fangs
Injected their fine venom in my blood,
How he enflamed the fever more and more!
Calmly and coldly he kept at me, drove me
Out to the farthest edge. O, you don't know him,
No, you don't know him, you will never know him!
I warmly offered him the finest friendship;
He threw my gift before my very feet.

And if my soul had not flamed up with passion,
It would forever be unworthy of
Your favor and your service. If I did
Forget the law and where I am, forgive me.
In no place can I ever be abject,
In no place can I bear humiliation.
Wherever it may be, if this heart fails you
And fails itself, then punish, cast me out,
And never let me see your face again.
ANTONIO: How easily this youth bears heavy burdens
And shakes off faults like dust out of a garment!
It would be quite amazing, if we weren't familiar
With poetry's magic power that so much loves
To play its games with the impossible.
I have some doubt, my Prince, that you and all
Your followers will look upon this deed
As being quite so insignificant.
For majesty extends its high protection
To all who come to it as to a goddess
And her inviolate dwelling place. And there,
As at the very altar steps, all passion
Will hold itself in check upon the threshold.
There no sword gleams, no threatening word is uttered,
Offense itself demands no vengeance there.
Broad fields provide sufficient open space
For anger and hostility. No coward
Threatens there, no man will flee. These walls
Your fathers founded on security,
And to reflect their dignity made strong
A sanctuary, wise and solemnly
Maintaining peace by heavy penalties.
There prison, death, and exile overtook
The guilty; neither did regard for person
Or clemency restrain the arm of justice.
The wicked man himself was terror-stricken.
Now after long and splendid peace we see
Raw fury lurching back again in frenzy,
Into the jurisdiction of right conduct.
Judge, Lord, and punish! Who can walk within

Set limits of his duty if the law
And if his Prince's power does not shield him?
ALFONSO: More than you both have said or ever could say
  My own impartial mind gives me to hear.
  You would have done your duty vastly better
  If I were not compelled to pass this judgment.
  For right and wrong are close-related here.
  Thus if Antonio has insulted you
  Then in some way or other he must grant
  Such satisfaction as you will demand.
  I would prefer it if you were to choose me
  As arbitrator. Meanwhile, your crime, Tasso,
  Makes you a prisoner. As I forgive you,
  I will alleviate the law for your sake.
  So leave us, Tasso. Stay in your own quarters,
  Your own sole guard and by yourself alone.
TASSO: Is this, O Prince, your sentence as a judge?
ANTONIO: Do you not recognize a father's lenience?
TASSO *(to Antonio):*
  To you I have no more to say at present.
                    (to Alfonso)
  O Prince, this solemn word of yours consigns me,
  A free man, to imprisonment. So be it!
  You deem it just. Honoring your sacred word,
  I bid my deepest, inmost heart be still.
  This is so new to me that I almost
  Do not know you, myself, or this fair place.
  But this man I know well—I will obey,
  Although I still could say a lot of things,
  And ought to say them, too. My lips fall silent.
  Was there a crime? It seems at least that I
  Am looked on as a criminal. Whatever
  My heart may say to me, I am a captive.
ALFONSO: You make more of it, Tasso, than I do.
TASSO: It's all incomprehensible to me.
  O, not incomprehensible exactly,
  I am no child. I almost think I must
  Have grasped it. Sudden light does dawn on me
  But in an instant closes up again.

I hear my sentence only, and I bow.
Too many useless words have passed already!
From now on get the habit of obeying.
You poor, weak mortal, you forgot your place.
The gods above seemed set on level ground
With you and now the steep fall overwhelms you.
Obey, and do so gladly; it befits
A man to do with goodwill what is painful.
First take this sword that you had given me
When I went with the Cardinal to France.
I've earned no fame in wearing it—nor shame,
Even today. This gift so full of hope
I yield up with a heart profoundly moved.
ALFONSO: You don't see clearly how I feel toward you.
TASSO: My lot is to obey, and not to think!
Unfortunately a splendid gift's refusal
Is what my destiny requires of me.
Nor does a crown befit a prisoner.
I take the mark of honor from my head
Myself; I thought it given for all time.
That finest fortune was vouchsafed too early
And, as if I had overreached myself,
Is torn from me, only too soon.
You take yourself what no one could take from you,
And what no god will give a second time.
We human beings have most wondrous trials;
We could not bear it, were it not that Nature
Endowed us with a blessed levity.
Distress invites us to play casually
And coolly with possessions beyond price,
And willingly we open up our hands
For such things to escape past all recall.
There is a tear united with this kiss,
Consigning you to transitoriness.
We are allowed this gentle mark of weakness.
Who would not weep when things immortal are
Themselves not proof against destruction? Come,
Join with this sword, which had no part, alas,
In winning you, and, twined about it, rest,

As on the coffin of the brave, upon
The tomb of my good fortune and my hope.
I willingly lay both before your feet,
For who is safely armed if you are angry,
And who is honored, Lord, if you misjudge him?
I go, a captive, to await my trial.
*(At a sign from the Prince, a page picks up
the sword and wreath and carries them away.)*

Scene 5

(Alfonso, Antonio.)

ANTONIO: Where are the boy's wild fancies taking him?
  In what hues does he paint his fate and merits?
  Limited, inexperienced, youth considers
  Itself unique, a chosen kind of being,
  To whom above all others all's allowed
  Let him feel punished; punishment is good
  For youth, the grown-up man will thank us for it.
ALFONSO: Punished he is: I only fear, too much.
ANTONIO: If you would be most lenient with him,
  Then give him back, O Prince, his liberty
  And let the sword then settle our dispute.
ALFONSO: If that's the general view, it may be done.
  But tell me, how did you provoke his anger?
ANTONIO: I cannot really tell you how it happened.
  Perhaps I hurt his feelings, as a man;
  As nobleman I gave him no offense;
  And at the height of anger not a crude
  Or vulgar word escaped his lips.
ALFONSO: So seemed
  Your quarrel to me, and what I thought at once
  Is all the more confirmed by what you say.
  When grown men quarrel, one may justly hold
  The wiser one responsible. You shouldn't
  Be angry with him; giving him your guidance
  Would more become you. But there still is time.
  This is no case that would require a duel.

As long as I am given peace I want
To have the pleasure of it in my house.
Restore the peace, you can do so with ease.
Lenore Sanvitale first will seek
With gentle lips to soothe his agitation.
Then go to him, and in my name give back
His total liberty to him and gain
His confidence with honest, noble words.
Accomplish this as soon as possible.
You'll talk to him as would a friend and father.
I want peace made before we go away,
And nothing is impossible to you
When once you will. Best we delay an hour,
Then let the ladies gently finish up
What you began; when we ourselves get back,
They will have wiped out every trace of this
Too quick impression. It appears, Antonio,
That there's no danger you'll get out of practice.
You've barely finished with one task, when back
You come and straightway get yourself another.
I trust that you'll succeed in this one also.

ANTONIO: I feel a sense of shame for in your words
I see my fault as in the clearest mirror.
It's easy for a man to obey a master
Who doesn't simply order but persuades.

Act 3

Scene 1

PRINCESS *(alone):* Where can Eleonore be? The worry
Deep in my heart with every passing moment
Pains more and more. I scarcely know what happened,
I scarcely know which one if them is guilty.
If she would only come! I should not like
To speak yet with my brother or Antonio
Till I am calmer, till I've heard how all
This matter stands, and what may come of it.

Scene 2

(Enter Leonore.)

What news do you bring, Leonore? Tell me,
How do things stand now with our friend? What happened?
LEONORE: I could not learn more than we know already.
They clashed in anger; Tasso drew his sword,
Your brother parted them. It seems, however,
That it was Tasso who began the quarrel.
Antonio walks about conversing with
His Prince, while Tasso on the other hand
Remains alone and banished in his room.
PRINCESS: I'm sure Antonio provoked him, cold,
Aloof, giving the high-strung youth offense.
LEONORE: I'm of the same opinion, for his brow
Was darkened by a cloud as he approached him.
PRINCESS: Alas, that we forget and can no longer
Observe the pure, mute signal of the heart!
A god speaks very softly in our bosoms,
Softly and very audibly, and shows us
What to accept and what we should avoid.
Antonio seemed to me this morning gruff
Beyond his wont, withdrawn into himself.
When Tasso went up there and stood beside him
My instinct warned me: Simply mark the outward
Appearance of the two, in face, in voice,
In look, in gait. In every point opposed;
The two of them can never share affection,
But that dissembler, Hope, persuaded me
And whispered: Both of them are rational men,
Both noble, erudite, and both your friends.
What bond is surer than what joins good men?
I urged the young man, he agreed completely;
How warm and fine his acquiescence was!
Had I but spoken with Antonio sooner!
I hesitated; there was little time,
I was reluctant to commend the youth
Warmly to him in the first words I spoke;

I trusted to good manners and politeness,
In social usage, which is interposed
So smoothly even between enemies,
Nor feared from so mature a man the passions
Of impetuous youth. But it is done.
The evil *was* far off, now it is here.
O give me counsel! What is to be done?
LEONORE: You feel yourself how difficult it is
To counsel after what you tell me. Here
Is no like-minded men's misunderstanding;
Words could set that aright—or weapons could,
If need be—easily and happily.
But these are two men, as I long have felt,
Who must be enemies because great Nature
Did not form one man from the two of them.
If they were well advised for their advantage,
They would ally themselves as friends together.
Then they would stand as one man and would walk
Along through life with joy and power and fortune.
So I had hoped, but now I see, in vain.
Today's dissension, be it as it may,
Can be composed, but that gives no assurance
For future times, not even for tomorrow.
It would be best for Tasso, I should think,
To travel for a time away from here.
Why, he could go to Rome, and Florence too;
There in a few weeks I could meet with him,
Could work upon his spirits as a friend.
Meanwhile, Antonio, who has become
So alien to us, you would be bringing
Closer to you and to your friends once more.
In that way time, that does so much, perhaps
Might grant what now seems quite impossible.
PRINCESS: You want the pleasure for yourself, my friend,
While I must do without. Is that quite nice?
LEONORE: You will not do without, except for what
You could not now enjoy in any case.
PRINCESS: So treat a friend? Just calmly banish him?
LEONORE: No, keep him! Banish only for appearance.

PRINCESS: My brother will not willingly release him.
LEONORE: When he sees it the way we do, he'll yield.
PRINCESS: Condemning oneself in a friend is hard.
LEONORE: Saving your friend you'll save yourself through him.
PRINCESS: I can't say yes to this and let it happen.
LEONORE: Then look for greater evil yet to come.
PRINCESS: You hurt me, and you can't be sure you're helping.
LEONORE: We soon shall learn which one of us is wrong.
PRINCESS: And if it is to be, ask me no more.
LEONORE: One who can make decisions, conquers sorrow.
PRINCESS: I cannot quite decide—but be it so,
  If he is not to be away for long.
  Let us protect his interests, Leonore,
  That he not lack for anything in future,
  And that the Duke may willingly advance
  His stipend to him even while abroad.
  Talk with Antonio, for with my brother
  He has much influence and will not hold
  This quarrel against us or against our friend.
LEONORE: Princess, one word from you would have more weight.
PRINCESS: I am not able, as you know, my friend,
  To ask things for myself and for my own
  The way my sister of Urbino can.
  I like to live my life in peace, accepting
  With gratitude whatever things my brother
  Is able or is willing to provide me.
  Once I used to reproach myself for this,
  But I have overcome that feeling now.
  A friend of mine would often scold me for it.
  "You are unselfish," she would say to me,
  "And that is fine; but you are so much so
  That you have no accurate perception
  Of what your friends may need." This I admit
  And must therefore put up with that reproach.
  Hence I am all the better pleased that I
  In fact can now be useful to our friend.
  My mother's legacy devolves on me,
  And I will gladly help toward his support.
LEONORE: Princess, my situation too is such

That I can come forth as a friend, and help.
He does not manage well, and where he's lacking
I shall be able to assist him nicely.
PRINCESS: Take him away, then, and if I must lose him,
Above all others you deserve to have him.
I see quite well: It will be best that way.
But must I once more praise this pain as good
And beneficial? That has been my fate
Since childhood; I am used to it by now.
The loss of happiness is less by half
If we'd not counted its possession certain.
LEONORE: I hope since you deserve it so, to see
You happy.
PRINCESS: Happy? O Eleonore!
O, who is really happy?—I might say
My brother is, for his great heart endures
His lot in life with equanimity,
But what he merits, never has been his.
And is my sister of Urbino happy?
That lovely woman, great and noble heart!
She bears no children to her younger husband
But he respects her, never holding it
Against her, but no joy dwells in their house.
What was the good of all our mother's wisdom,
Her learning of all kinds, and her great mind?
Could it protect her from mistakes of others?
They parted us from her; now she is dead.
She did not leave us children with the comfort
Of knowing she died reconciled with God.
LEONORE: O do not look at what a person lacks,
Consider what each one still has, Princess,
Think of all that you still have.
PRINCESS: Still have?
Patience, Eleonore! I could practice that
From childhood on. While sister, brothers, friends
Enjoyed their parties and their games together,
My illness kept me shut within my room,
And in the company of many ailments
I early had to learn to do without.

One thing there was that charmed my solitude,
The joy of song; I entertained myself
All by myself, I lulled to sleep my yearning,
My pain, my every wish, with gentle tones.
Grief often turned to pleasure then, the sense
Of sadness even turned to harmony.
That happiness was not allowed me long,
The doctor took that too away; his strict
Command bade me be still. I was to live,
To suffer, to renounce this sole, small comfort.
LEONORE: Yet many friends came by to visit you;
And now you're well and take delight in life.
PRINCESS: Yes, I am well, which means I am not ill;
And I have many friends whose loyalty
Does make me glad. I also had a friend—
LEONORE: You have him still.
PRINCESS: But I shall lose him soon.
The moment when I first caught sight of him
Meant much to me. I hardly had recovered
From many sufferings, my pain and illness
Had only just departed; timidly
I looked at life again, joyed in the daylight
And in my family. With strength regained
I breathed the purest fragrance of sweet hope.
I dared to look ahead and into life
More deeply, and from the far distance came
Figures of friends to meet me. Then it was,
Eleonore, that my sister came,
Leading this youth to me; she introduced him,
And, to confess quite freely, my soul seized
Upon him and will hold him fast forever.
LEONORE: For that you need have no regret, my Princess!
To recognize what's noble is pure gain,
A gain that never can be wrested from us.
PRINCESS: Things beautiful and excellent are to be feared,
Much like the flame, that serves so splendidly
So long as it burns only on your hearth,
Or in a lantern lights your way. How lovely!
Who can do without it; who would want to?

And once it eats its way afar, unguarded,
How wretched it can make us! Leave me now.
I talk and talk. Better I should conceal,
Even from you, how weak I am, and ill.
LEONORE: The illness of the spirit is relieved
  Most easily by grieving and confiding.
PRINCESS: I'll soon be healed then, if confiding heals:
  You have my confidence, complete and pure.
  Alas, my friend, it's true, I've made my mind up:
  Let him depart. But I already feel
  The long protracted suffering of those days when I
  Shall be deprived of what gave me delight.
  No longer will the sun lift from my eyelids
  His beautifully transfigured dream-borne image.
  No longer will the hope of seeing him
  Fill my scarce wakened mind with joyous yearning;
  My first glance down into our gardens will
  Seek him in vain amid the dewy shadows.
  How pleasingly my wishes were fulfilled,
  Being with him on every cheerful evening!
  How our companionship increased the longing
  To know and understand each other better.
  Each day our spirits were attuned more truly
  In pure and ever purer harmonies.
  But what a twilight now descends before me!
  The sun's resplendency, the happy sense
  Of the high day, the world a thousandfold
  In bright and radiant presence—all are empty,
  Veiled deep within the mist that is around me.
  Before, each day was a whole life to me;
  Care was stilled, even foreboding mute
  And under joyous sail, the river bore us
  Along on gentle waves, without a rudder.
  Now terrors of the future overwhelm
  My secret heart amid the dismal present.
LEONORE: The future will return your friends to you
  And bring new joy and happiness as well.
PRINCESS: Whatever I possess I like to keep.
  Change brings diversion but does little good.

I never reached with youthful greed and yearning
Into some stranger's urn of fate, to seize
By chance upon some object for my own
Impoverished and inexperienced heart.
I had to honor him, therefore I loved him;
I had to love him, for with him my life
Became a life such as I'd never known.
At first I told myself: Stay far away
From him. I fled and fled and kept on coming
Closer—so sweetly lured, so harshly punished.
I lose a pure and true possession; joy
And happiness are gone—an evil spirit
Defrauds my longing with their kindred sorrows.

LEONORE: If the words of a friend cannot console you
  The quiet power of time, of the fair world,
  Will imperceptibly restore your spirits.

PRINCESS: The world is fair indeed, its wide expanse
  Traversed both far and near by so much good.
  How sad that it forever seems to draw
  Away from us by just a single step
  And lure our anxious yearning on through life,
  Step after step, up to our very graves!
  It is so rare that human beings find
  What seemed to have been theirs by destiny,
  So rare that they can ever hold and keep
  What once their fortunate hands have seized upon!
  What first submitted to us, wrenches free
  And we relinquish what so avidly
  We grasped. There is a happiness; we know
  It not, or knowing, know not how to prize it.

                    (Exit.)

Scene 3

LEONORE *(alone):* How sad I feel for that pure, noble heart!
  How sad the lot that now falls to Her Highness!
  She loses—and what makes you think you'll gain?
  Is it so necessary that he leave?
  Or do you make it so, for sole possession

Of talents and a heart which up to now
You've had to share—and share unequally—
With someone else? Is this an honest act?
Are you not rich enough? What do you lack?
Husband and son, possessions, rank and beauty,
All these you have, and still you want him too,
With all the rest? Are you in love with him?
Why else can you not get along without him?
You can admit it freely to yourself—
How charming to behold one's image mirrored
Within his generous mind! Is happiness
Not doubly great and splendid when his verse
Exalts and carries us as if on clouds?
Then only are you enviable! You *are*—
Not merely *have*—the thing that many wish for;
Everyone knows exactly what you have.
Your country speaks your name and looks at you,
That is the pinnacle of happiness.
Must *Laura* be the one and only name
That is to sound upon all tender lips?
Did only Petrarch have the right to raise
An unknown beauty to the rank of goddess?
Where is there any man to be compared
With them, my friend? The world reveres him now,
Posterity will reverence him as well.
How wonderful it is to have him at
One's side amid the splendor of this life
And with light step move with him toward the future!
Nothing will have the power to affect you:
Not time nor age, not vaunting reputation
Which drives the waves of public favor back
And forth; his verses will preserve the transient.
You are still beautiful, you are still happy,
Though you've been swept along in tides of change.
You must have him, and you take nothing from her,
For her affection for so fine a man
Is just the same as all her other passions.
They shed a meager gleam like quiet moonlight
Upon the traveler's pathway in the night.

They give no warmth and cast no pleasure round
About, nor joy of life. She will be glad
Once she knows he is gone, knows he is happy,
The same way she rejoiced when she saw him
Each day. Besides, I won't exile my friend
And me, either from her or from this court,
I will come back, and bring him back as well.
So let it be!—Here comes our rude friend now.
We shall find out if we can tame him down.

Scene 4

(Enter Antonio.)

You bring us war instead of peace; it seems
As if you came from camp or from a battle
Where violence prevails and force decides,
And not from Rome, where solemn wisdom lifts
Its hands in blessing and before its feet
Beholds a world that gladly hears and heeds.
ANTONIO: My lovely friend, I must accept this censure,
But my excuse lies no great distance off.
There's peril in it when one must behave
Wisely and moderately too long a time.
The evil spirit lurks beside you, goading
Demanding sacrifice from time to time.
On this occasion it was my misfortune
To yield and give it him at friends' expense.
LEONORE: You have so long directed all your efforts
Toward strangers, taking cues from their intentions,
That, now you see your friends again, you quite
Mistake them and dispute as if with strangers.
ANTONIO: There lies the danger, my beloved friend!
With strangers one will pull oneself together,
Be on one's guard, and in their favor seek
One's purpose, so that they may be of use.
But with our friends we let ourselves go freely,
We rest upon their love, permit ourselves
Caprice, and passion has a more untamed

Effect; and thereby we offend first off
The very ones we love most tenderly.
LEONORE: In this contemplative repose, dear friend,
I'm glad to find you your true self again.
ANTONIO: Yes, I'm distressed—and willingly confess it—
At having strayed so out of bounds today.
Grant me, however, when an honest man,
His brow all hot, comes home from heavy labors
And thinks late in the evening he will rest
In longed-for shade, before his new exertions,
And finds the shady place all taken up
By some poor idler, is he not to feel
Some very human stirrings in his heart?
LEONORE: If he is truly human he will share
The shady spot quite gladly with a man
Who sweetens his repose, lightens his work,
By conversation and by lovely music.
The tree is broad, my friend, that gives the shade,
And neither needs to drive the other out.
ANTONIO: O, Eleonore, let's not play this game,
This back and forth exchange of metaphor.
This world contains so many things that one
Will grant to someone else or gladly share.
But there is one thing precious which we won't
Grant gladly but to those of special merit,
Another one which with the best of will
We'll never share, not with the most deserving.
And if you ask what these two treasures are,
They are the laurel leaf and women's favor.
LEONORE: Did that wreath on our young man's head offend
This earnest-minded man? But you yourself
Could not have found a more discreet reward
For all his work and for his splendid poem.
Accomplishments transcending earthly bounds,
Hovering in air, their magic voiced in music,
In gentle images alone, as they
Enthrall our minds—these cannot be rewarded
Except by a lovely symbol and fair image.
And if he barely touches earth himself,

His head is barely touched by highest praise.
It is no better than a sterile branch,
The gift that sterile admiration brings
From people eager to discharge a debt
The cheapest way. I doubt that you'd begrudge
The golden halo in the martyr's portrait,
On his shorn head; surely the laurel crown,
No matter in what place you chance to see it,
Is more a sign of suffering than of joy.

ANTONIO: Is this what your delightful lips would do:
Teach me contempt for worldly vanity?

LEONORE: I do not need to teach you how to value
All things at their just worth. And yet it seems
That wise men need as much as others do
To have someone from time to time display
The things that they possess in their true light.
You, as a noble man, will not assert
A claim for phantom honors and rewards.
The bond of service which you owe your Prince,
The bond which likewise binds your friends to you,
Is vital and effective; its reward
Must also be effective and alive.
Your laurel is your Prince's confidence,
Which rests upon your shoulders as a weight
Beloved, lightly borne; your fame consists
Of people's universal trust in you.

ANTONIO: And you say nothing still of women's favor?
Don't tell me you think *that* is unimportant.

LEONORE: That all depends. You do not lack for it,
And you could sooner get along without it
Than could that kindly man of whom you speak.
For what success would any woman have,
Tell me, if in her fashion she should try
To care for you, to show concern for you?
With you, all is security and order;
You take care of yourself and others too;
You have what one would like to give you. He
Engages us in our own special field.

He lacks a thousand little things, which women
Gladly will bend their efforts to provide.
He likes to wear the finest linen, or
A silken garment with embroidery.
He likes to see himself well dressed—or rather
He cannot stand the touch of ill-made clothing
Which marks the lackey; everything of his
Must suit him well: fine, and good, and noble.
And yet he has no skill in getting all
These things himself, or keeping them if once
They should be his; he always lacks for money,
For prudent care. He'll leave one thing in this place,
Another one in that—he can't return
From any trip but that one third of all
His things are missing—then again his servant
Will steal from him. And so, Antonio,
One must take care of him the whole year long.

ANTONIO: And that care makes him lovable all the more.
Lucky young man, to have his imperfections
Called virtues, be so handsomely allowed
To play the boy when he's long since a man,
To boast about his charming weaknesses!
You'll have to pardon me, my lovely friend,
If here as well I grow a trifle bitter.
You leave out much—how he presumes, for instance,
And that he's cleverer than people think.
He boasts two flames of love! He ties and unties
The knots, first one way, then another, thus
By *such* arts wins *such* hearts! Would anyone
Believe it?

LEONORE: Good! That very fact will prove
That it is only friendship that impels us.
And even if we traded love for love,
Would it not be cheap payment for a heart
So dear, that quite forgets itself and, dreaming
Sweetly, lives for its friends in full devotion?

ANTONIO: Go on and spoil him, more and more; allow
His selfishness to pass for love; offend

All friends who dedicate themselves to you
With loyal hearts, pay voluntary tribute
To that proud man and thus destroy completely
The worthy circle of a common trust!
LEONORE: We are not quite so partial as you think.
We reprimand our friend in many cases;
We wish to educate him so that he
Can take more pleasure in himself and give
Others more pleasure. We can criticize him,
His defects are by no means hidden from us.
ANTONIO: Yet you praise much that should be criticized.
I long have known him, for he is so easy
To know, and too proud to conceal himself.
He sinks into himself as if the world
Were all inside his heart and he were wholly
Sufficient to himself within his world,
And everything around him disappears.
He drops it, lets it go, thrusts it away,
And rests within himself.—Then suddenly,
As an unnoticed spark ignites a mine,
In joy, grief, whim, or rage, he can explode.
Then he must seize on everything and hold it.
What ought to be prepared for through the years
Within a moment's space must come to pass.
What hard work scarcely could resolve in years
Must be decided in a moment's space.
He sets himself impossible demands,
To warrant making like demands of others.
His mind is drawn to seek the final causes
Linking all things, a task where one in millions
Of human beings scarcely could succeed.
And he is not the man. He falls at last,
In no way better, back into himself.
LEONORE: He harms himself; he does no harm to others.
ANTONIO: He does hurt other people, all too much.
Can you deny that in the many moments
Of passion that so suddenly assail him
He will presume to blaspheme and abuse

The Prince, even the Princess—anyone,
Just momentarily, of course. However,
That moment will recur, for he controls
His mouth as little as he does his heart.
LEONORE: I should imagine, if he were to go
  Away for a short time, it would no doubt
  Be good for him and good for others too.
ANTONIO: Maybe, and maybe not. Now's not the time
  To think of it; because I do not want
  The burden of the error on my shoulders.
  It might appear that I drove him away,
  And I'm not driving him away. For all
  I care, he can remain at court in peace.
  And if he wishes to be reconciled
  With me, if he can follow my advice,
  Then we can get along quite tolerably.
LEONORE: So now you hope to influence a spirit
  That recently you thought beyond all hope.
ANTONIO: We always hope, and in all things it's better
  To hope than to despair. For who can tell
  The limits of what's possible? Our Prince
  Has high regard for him. He must stay with us.
  If our attempt to educate him fails,
  He's not the only one we must put up with.
LEONORE: I did not think you so impartial, so
  Dispassionate. You've quickly changed your mind.
ANTONIO: Age must have one advantage, after all;
  That is, if it cannot escape from error,
  It can control itself immediately.
  It was your first concern to reconcile
  Me with your friend. Now I ask that of you.
  Do what you can so he may find himself,
  And everything return again to normal.
  I plan to go and see him just as soon
  As you have let me know that he's calmed down,
  As soon as you consider that my presence
  Will not make matters worse. But what you do,
  Must still be done within the hour. Alfonso

Returns this very evening, and I shall
Accompany him back. Meanwhile, farewell.
                    (Exit.)

Scene 5

LEONORE *(alone):* This time, my friend, we are not in agreement.
My own advantage won't go hand in hand
With yours today. I mean to seize the moment,
Try to win Tasso over. Quickly now!

Act 4

Scene 1

A room.

TASSO *(alone):* Are you awakened from a dream; has fair
Illusion suddenly deserted you?
And on a day of utmost joy did sleep
Subdue you? Does it hold and vex your soul
With heavy fetters? Yes, you are awake,
And yes, you dream. Where have the hours gone
That played about your head with wreaths of flowers,
The days in which your mind, its yearnings freed,
Transfixed the far-flung blueness of the sky?
Yet you are still alive, you touch yourself,
You touch yourself and are not sure you live.
Is it my fault, is it another's fault
That I now find I'm here a man condemned?
Have I transgressed, that I must pay in suffering?
Is not my whole mistake in fact a merit?
I looked at him, and I was swept away
By goodwill and the heart's fond hope, that one
Who bore a human likeness must be human.
Thus I went up to him with open arms—
And I encountered locks and bolts, no heart.
O, I had thought it out so cleverly

How I would treat this person who from times
Long past had seemed to me suspicious, yet,
No matter what may have befallen you,
Hold fast to this one certainty: I did
See *her!* She stood before me, and she spoke
To me, and I heard what she said! Her glance,
Her tone, the lovely message of her words,
They are forever mine, not to be stolen,
Whether by time or fate, or by wild fortune!
And if my spirit soared too high, too fast,
And if I was too quick to give full vent
To flames within my heart which now consume
My very self, I still cannot regret it,
Though my life's fate were thereby lost forever.
I would devote myself to her and gladly
Follow her bidding though it summoned me
To ruin. So be it! I've still proved worthy
Of that exquisite trust that gives me life,
That gives me life now at the very hour
That with rude force throws open the black gates,
The portals of long grieving—Yes, it's done!
The sun of fairest favor sets for me
So quickly now. The Prince averts from me
His gracious glance and leaves me standing here
Upon a dismal, narrow path, forlorn.
Those ugly winged things of double omen,
The loathsome retinue of ancient Night,
Come swarming out and buzz about my head.
O where, O where shall I direct my step
To flee the abomination whirling round me,
To save myself from the abyss before me?

Scene 2

(Enter Leonore.)

LEONORE: What's happened now? Dear Tasso, did your zeal,
Did your suspicious thoughts so goad you on?
How did it come about? We're all dismayed.

Your gentle temper, your complaisant way,
Your rapid insight, your just understanding,
Which let you give to everyone his due,
Your even mood that bears what noblemen
Soon learn to bear but vain men seldom do
The well-advised control of tongue and lip—
Dear friend, I almost fail to recognize you!

TASSO: And what if now all that were lost and gone?
What if you came upon a friend whom you
Thought rich and found him suddenly a beggar?
You are quite right, I am myself no longer,
And yet I am, just as I ever was.
It seems to be a riddle, but is not.
The quiet moon that in the night gives joy
And with its shining irresistibly
Entices eye and spirits, floats by day
An insignificant, pale, small cloud. I am
Outshone, the splendor of the day outshines me.
You don't know me, I know myself no longer.

LEONORE: I cannot grasp what you are saying, friend,
The way you say it. Please explain yourself.
Are you so hurt by that brusque man's offense
That you completely fail to recognize
Yourself and us as well? Confide in me.

TASSO: I'm not the one offended; you see me
Punished because I gave offense. The sword
Would cut the knotted web of many words
Quite easily and fast, but I am captive.
You may not know it—don't, dear friend, be frightened
But here you find your friend in jail. The Prince
Is disciplining me like any schoolboy.
I will not argue with him and I cannot.

LEONORE: You seem to be upset, unduly so.

TASSO: Do you think me so weak, so much a child,
That such a fall could shatter me at once?
The thing that happened does not hurt me deeply;
What hurts is rather what it means to me.
Just give my foes and those who envy me
Free rein. The field is clear and open to them.

LEONORE: Many of them you hold in false suspicion.
  Of that I have convinced myself already.
  Nor does Antonio bear you such ill will
  As you imagine. And today's vexation—
TASSO: I set that quite aside, and only take
  Antonio as he was and still remains.
  His stiff-necked wisdom always did annoy me,
  His everlasting playing of the master.
  Instead of seeing if his hearer's mind
  Is not already on the proper track,
  He lectures you on things that you yourself
  Felt better and more deeply, does not hear
  A word you say, and will misjudge you always.
  To be misjudged, misjudged by a proud man
  Who smiles and thinks he's better than you are!
  I am not old enough or wise enough
  That I could merely smile back and endure it.
  Sooner or later, it would have to stop,
  We had to break; if later, it would only
  Have got just that much worse. I recognize
  One master only, that's the one who feeds me;
  Him I will gladly follow, but no other.
  I must be free in what I *think* and *write*;
  Life limits us enough in what we *do*.
LEONORE: He often speaks of you with great respect.
TASSO: Forbearingly, you mean, subtly and shrewdly.
  And that's what vexes me: The words he speaks
  Are all so smooth, so qualified, that praise
  Becomes in fact disparagement, and nothing
  Hurts you more surely or more deeply than
  Praise from his lips.
LEONORE: If only you had heard,
  My friend, the way he used to speak of you
  And of the talent gracious Nature gave you,
  Beyond so many men. He surely knows you
  For what you are and have, and he respects it.
TASSO: A selfish spirit, O believe me, can't
  Escape the torments of its narrow envy.
  A man like that may well forgive another

His fortune, rank, and honor; for he thinks:
You may have that yourself if you so wish,
And persevere, and Fortune favors you.
But that which only Nature can bestow,
Which lies beyond the reach of all exertion,
Forever unattainable by effort,
What neither gold, nor sword, nor shrewdness, nor
Persistence can achieve, he'll not forgive.
He'll grant me my success, you say? That man
Who, stiff-necked, thinks to force the Muses' favor?
Who strings together thoughts of many poets,
Then seems in his own eyes a poet too?
He'd sooner grant to me the Prince's favor,
Which he would like to limit to himself,
Than grant the talent which those Heavenly Muses
Have given to a poor and orphaned youth.

LEONORE: I wish you saw as clearly as I see it!
You judge him wrongly; he is not like that.

TASSO: If I misjudge him, I misjudge him gladly!
I see him as my worst of enemies.
And I'd be wretched if I had to think
More kindly of him. It's a foolish thing
To be fair-minded all the time; that means
Destruction of oneself. Are people then
So fair of mind toward us? O no! O no!
The human being in his narrow nature
Requires the double feeling: love and hate.
Does he not need the night as well as day
And sleep as well as waking? No, I must
From this time onward hold that man to be
The object of my very deepest hatred;
Nothing can ever take from me the pleasure
Of thinking worse and worse of him.

LEONORE: Dear friend,
If you won't change your attitude, I don't
See how you can expect to stay at court.
You know how much he counts for—as he must.

TASSO: I know full well how quite superfluous
I have long since become at court, fair friend.

LEONORE: That you are not, that you can never be!
　Instead, you know how glad the Prince, how glad
　The Princess is, to live with you; and when
　Their sister from Urbino comes, she comes
　Almost as much for your sake as for theirs,
　Her brother and sister. All alike think well
　Of you, and each has total trust in you.
TASSO: O Leonore, what kind of trust is that?
　When has he ever said a word to me,
　A serious word, about his state? If ever
　There was a special case where, even in
　My presence, he consulted with his sister
　Or others, he did not ask my opinion.
　Always it was: "Antonio will be coming!
　We must write to Antonio! Ask Antonio!"
LEONORE: Instead of thanking, you complain. If he
　Is pleased to give you total liberty,
　He honors you the finest way he can.
TASSO: I'm left in peace, because he thinks me useless.
LEONORE: *Because* you're left in peace you are not useless.
　How long you've nurtured worry and annoyance.
　Like some beloved infant, at your breast.
　Often I have considered this and still,
　Consider as I will: On this fair soil
　Where Fortune had, it seemed, transplanted you,
　You do not thrive. O Tasso!—Shall I say it?
　Dare I advise you?—You should go away.
TASSO: O do not spare the patient, dear physician!
　Give him the remedy, do not consider
　Whether it's bitter.—Rather ask yourself,
　My wise, good friend, if he can still recover.
　I see it all myself, it's over now.
　I can forgive him, he can not forgive me.
　They need him, and, alas, they don't need me.
　And he is shrewd, and I, alas, am not.
　He works against my interests; I can not
　Retaliate, I won't do so. My friends,
　They let it pass—they see it otherwise—
　Barely resist when they should fight for me.

You think that I should leave. I think so too—
So then, farewell. I will endure that also.
You parted with me—may the strength and courage
Be granted me to part with you as well.

LEONORE: Ah, from a distance everything looks clearer
Which from nearby we only find bewildering.
Then you will realize perhaps what love
Surrounded you on every side, what value
The loyalty of true friends has, and how
The wide world can't replace those closest to you.

TASSO: That we shall see. From childhood I have known
The world, the way that, quite without concern,
It leaves one lonely, destitute, and goes
Its way like sun and moon and other gods.

LEONORE: Listen to me, my friend, and you shall never
Go through this sad experience again.
If you take my advice, you first will go
To Florence, there you'll find a friend who will
Take friendly care of you. Be of good cheer.
I am that friend. Within the next few days
I go to meet my husband there; for him
And for myself I can't cause greater joy
Than if I bring you with me to our midst.
I shall not say a word, you know yourself
What kind of Prince you will be coming to,
What kind of men that lovely city holds
Within its bosom, and what kind of women.
You do not speak? Consider well! Decide.

TASSO: It is delightful, what you say, so much
In keeping with the wish I entertain.
Only it is too new. I beg of you,
Let me consider. I will soon decide.

LEONORE: I go away now with the fairest hopes
For you and us and also for this house.
Consider, and if you consider rightly,
You hardly can conceive a better plan.

TASSO: Just one more thing, beloved friend! Tell me,
How does the Princess feel about me now?
Was she annoyed with me? What did she say?—

She must have found great fault with me? Speak freely.
LEONORE: She knows you, so she easily excused you.
TASSO: Have I lost in her eyes? Don't flatter me.
LEONORE: A woman's favor's not so lightly lost.
TASSO: Will she release me gladly if I go?
LEONORE: If it is for your welfare, certainly.
TASSO: Am I not going to lose the Prince's favor?
LEONORE: Rest safely in his magnanimity.
TASSO: And will we leave the Princess all alone?
   You're leaving too, and though I count for little
   I still meant something to her, that I know.
LEONORE: Friendly companionship we still can feel
   With distant friends, if we know they are happy;
   It will be so, for I see you made happy;
   You will not leave this place unsatisfied.
   The Prince so ordered, and Antonio
   Will come to see you. He himself reproves
   His bitterness in hurting you. I beg you,
   Receive him as he comes to you—in calm.
TASSO: I can stand up to him in every sense.
LEONORE: And Heaven grant I may, before you go,
   Open your eyes, dear friend, and make you see
   That nobody in all our country hates,
   Taunts, persecutes, or works you secret harm.
   You're surely wrong, and just as once you wove
   Verses for others' joy, so now, alas,
   You have in this case spun the strangest web,
   For your own harm. I shall do everything
   To rip that web asunder, so that you
   May walk the fair pathway of life in freedom.
   Farewell to you. I hope for good word soon.
              (Exit.)

Scene 3

TASSO *(alone):* I am to recognize that no one hates me,
   That no one persecutes me, that these wiles
   And all the secret webs were solely spun
   And woven of themselves inside my head!

I'm to confess that I am in the wrong,
That I to many do injustice, who
Have not deserved it of me! At an hour
When my undoubted right lies clear before
The countenance of the sun, as does their guile.
I am to feel profoundly how the Prince
Grants me his favor with an open heart,
Apportions gifts to me in bounteous measure,
When at the very time, weak as he is,
He lets his eye be dulled by enemies
Of mine and lets his hands be fettered too.

I'm sure he cannot see he's being duped,
And I can't show him they are the deceivers.
So that he may be quietly deceived,
So that they may deceive him at their leisure,
I am to stand aside, even retreat.

And who gives me this counsel? Who so shrewdly
Urges me on with true and fond intent?
Lenore herself, Lenore Sanvitale,
My tender friend! Aha! I know you now!
Why did I ever trust those lips of hers?
She was not honest—no, whatever favor,
Whatever tenderness she showed to me
With her beguiling words! O no, she was
And still remains a scheming heart; she turns
Toward favor with a soft and clever tread.

How often I've indulged in self-deception—
About her too! Yet fundamentally
My vanity alone betrayed me. Good!
I knew her, yet kept flattering myself;
She is this way with others, I would say,
With you, though, her intent is frank and loyal.
And now I see it, see it all too late.
Then I was favored, and she clung so softly
To one so fortunate. Now that I fall,
She turns her back on me, as Fortune does.

And now she comes as agent of my foe,
Glides up to me and with a honeyed tongue
The little serpent hisses magic tones.
She seemed so lovely! Lovelier than ever!
How good it felt, each word that left her lips!
Yet flattery could not long conceal from me
Her false intentions, for the opposite
Of everything she said appeared too clearly
Written upon her brow. I quickly sense
When someone seeks the pathway to my heart
And does not mean it from the heart. I am
To leave? For Florence, as soon as I can?

And why for Florence? I see that quite well.
The new house of the Medici rules there;
True, not overtly hostile to Ferrara,
But still the chilling hand of silent envy
Prevents the meeting of the finest minds.
Should I receive distinguished signs of favor
From those great princes there, as I could surely
Expect to do, some courtier soon would try
To cast suspicion on my gratitude
And loyalty, and he might well succeed.

Yes, I will leave, but not the way you wish.
Yes, I will go, and farther than you think.
What's for me here? Who holds me back? O yes,
I understood too well each word I drew
From Leonore's lips! But syllable
To syllable I barely caught it—now
I know the whole of what the Princess thinks—
Yes, yes, that too is true, do not despair!
"She will release me gladly if I go,
Since it's for my own welfare." How I wish
She had a passion in her heart that would
Destroy me and my welfare both! I'd welcome
Far more the touch of death than of this hand
That, stiff and cold, dismisses me—I go!—
Be on your guard now and let no appearance

Of friendship or goodwill deceive you. No one
Betrays you unless you betray yourself.

Scene 4

(Enter Antonio.)

ANTONIO: I've come to have a word with you, Tasso,
 If you can hear me calmly and will do so.
TASSO: Action, you know, is still forbidden me.
 It's only fitting that I wait and listen.
ANTONIO: I find you tranquil, just as I had hoped.
 I'm glad to say this freely from the heart:
 First in the Prince's name I here dissolve
 The tenuous bond that seemed to hold you captive.
TASSO: Caprice now sets me free, as once it bound me.
 This I accept and do not ask for trial.
ANTONIO: Then speaking for myself, let me say this:
 It seems that words of mine have hurt you deeply,
 More than I realized, stirred as I was
 By many passions. Yet no word of insult
 Escaped my lips, even through inadvertence.
 As nobleman you've nothing to avenge,
 And as a man you won't refuse forgiveness.
TASSO: Which one would hit the harder, hurt or insult,
 I won't pursue that now. The former pierces
 The inner marrow, the latter cuts the skin.
 The dart of insult turns back on the man
 Who thought to wound; a deftly wielded sword
 Quickly allays most other men's opinion.
 But an offended heart recovers slowly.
ANTONIO: Now it's my turn to say most urgently,
 To you: Do not draw back, grant me my wish,
 Which is the Prince's wish, who sends me to you.
TASSO: I know my duty, and I will give in.
 As far as possible, all is forgiven.
 The poets tell a story of a spear
 That could by friendly application cure
 A wound which it had once itself inflicted.

The tongues of human beings have that power;
I shall not spitefully resist it now.
ANTONIO: I thank you, and I wish that you would put me,
And put my will to serve you, to the test,
Immediately, with confidence. Tell me,
How can I help you? I will gladly do so.
TASSO: You offer just what I myself was wishing.
You brought me back my liberty again;
Now get for me, I pray, the use of it.
ANTONIO: What can you mean by that? Explain yourself.
TASSO: You know I've brought my poem to an end.
It still lacks much of being truly finished.
Today I did present it to the Prince,
But hoped to ask a favor as I did so.
I find a number of my friends are now
Gathered in Rome; and certain ones have written
Letters to me expressing their opinions
Of certain passages; I have been able
To make good use of many things, but much
Seems still to need review; some passages
I should not like to change unless I were,
More than thus far, convinced by what they say.
That kind of thing cannot be done through letters;
Their presence would resolve the problem quickly.
I meant to ask the Prince myself today;
I found no chance and now I dare not try it.
So now I hope to gain this leave through you.
ANTONIO: It does seem ill-advised for you to leave
Just at the moment when your finished work
Commends you to the Prince and to the Princess.
A day of favor's like a day of harvest,
One must be busy as soon as it ripens.
If you should go away you will gain nothing
And maybe lose what you have gained already.
The present moment is a mighty goddess.
Learn to perceive her influence: Stay here.
TASSO: There's nothing that I need to *fear*. Alfonso
Is noble, he has always shown himself
Magnanimous to me. And what I *hope* for,

I want to owe to his good heart alone,
Not purloin favors or take anything
From him that he'd regret he ever gave.
ANTONIO: Then do not ask him to release you now.
He'll do so with reluctance, and I fear
Almost that he will not do it at all.
TASSO: He'll do so gladly, if the approach is right—
And you can do it any time you wish.
ANTONIO: But tell me please, what grounds am I to cite?
TASSO: Just let my poem speak from every stanza!
What I intended merits praise, although
The goal surpassed my powers of attainment.
There was no lack of industry and effort.
The cheerful course of many lovely days,
The quiet spaces in the depths of night,
Were all devoted to that hallowed poem.
My hopes lay, modestly, in coming close
To the great master poets of ancient times,
Boldly, in summoning men of our own times
Out of long sleep, to accomplish noble deeds,
Perhaps in sharing then the fame and peril
Of holy war with noble Christian armies.
And if my poem is to rouse the best
Of men, it must be worthy of the best.
What I've produced thus far I owe to Alfonso;
I'd like to owe him its fulfillment too.
ANTONIO: And that same Prince is here, and others too,
Who'll guide you just as well as Romans can.
Complete your writing *here,* here is the place,
Then off to Rome to see your work in action.
TASSO: Alfonso first inspired me; he will be
Surely the last to tell me what to do.
Advice from you and from the men of wisdom
Whom our court has assembled, I prize highly.
You shall decide in case my friends in Rome
Fall short of totally persuading me.
But I must see them all the same. Gonzaga
Has formed a court for me, to which I must
Present myself, and I can hardly wait.

Flaminio de' Nobili, Angelio
Da Barga, Antoniano and Speron Speroni!
You surely know these men.—What names those are!
They fill my heart, which gladly bows before them,
With confidence and yet with trepidation.
ANTONIO: You think of yourself only, not the Prince.
 I tell you he will not release you now;
 Or if he does, it will be with reluctance,
 Surely you will not ask what he would not
 Grant willingly. Must I be intercessor
 For something I myself cannot approve?
TASSO: Will you refuse me the first thing I ask
 When I put to the test your proffered friendship?
ANTONIO: True friendship shows itself in saying no
 At proper times, and often love confers
 A harmful gift by thinking more about
 The asker's wishes than about his welfare.
 Right now you seem to think extremely well
 Of what you eagerly desire, to ask
 That what you want be given you straightway.
 An erring man makes up by vehemence
 For what he lacks in truth and strength. My duty
 Bids me to do whatever I can do
 To moderate this haste that guides you wrong.
TASSO: I'm well acquainted with this tyranny
 Of friendship, which of all the tyrannies
 Seems most intolerable to me. You think
 A different way, and therefore you believe
 You're right in what you think. I quite agree:
 You wish for my well-being; only don't
 Ask me to seek it on the path you set.
ANTONIO: Am I to do you harm right at the start,
 Cold-bloodedly, in full and clear awareness?
TASSO: Let me free you from any such concern!
 You will not hold me back by what you're saying.
 You did pronounce me free; this door, which now
 Stands open for me, leads me to the Prince.
 I leave the choice to you now. You, or I!
 The Prince is leaving. This is not the moment

For hesitation. Choose, but fast. If you
Don't go, I'll go myself, let come what may.
ANTONIO: A brief postponement's all I hope to gain
From you: to wait until the Prince returns.
Just not today!
TASSO: No! In this very hour
If possible! My feet are burning on
This marble pavement, and my mind cannot
Find rest until the dust of the open road
Swirls all around me as I hurry on.
I beg of you! You see how very awkward
I'd be in speaking with my lord at such
A moment. You see—How can I conceal it?—
That at this moment I cannot compel
Myself; nor is there any power in all
This world that can. No, chains alone could hold me!
Alfonso is no tyrant, he has freed me.
How gladly I obeyed him once! Today
I cannot so obey. Only this day
Leave me in freedom, so my mind can find
Itself. I will return to duty soon.
ANTONIO: You make me hesitate. What shall I do?
I clearly see that error is contagious.
TASSO: If I am to believe you wish me well,
Get what I want, as far as you are able.
The Prince will then release me, and I will
Not lose his favor, will not lose his help.
That I will owe to you, and I will thank you.
But if you hold an old grudge in your heart,
If you prefer me banished from this court,
And if you want to warp my fate forever
And drive me out into the wide world, helpless,
Then stick to your opinon and oppose me!
ANTONIO: Because I am to harm you anyway,
I will, O Tasso, choose the way you've chosen.
The outcome will decide who was in error!
You want to leave! I tell you this beforehand:
When you have barely turned your back upon
This house, your heart will long to come back to it.

Your stubbornness will drive you on. In Rome,
Perplexity and grief and pain await you.
And you will fail your purpose there as here.
I say this now no longer to advise you.
I am foretelling only what will happen,
And I invite you now before the fact
To trust in me when worst has come to worst.
I shall speak to the Prince now, as you ask.

(Exit.)

Scene 5

TASSO *(alone):* Yes! Go ahead and go with the conviction
That you've persuaded me to what you will.
I'm learning to dissimulate, for you
Are a past master, and I catch on quickly.
Life forces us to seem, in fact to be,
Like those whom we could, boldly and with pride,
Despise. Now I can see quite plainly all
The artfulness of court intrigue! Antonio
Wishes to drive me out of here—and does
Not wish to seem as if he drove me out.
He plays the wise, considerate one, so that
I may be found inept and sick, appoints
Himself my guardian so as to debase
Me to the level of a child, me whom
He couldn't force as lackey. Thus he clouds
The Prince's brow, the vision of the Princess.
They should keep me, he says: For after all
Nature did give me quite commendable talents,
A noble gift, which she, to my great loss,
Alas, combined with many weaknesses:
Unbounded pride, excessive sensitivity,
My own peculiar kind of somber mood.
There's nothing for it; destiny so formed
This one particular man this way, so people
Must take him just the way he is, endure him,
Put up with him, and some fine day, maybe,
Enjoy from him, as unexpected gain,

Some thing or other which can give them pleasure.
But as for other matters, he must be
Allowed to live and die as he was born.

Do I still see Alfonso's steadfast mind?
Defying foes and stoutly shielding friends,
Do I see him as he confronts me now?
Oh yes, I now see fully my disaster!
It is my fate that everyone will change
Toward me alone, but toward all others will
Stand firm and true and sure—will lightly change
With one small breath, and in a moment's time.

Did not this man's arrival of itself
Destroy my fate completely, in one hour?
Did he not overthrow the structure of
My happiness from its most solid footing?
O must I live through this, must I, today?
Yes, just as everyone once thronged to me,
So everyone deserts me now; as each one
Sought to attract me to himself and hold me,
So now they cast me off and all avoid me.
And why is that? Does he alone outbalance
The weight of my worth in the scales and all
The love that I once had in such abundance?

Yes, everyone flees from me now. You too,
Beloved Princess, you draw back from me!
In all these dismal hours she's not sent
A single token of her favor to me.
Have I deserved that at her hands?—Poor heart,
For whom it was so natural to adore her!—
When I but heard her voice, how my breast was
Suffused with inexpressible emotion!
When I beheld her, day's bright light was dimmed
For me; her eyes, her lips would draw me on
Past all resistance and my knees would barely
Support me, and I needed all
My strength of mind in order to stand upright

And not fall down before her feet; I barely
Was able to dispel that ecstasy.
Hold fast, my heart! And my clear mind, don't let
Yourself be overclouded here! She too!
Yes! Dare I say it?—I can scarce believe it;
I do believe it and I want to hide it.
She too! She too! Excuse her fully, but
Don't hide it from yourself: She too! She too!

O these words, which I ought to doubt as long
As any breath of faith still lives within me,
Yes, these words in the end they stand engraved,
Like one of Fate's decrees, on the bronze margin
Of the full-written tablets of my torment.
Now only are my enemies made strong,
Now I am robbed forever of my strength.
How can I fight if *she* is in the army
Against me? How can I endure in patience
If *she* does not lend me her hand from far?
If *her* glance does not touch the suppliant?
You dared to think it, yes, you even said it,
And here, it's true, before your fears imagined.
And now before despair with claws of bronze
Destroys your senses, tearing them asunder,
Accuse the bitter destiny, repeat
And then repeat again: She too! She too!

Act 5

Scene 1

A garden.
(Alfonso, Antonio.)

ANTONIO: At your behest I went a second time
  To Tasso; I've just come from seeing him.
  I spoke to him, indeed entreated him,
  But he will not give up his point of view:

He begs you fervently to give him leave
That for a brief time he may go to Rome.
ALFONSO: I must admit to you that I'm annoyed
And I would rather tell you that I am
Than hide it all and make the annoyance greater.
He wants to leave us. Good! I will not keep him.
He wants to go away, to Rome. So be it!
As long as Scipio Gonzaga doesn't
Steal him from me—or that shrewd Medici!
That's what has made our Italy so great,
Each neighbor vying with the rest to gain
The better men and make good use of them.
A Prince who does not gather talents round him
Is in my eyes a General with no army,
And one who fails to hear the voice of poetry,
No matter who he is, a mere barbarian.
I found this man, I chose him, and I'm proud
Of him and proud to have him as my servant,
And since I've done so much for him already,
I should not like to lose him without cause.
ANTONIO: I feel embarrassed, for I bear the blame
Before you for what happened here today.
I'm also willing to admit my error;
Forgiveness now depends upon your mercy,
But if you were to think that I'd not made
The utmost effort to conciliate him,
I would be inconsolable. O speak
To me with gracious mien so that I may
Regain composure and my confidence.
ALFONSO: Antonio, no, on that score rest assured.
By no means do I put the blame on you.
I know this man's true temper all too well,
And all too clearly I know what I've done,
How often I indulged him, how much I
Forgot that it was actually for me
To give the orders. Man can make himself
Master of many things; true temper scarcely
Bends to necessity or time's long passage.
ANTONIO: When others do a great deal for one man,

It's fitting that in turn this man be quick
To ask himself what help the others need.
One who has trained his mind so well and who
Shrewdly stores up all sciences and all
Knowledge vouchsafed to us to comprehend,
Should he not doubly be obliged to hold
Himself in check? And does he think of that?

ALFONSO: It seems we are not meant to be at peace!
As soon as we plan to enjoy ourselves,
A foe is given us to test our valor,
A friend is given us to test our patience.

ANTONIO: Man's first and foremost duty, choosing food
And drink—since Nature has not bounded him
So tightly as the beasts—does he fulfill it?
Does he not rather let himself be lured
As children are by all that suits his palate?
When does he ever mix his wine with water?
Sweet things, spices, strong drink, one after the other
He swallows down in headlong fashion, then
Complains about his clouded mind, his blood
Afire, about his all-too-violent manner—
And puts the blame on Nature and on Fate.
How often I have seen him with his doctor
Arguing bitterly and foolishly—
Comic almost, if anything is comic
That must torment a man and vexes others.
"I have this trouble," he says plaintively
And much chagrined: "Why do you vaunt your skill?
Make me get well!"—"All right!" replies the doctor,
"Then don't eat this and this."—"I can't do that."—
"Then take this medicine."—"Oh no; it tastes
So vile, my system just revolts at it."—
"Well, then, drink water."—"Water? That I won't!
I am as water-shy as rabid people."
"Well, then, there is no help for you."—"Why not?"
"Your trouble will go on and gather trouble,
And if it doesn't kill you, it will plague you
More and more every day."—"O fine! Then what
Are you a doctor for? You know my trouble,

And you should know the remedies as well,
And make them palatable so that I need
Not suffer first to end my suffering."
You smile yourself, but isn't it the truth
That you have heard him say these very things?

ALFONSO: I've heard them often and excused them often.

ANTONIO: It is most sure that an intemperate life,
Just as it gives us wild, oppressive dreams,
Will finally make us dream in broad daylight.
What else is his suspicion but a dream?
Walk where he may, he thinks he is surrounded
By enemies. No one can grant his talent
But that "he's envious"; none can envy him
But that he "hates and fiercely persecutes" him.
He's often burdened you with such complaints:
Forced locks and intercepted letters; yes,
Poison and daggers! What all won't he fancy?
You had these things investigated—tried yourself;
Did you find anything? Hardly a semblance.
No Prince's patronage will make him safe,
No friend's devotion can assuage his feelings,
And will you promise peace and happiness
To such a man, and look for joy from him?

ALFONSO: You would be right, Antonio, if I looked
To find in him my own direct advantage.
But it is my advantage that I don't
Expect the gain to be direct and total,
Not all things serve our purposes alike.
Wanting the use of many things one must
Use each thing in its fashion. Thus he'll be
Well served. The Medicis have taught us that.
And so the Popes themselves have demonstrated.
With what consideration, princely patience,
And great forbearance they have got along
With many men of talent who seemed not
To need their wealthy favor, yet did need it!

ANTONIO: Who's not aware of that, my Prince? Life's pains
Alone teach us to value life's rewards.
While still so young he has attained too much

For him to savor it contentedly.
O, if he were obliged to work and earn
What now is offered him with open hands,
He would exert his powers like a man
And would from step to step be satisfied.
A nobleman of little means already
Has gained the goal of his most cherished wish
When a great Prince selects him as his courtier
And with a generous hand delivers him
From penury, if he gives him as well
His confidence and favor, and is willing
To raise him over others, to his side,
Be it in war, in business, or in talk,
Then I should think a modest man might honor
His happiness by silent gratitude.
And Tasso has, on top of all of this,
A young man's finest happiness: His country
Has recognized him and has hopes for him.
Believe me, his capricious discontent
Rests on an ample cushion of good fortune.
He's here; release him graciously, and give
Him time in Rome, in Naples, or wherever,
To look for what he felt the lack of here
And only here can ever find again.

ALFONSO: Does he first want to go back to Ferrara?

ANTONIO: He wants to stay on here in Belriguardo.
The things most necessary for his trip
He'll have delivered to him through a friend.

ALFONSO: I am content. My sister will go back
Directly with her friend, and I on horseback
Will still reach home before them. You will follow
As soon as you have tended to his needs.
Give orders to the castellan for what
He needs so he can stay here at the castle
As long as he may wish, until his friends
Have sent his luggage to him, till we send him
The letters I intend to give to him
To take to Rome. But here he comes. Farewell.

(Exit Antonio; enter Tasso.)

Scene 2

TASSO *(with reserve):* The gracious favor you've so often shown
　　me
　　Today reveals itself in its full light.
　　You have forgiven what I thoughtlessly
　　And wantonly committed at your court,
　　And you have reconciled my adversary.
　　Now you permit me to absent myself
　　From you a while, yet generously consent
　　Still to preserve my place in your good graces.
　　I now depart in total confidence,
　　And in the quiet hope that this brief respite
　　Cures me of all that now oppresses me.
　　My spirit shall uplift itself anew,
　　And on the path where, heartened by your glances,
　　I first set forth, joyful and bold, again
　　Shall make itself deserving of your favor.
ALFONSO: I wish you happiness upon your journey
　　And hope that you'll come back to us all cured
　　And in a cheerful mind. Contented then,
　　You will be bringing us twofold reward
　　For every hour you now deprive us of.
　　I shall write letters for you to my people
　　And friends of mine in Rome, and I much wish
　　That you will everywhere keep in close touch
　　With them in confidence, as I most surely
　　Consider you, though absent, still my own.
TASSO: O Prince, your favor overwhelms a man
　　Who feels himself unworthy and cannot
　　So much as thank you at the present moment.
　　Instead of thanks I bring to you a plea!
　　My poem lies most closely at my heart.
　　I've made much progress, sparing neither toil
　　Nor diligence, but still too much of it
　　Remains imperfect. Therefore I should like
　　To put myself to school once more down there
　　Where spirits of great men still soar above,
　　And soaring spur us on. My song would then

Deservedly rejoice in your approval.
O give me back those pages which I know
Now only to my shame are in your hands.
ALFONSO: You will not take away from me today
What you have barely given me today.
Between you and your poem let me step
As intercessor. Take care not to injure
By rigorous industry the natural grace
That now lives in your verses. Do not listen
To the advice you hear from every side!
The thousandfold ideas of as many
Different men, who contradict each other
In life and in opinions, these the poet
Will wisely gather all in one and never
Shrink from displeasing many so that he
May that much better please so many others.
Yet I don't say that here and there you shouldn't
Make modest use of file or shears. Herewith
I promise you, in very little time
You shall receive a copy of your poem.
What's in your hand will stay in my hands; thus,
Together with my sisters, I may first
Have some real pleasure in it. If you bring
It back more fully perfect, we shall then
Enjoy the heightened pleasure and express,
Only as friends, our doubts at certain places.
TASSO: Embarrassed, I can only beg again:
Let me have the copy quickly. My mind
Dwells wholly now upon this work, for now
It must become the thing it can become.
ALFONSO: I do approve the impulse that inspires you!
And yet, if it were possible, good Tasso,
You ought to first enjoy the world in freedom
Awhile, amuse yourself, improve your blood
By taking of a cure. For then you'd find
The harmony of senses thus restored
Would give you everything you now are seeking,
Seeking in vain in all your gloomy zeal.
TASSO: My Prince, it seems that way; yet I am well

230 · *Johann Wolfgang von Goethe*

When I can yield to my own thirst for work,
Hence my own thirst to work will make me well.
You've noticed long ago; I do not thrive
In easy luxury. Quiet and peace
Can give me peace and quiet least of all.
My temperament, I feel, alas, is not
By Nature meant to drift upon the days'
Soft element to the broad seas of time.

ALFONSO: All that you think and do leads you deep down
    Into yourself. On every side of us
    There lie abysses dug by destiny,
    The deepest being here within our hearts,
    And we are pleased to cast ourselves into it.
    I beg you, tear yourself away from *you*.
    The man will profit what the poet loses.

TASSO: It's all in vain that I repress that impulse
    Which surges day and night within my bosom.
    When I can neither write nor meditate,
    Life is no longer any life for me.
    Forbid the silkworm to continue spinning
    Though it is spinning on to its own death!
    It will evolve its precious weft from deep
    Within its inner self and will not cease
    Till it has cased itself in its own coffin.
    O would that some kind god would give us too
    The destiny of that most enviable worm,
    Swiftly and joyously to spread our wings
    In a new valley of the sun!

ALFONSO: Hear me!
    You give so many people double pleasure
    In living; learn to know, I beg of you
    The value of the life that you still have,
    And now tenfold enrich. And so, farewell!
    The sooner you return to us, the more
    Gratefully welcome you will be to us.

                    (Exit.)

Scene 3

TASSO *(alone):* So now hold firm, my heart, for that went well!
It's hard for you—the first time you are able,
And also choose, to play the double game.
You heard it; that was not his nature speaking,
Those weren't his words; rather it seemed to me
Only an echo of Antonio's voice.
Be watchful now! From this point on you'll hear it
From every side. Be firm, be firm! It's still
Only a matter of a moment yet,
And one who learns dissembling late in life
Brings from the past his earlier honest image.
It's sure to work, just practice it on them.
> *(after a pause)*
Your gloating's premature, for there she comes.
The gracious Princess comes! O what emotion!
She enters; in my heart all my distress
And my suspicion are dissolved in sorrow.

Scene 4

(Enter the Princess.)

PRINCESS: You plan on leaving us, rather you mean
To stay behind a while in Belriguardo,
Tasso, and you will then depart from us?
I hope it will be for a short time only.
You go to Rome?
TASSO: That's where I'll first direct
My steps, and if my friends receive me kindly,
The way I hope they will, then while I'm there
I may perhaps with patience and great care
Apply the final touches to my poem.
I'll find, assembled there, numbers of men
Who in all fields may well claim mastery.
In that first city of the world does not
Each place, each stone, speak audibly to us?

232 • *Johann Wolfgang von Goethe*

How many thousand silent teachers beckon
In friendliness and solemn majesty.
If I do not complete my poem *there,*
I never can. And yet, alas, I feel
No luck attends on any enterprise
Of mine. Change it I will, but never finish.
I feel, I truly feel, the mighty art
That nourishes us all, that so enlivens
And strengthens healthy minds, will ruin me,
Will drive me off; I leave in haste. I mean
To go to Naples.

PRINCESS: Can you take that risk?
  They have not lifted yet the strict proscription
  Issued against you and your father both.
TASSO: You're right to warn me, I have thought of that.
  I shall go in disguise. I shall assume
  The poor coat of a pilgrim or a shepherd.
  Slip through the city streets where thronging thousands
  Will easily conceal one single person.
  And I shall hurry to the shore and find
  At once a boat with willing, kindly people,
  Peasants, who having come from market now
  Are going home, with people of Sorrento.
  For I must hurry over to Sorrento.
  There lives my sister, who along with me
  Was once my parents' joy amid their sorrow.
  I shall be silent in the boat and still
  In silence step on land and softly then
  Go up the path, and at the door shall ask:
  "Where does Cornelia live? Would you please show me?
  Cornelia Sersale." Graciously
  Some spinstress will point out the street for me
  And indicate the house. I shall climb higher.
  The children will run after me and stare
  At my wild hair and at the somber stranger.
  I shall approach the threshold. Open stands
  The door, and I shall step into the house—
PRINCESS: Look up, if that is possible, O Tasso,
  And recognize the danger you are in!

I spare your feelings, otherwise I'd ask you:
Is it a noble thing to speak as you do?
Noble to think of your own self alone,
As if you had no friends whose hearts were hurt?
Is what my brother thinks concealed from you?
Or how my sister and I both value you?
Have you not noticed that, not understood it?
Has everything been changed in so few minutes?
O Tasso, if you want to go away,
Do not leave pain and grief behind for us.

(Tasso turns away.)

What comfort it affords, when some friend is,
For a brief time, about to go away
To give him some small present, be it only
A new cloak or a sword! There's nothing more
That one can give to you—you throw away
In anger everything that you possess.
You choose the black smock and the pilgrim's purse
And the long staff, and of your own free will
Go off in poverty and take from us
What you could so enjoy with us alone.

TASSO: Then you are not rejecting me completely?
O what sweet words, what fair and precious comfort!
Speak for me! Take me under your protection!—
Leave me in Belriguardo here, transfer
Me to Consandoli, or where you will!
The Prince is owner of so many castles,
So many gardens, tended all year long,
In which you hardly walk *one* day, and that
Perhaps no more than for a single hour.
Yes, choose the most remote of them, one which
You'll not be visiting for years on end
And which perhaps is lying now untended,
And send me there! And there let me be yours!
What care I'll take of all your trees; I'll cover up
The lemon trees with boards and tiles in autumn
And I'll protect them well with bundled rushes.
The lovely flowers in the flowerbeds
Will spread their roots abroad, each little spot,

Each path shall be kept beautiful and neat.
The palace too—let me take charge of that.
I'll open windows at the proper times
So dampness will not damage all the paintings;
The walls adorned with lovely stucco work.
I'll clean them with a gentle feather duster,
The pavement floor will gleam, spotless and bright,
No one stone, not one brick shall be displaced,
No grass shall grow from any single crack.
PRINCESS: I find no word of counsel in my heart,
 I find no reassuring hope for you—
 Or us. I look around to see if somehow
 Some god might send us help, reveal to me
 A healing herb, a potion that could bring
 Peace to your mind, and peace to us as well.
 The truest word that issues from my lips,
 The best of curatives no longer works.
 I have to leave you, and my heart cannot
 Abandon you.
TASSO: So it is she, ye gods,
 The one who speaks with you, takes pity on you!
 And how could you mistake this noble heart?
 And was it possible that in her presence
 Faint heartedness once seized and overwhelmed you?
 No, it is *you*, and I am now myself.
 O go on speaking and from your own lips
 Let me hear all my comfort! Don't withdraw
 Your counsel from me! Speak: What shall I do
 In order that your brother might forgive me,
 That you yourself could willingly forgive me,
 That all of you might once again, and gladly
 Count me among your own? O tell me that!
PRINCESS: It is but little that we ask of you.
 And yet it seems to be too much by far.
 You should entrust yourself to us in friendship.
 We want no more from you than what you are
 When once you are contented with yourself.
 When you yourself are pleased, you give us pleasure,
 You only sadden us when you avoid it.

And though you do make us impatient, still
It's only that we'd like to help you out—
And then we see, alas, there is no help,
If you yourself won't take the friendly hand
That reached out longingly but could not touch you.

TASSO: You are your own true self, and just the way
I first encountered you, a holy angel.
Forgive the clouded vision of a mortal
If for a time he failed to recognize you.
He knows you now once more! His soul is opened
Fully, adoring none but you forever.
This heart is wholly filled with tenderness—
She, she stands before me. What emotion!
Is it confusion which draws me to you?
Or madness? Or some heightened sense, alone
Able to grasp the highest, purest truth?
Yes, it is this emotion, only this,
That on this earth can give me happiness,
And which alone made me so miserable
When I resisted it and tried to bar
My heart against it. I had meant to fight
This passion, and I fought and fought with my
Profoundest being, impiously destroyed
My very self, which you belonged to wholly—

PRINCESS: If I'm to listen to you further, Tasso,
Then calm these fiery words, which frighten me.

TASSO: But will a goblet's brim retain the wine
That foams and swells and, boiling, overflows?
With every word you lift my happiness,
With every word your eyes more brightly shine.
I feel myself in inmost soul transformed,
I feel myself unburdened of all pain,
Free as a god—I owe it all to you!
The power ineffable that masters me
Streams from your lips. Yes, you make me completely
Your own, and nothing of my total self
Henceforward will belong to me again.
My eye grows dim with light and happiness,
My senses fail, my limbs no longer bear me.

You call me to you irresistibly,
My heart is drawn to you beyond recall.
You've won me to you wholly and forever,
So take me, all I am, my very being!
    (He falls into her arms and presses her to him.)
PRINCESS *(thrusting him aside and hurrying off)*:
    Away!
LEONORE *(who for a time has been visible in the background, coming quickly nearer)*:
        O Tasso, what has happened? Tasso!
            (She follows the Princess.)
TASSO *(on the point of going after them)*:
    My God!
ALFONSO *(who for a time has been seen approaching with Antonio)*:
        He's lost his reason! Seize and hold him!
           (Exit.)

Scene 5

ANTONIO: O if some enemy—as you imagine
    That you are always ringed about by foes—
    Were standing by you now, how he would gloat!
    Unhappy man, I hardly catch my breath
    When something wholly unexpected happens,
    When our eyes chance upon some monstrous thing,
    Our minds are rendered motionless awhile
    For we have nothing to compare it with.
TASSO *(after a long pause)*:
    Fulfill your office, I see who you are!
    Yes, you deserve your prince's confidence.
    Fulfill your office, torture me to death,
    Slowly, for over me the staff is broken.
    So go ahead and draw, draw out the arrow,
    So I may cruelly feel the barbed hook
    That tears my flesh!
    You are the tyrant's precious instrument;
    Be prison keeper, be the torturer,

How well, how very aptly both become you!
(*toward offstage*)
Yes, go ahead then, tyrant! You could not
Wear your disguise forever—gloat in triumph!
You have the slave now well in chains, you have him
Well saved and set aside for torments planned.
I hate you! Go ahead! I feel completely
The loathing that superior force engenders
When it lays hold unjust and wantonly.
(*after a pause*)
So in the end I see myself now banished,
Driven away and banished like a beggar.
They crowned me—to be led before the altar
Adorned like any sacrificial victim!
And they enticed from me on this last day
The sole thing that belonged to me, my poem,
With smooth words got it for themselves and kept it!
In your hands is my sole possession which,
In any place, could have commended me
And which alone could save me from starvation!
I see why I'm supposed to take this leave.
It is a plot, and you're the leader of it.
So I've no chance to make my poem better,
So that my name won't be more widely known,
So enviers may find a thousand flaws,
So I at last may be forgotten wholly,
That's why I should get used to idle living,
That's why I should indulge myself, my senses.
What worthy friendship, sweet solicitude!
I thought it loathsome, your conspiracy
Spun ceaselessly, invisibly about me,
But now it has become more loathsome still.

And you, the Siren, who so tenderly,
Divinely lured me on, now suddenly
I see you. Yes, but why, O God, so late!

Yet we so willingly deceive ourselves
And honor the depraved who honor us.

No, human beings do not know each other;
It's only galley slaves know one another,
Who pant for breath, chained to a single bench;
Where none has anything to ask and none
Has anything to lose—they know each other;
Where every man admits he is a scoundrel
And takes his fellow men for scoundrels too.
But we politely misjudge other people
So that they will misjudge us in their turn.

How long your sacred image hid from me
The courtesan who plays her little tricks.
The mask now falls, and I behold Armida
Stripped bare of all her charms—Yes, that is you!
Foreknowingly my poem sang of you!

And then the wily little go-between!
What deep disgrace I see her in before me!
I hear her rustle of light footsteps now,
I know the circle now round which she stole.
I know you all! Let that suffice for me!
If misery has robbed me of everything,
I praise it still; it teaches me the truth.

ANTONIO: I hear you, Tasso, with astonishment,
Much as I know how quickly your rash mind
Can swing from one far boundary to the other.
Stop and reflect, master your rage. You blaspheme,
And you permit yourself word after word
Which in your grief can be forgiven you
But which you never can forgive yourself.

TASSO: Don't talk to me with soft and gentle lips,
From you I want to hear no words of wisdom!
Leave me this hollow happiness, so that
I don't reflect, only to lose my mind.
I feel my bones all broken deep inside
And I am still alive to feel the pain.
Despair in all its fury seizes me
And in the hellish torment that consumes me

Blaspheming is a muffled sound of pain.
I want to leave! If you are honorable,
Then show me, let me go immediately!

ANTONIO: I won't abandon you in your distress.
Though you may lose your self-control completely,
You may be sure I'll show no lack of patience.

TASSO: Then I must make myself your prisoner?
I do give myself up, and so it's over.
I offer no resistance, that is best—
Then let me painfully repeat once more
How beautiful it was, what I have squandered.
They're leaving now—O God, I see the dust
Already rising from their carriage wheels—
Foreriders out ahead—So there they go,
And disappear! Did I not come from there?
Now they are gone, and they are angry with me.
If I could only kiss his hand once more!
If I could only say farewell again!
To have the chance to say again: "Forgive me!"
And just to hear him say: "Go, you're forgiven!"
I do not hear it, though, and never will.
Yes, I will go! Just let me say farewell,
Just say farewell! But give, O give me back
The here and now for just a moment more!
Perhaps I will get well again. No, no,
I'm cast aside, I'm banished, I have banished
Myself, and I will never hear that voice
Again, and I will never meet that glance
Again, no, never—

ANTONIO: Listen and be reminded by the voice
Of one who stands beside you, not unmoved:
You are not quite so wretched as you think.
Be strong! You give in to yourself too much.

TASSO: And am I then as wretched as I seem?
Am I as weak as I appear before you?
Has everything been lost? Has sorrow not,
As if the earth had quaked, transformed this structure
Into an awful heap of shattered rubble?
Have I no talent left now to divert me

A thousandfold, and to sustain me?
Is all the strength extinguished which once stirred
Within my heart? Have I then come to nothing,
Nothing at all?
No, everything is here, and I am nothing!
I'm cut off from myself, and she from me!
ANTONIO: However wholly lost you think to be,
    Take stock and see yourself for what you are!
TASSO: Yes, you remind me at the proper time!—
    Will no example out of history help?
    Won't any noble man come to my mind
    Who suffered more than I have ever suffered,
    So by comparison I may be steadied?
    No, all is lost!—One thing alone remains:
    The gift of tears is given us by Nature,
    The cry of anguish, when at last a man
    Can bear no more—to me above all else—
    In grief she left me melody and speech
    To cry the fullest measure of my anguish.
    If mankind in its torment must be mute,
    Some god gave me the power to tell my pain.
                    (*Antonio steps up to him and takes*
                            him by the hand.)
    O noble man! You stand secure and quiet,
    It's only I who seem the storm-tossed wave.
    Reflect, however; don't be overproud
    Of all your power! Mighty Nature, who
    Gave firm foundation to the rock, has also
    Conferred mobility upon the wave.
    She sends her storm winds out; the wave gives way
    And rolls and swells and, foaming, arches over.
    And on that wave the sun was mirrored once
    In beauty, and the stars in constellations
    Rested upon its gently swaying bosom.
    The splendor now has vanished, peace has fled.—
    I know myself no longer, in my peril.
    And I'm ashamed no longer to confess it.
    The helm is shattered and the ship is breaking
    In every part of it. The ground is sundered;

Bursting, it opens up beneath my feet.
And so I throw my arms around you now—
Thus at the very last the helmsman clings
Fast to the rock on which he nearly foundered.

Translated by Charles E. Passage;
adapted by Frank G. Ryder

THE GERMAN LIBRARY
in 100 Volumes

Wolfram von Eschenbach
Parzival
Edited by André Lefevere

Gottfried von Strassburg
Tristan and Isolde
Edited and Revised by Francis G.
  Gentry
Foreword by C. Stephen Jaeger

German Medieval Tales
Edited by Francis G. Gentry
Foreword by Thomas Berger

German Mystical Writings
Edited by Karen J. Campbell
Foreword by Carol Zaleski

German Humanism and Reformation
Edited by Reinhard P. Becker
Foreword by Roland Bainton

Immanuel Kant
Philosophical Writings
Edited by Ernst Behler
Foreword by René Wellek

Friedrich Schiller
*Plays: Intrigue and Love and Don
  Carlos*
Edited by Walter Hinderer
Foreword by Gordon Craig

Friedrich Schiller
Wallenstein and Mary Stuart
Edited by Walter Hinderer

Johann Wolfgang von Goethe
*The Sufferings of Young Werther
and Elective Affinities*
Edited by Victor Lange
Forewords by Thomas Mann

German Romantic Criticism
Edited by A. Leslie Willson
Foreword by Ernst Behler

Friedrich Hölderlin
Hyperion and Selected Poems
Edited by Eric L. Santner

Philosophy of German Idealism
Edited by Ernst Behler

G. W. F. Hegel
*Encyclopedia of the Philosophical
  Sciences in Outline and Critical
  Writings*
Edited by Ernst Behler

Heinrich von Kleist
Plays
Edited by Walter Hinderer
Foreword by E. L. Doctorow

E. T. A. Hoffmann
Tales
Edited by Victor Lange

Georg Büchner
Complete Works and Letters
Edited by Walter Hinderer and
  Henry J. Schmidt

German Fairy Tales
Edited by Helmut Brackert and
  Volkmar Sander
Foreword by Bruno Bettelheim

German Literary Fairy Tales
Edited by Frank G. Ryder and
  Robert M. Browning
Introduction by Gordon Birrell
Foreword by John Gardner

F. Grillparzer, J. H. Nestroy,
  F. Hebbel
Nineteenth Century German Plays
Edited by Egon Schwarz
  in collaboration with
  Hannelore M. Spence

Gottfried Benn
Prose, Essays, Poems
Edited by Volkmar Sander
Foreword by E. B. Ashton
Introduction by Reinhard Paul
  Becker

German Essays on Art History
Edited by Gert Schiff

German Radio Plays
Edited by Everett Frost and Margaret
  Herzfeld-Sander

Hans Magnus Enzensberger
Critical Essays
Edited by Reinhold Grimm and
  Bruce Armstrong
Foreword by John Simon

All volumes available in hardcover and paperback editions at your bookstore or from the publisher. For more information on The German Library write to: The Continuum Publishing Company, 370 Lexington Avenue, New York, NY 10017.

PT 2026 .A5 1993
Goethe, Johann Wolfgang von
Plays